THE
LOST
FENS

THE
LOST
FENS

ENGLAND'S GREATEST ECOLOGICAL DISASTER

IAN D. ROTHERHAM

The
History
Press

First published 2013

The History Press
The Mill, Brimscombe Port
Stroud, Gloucestershire, GL5 2QG
www.thehistorypress.co.uk

British Library Cataloguing in Publication Data.
A catalogue record for this book is available from the British Library.

ISBN 978 0 7524 8699 4

Typesetting and origination by The History Press
Printed in Great Britain

CONTENTS

ACKNOWLEDGEMENTS

Many people have supplied information and images for the book and others have simply encouraged the work. My wife Liz is thanked for her endless patience and my colleague Joan Butt produced many of the maps. The History Press and their editors are thanked for their encouragement and support. Acknowledgement is also given to the National Archives, ref. MPC1/56, for the use of the Inclesmoor Map.

FOREWORD

It is my great pleasure to write the Foreword for this book. Until I read it my knowledge of the Fens – both the Northern Fens of South Yorkshire and north Lincolnshire and the Southern Fens of south Lincolnshire and Cambridgeshire – was bitty and incomplete. I had dipped into one book, carried in my head a short vivid description from a second book, and read a third book from cover to cover. Now, having read Ian Rotherham's *The Lost Fens*, I feel that my fenland education is much more complete.

The book that I had dipped into was Jack Ravensdale's *Liable to Floods* (1974), the history of three villages on the edge of the Cambridgeshire Fens between AD 450 and 1850. The description that I carry around in my head is of the last royal deer hunt that took place in the Northern Fens in South Yorkshire in 1609. The description is by the antiquarian and diarist Abraham De La Pryme (1671–1704), and was quoted in the Revd Joseph Hunter's *South Yorkshire* (Vol. 1, 1828, p. 156). The occasion was a visit to Hatfield Chase by Prince Henry, Prince of Wales. The royal party embarked in almost 100 boats, having frightened about 500 deer to take to the water. They pursued them into Thorne Mere 'and there being up to their very necks in water, their horned heads raised seemed to represent a little wood'. Ian quotes the piece in full in Chapter 2.

On the subject of fenlands, a book that I have read from cover to cover is a very short book, of just sixty-seven pages: Eric Ennion's *Adventurers Fen*, published in 1942. It contains a vivid account of this small fenland remnant over a period of forty years, from 1900 to 1940. During this time it changed from being a working fen (with litter cutting for coarse hay, turf cutting for domestic fuel, reed cutting for thatching, and osiers for making wicker baskets and eel traps), to being drained and farmed. It then reverted to nature during the Depression years of the 1930s and then, at the outbreak of the Second World War, it was lost to agriculture forever. As Brian Vesey-Fitzgerald says in his Foreword to Ennion's book, it is a love story 'the headstone over the grave of a part of Britain … where but a short while ago the bittern nested is sugar beet'.

This quotation says it all. Visitors to the former fenland regions today, and many of their residents, see a tamed landscape. They are quite unaware of what the Fens once looked like, how their resources were exploited for thousands of years, of the rich plant life and animal life that once abounded there, and how they were destroyed. All they see is a rich agricultural landscape, Britain's 'bread basket', full of flat fields of wheat, sugar beet, potatoes and other vegetables that replaced around 2,500 square miles (4,000km²) of ancient fenland landscape in the Southern Fens of Lincolnshire, Cambridgeshire, and East Anglia, and 1,900 square miles (3,000km²) in the Northern Fens of South and East Yorkshire and north Lincolnshire. This book tries to set the record straight. It looks at the landscape and wildlife before drainage, the piecemeal and then highly organised drainage of the wetlands and the consequences of the land 'improvement', and then brings the story up to date in the context of twenty-first century environmental issues.

Ian has been called a 'take-no-prisoners environmentalist'. He has campaigned hard and long for countryside management and environmental responsibility in his native South Yorkshire. Here he takes a much wider view and has written a compelling book about a subject that has been very close to his heart for many years. The book has everything. First, it covers both the major former fenland areas, not only the well-known Cambridgeshire Fens and their extension into south Lincolnshire but also the less well-known former fenland landscapes of South Yorkshire and neighbouring north Lincolnshire. Secondly, it covers a vast sweep of time from the very beginnings of fenland environments, through the 2,000 years of draining and 'improvement', to their virtual disappearance, and then on to current projects to stabilise remaining fenland remnants and reinstate others. There is also a telling chapter about the wildlife and lost flora of the un-drained Fens, and a fascinating chapter on the impact of peat extraction. Finally, having dealt with the attitudes of mind that led to the destruction of the ancient fenlands, there is a powerful last chapter about the future and about environmental sustainability in general. It is a story of great loss, of a great ecological catastrophe, but also a vision for the future, a vision for restoration.

His audience is very wide; it not only embraces the general reader, such as local historians and amateur naturalists, and specialists such as landscape historians and ecologists, but also planners, local politicians and national politicians – indeed, anyone who cares or should care about fenland environments and environmental concerns generally.

This is a powerful book with a number of powerful messages. It is timely and deserves to find a permanent place in the literature on the Fens.

Melvyn Jones,
Kirkstead Abbey Grange,
Thorpe Hesley, 2013

INTRODUCTION

About a quarter of the British Isles is, or has been, some kind of wetland.

Oliver Rackham (1986)

A LOST WORLD AND A FORGOTTEN LANDSCAPE

To stand inside the dykes and banks of the Wicken Sedge Fen is to take a step back in history. Suddenly you become Hereward the Wake, the last Saxon warlord, gazing out over an English kingdom squeezed in the grasp of Norman steel and a culture battered and broken. Our view today is across a largely barren, dry vista of intensive agri-industry; devoid of its ecology and deprived of its native peoples. Yet history tells us that this was once the richest landscape for people and for wildlife in Britain. Such an observation begs the questions of when and why it disappeared. What did it look like and exactly what was its ecology? These basic questions are hard to answer since there are few written records, and this Fen was mostly destroyed before anyone bothered to identify and catalogue its animals and plants. We know that much of the great wetland was still here in 1600, but was virtually annihilated by 1900. By whom and why did this happen?

Recent conservation work, at great expense, has begun the slow process of recovery of areas immediately around the handful of fen sites that remain. However, even here and with the largest conservation grants ever allocated by the Heritage Lottery Fund, the recovery is habitat re-creation not restoration. The fen, its ecology, and its people are so changed that it can never be restored, but we must still try to create something new and perhaps a mirror of sorts to the past. Here at Wicken there are great plans afoot to reverse the worst of farming's atrocities and to try to restore at least a veneer of respectability to England's last true fenland. However, step outside the protective banks and ditches of the old fen, and the land, though reverted from intensive farming to a broad, open, grazed landscape, is still dry. For technical and social (adjacent farming) reasons this land will never again be wet. Some areas of the most-recently drained fen have been restored with a degree of success, but the bigger landscape,

How the old fen might have looked. (Victorian print)

like Hereward's Saxon England, remains under the firm grip of its new master. The land is dry and the waters have been banished.

What do we know of the lost ecology? We can gain some insight into former vegetation and wildlife from meticulous analysis of pollen and animal remains preserved in peat or other anaerobic sediments because the lack of oxygen impedes the processes of decomposition. Remarkable discoveries at prehistoric sites provide a vision of the larger animals hunted and eaten by early settlers, but the living ecology eludes us. This was a vast landscape on a scale similar to the intractable wildernesses viewed by European settlers when they first arrived in North America. We get an idea of what they faced in the names they gave the landscape – such as the 'Great Dismal Swamp' – and yet they wrote too of the unimaginably rich wildlife, the flocks of birds and the super-abundant fish. This image is a starting point for our journey of discovery in search of the lost fens.

Along the eastern seaboard of England, the Fens stretched almost continuously from East Anglia to North Yorkshire. Beyond them were extensive heaths, moors, dunes, woods and forests, and great open sheep-walks, and the whole was linked by arteries and veins of rivers great and small, meandering across vast floodplains, curving, spilling, slow and tortuous; the life-blood of this remarkable ecology. Its loss represents the single most dramatic transformation of nature in British history, and yet today it barely merits a footnote in our accounts of England and the English. Just as David Lowenthal described the past as a 'foreign country', the lost fens were a different world.

SETTING THE SCENE

In 1536, the commoners of Lincolnshire made a complaint to King Henry VIII about the selection of his ministers and advisors, and through this the suppression of the monasteries and abbeys and other religious houses. Henry replied in his 'Answer to the Petition of the Rebels and Traitors of Lincolnshire'. In this response he described them as 'the rude commons of one shire' and Lincolnshire itself as 'one of the most brute and beastly of the whole realm'. This gives some insight into how the region was viewed both from within and from the outside. The vast areas of farming commons and often-extensive wetlands retained independence and even a stubbornness and resistance to change or innovation. Early writers put this down to a deep retention of their Anglo-Saxon roots. It was around Ely, for example, that Hereward the Wake held out against the Norman invasion until he was betrayed by the Church. So it is an amazing transformation which, in a little over 500 years, has turned this region both in the Northern Fens and the Southern Fens into one of the world's most productive farming landscapes. Even more surprising perhaps, is how the earlier landscapes and cultures have been erased almost entirely from the regions, and even from the cultural memory.

The reclamation of marsh and fen has been described as one of the most spectacular feats of colonisation of the landscape, as farmers and others moved onto lands wrested from the water. In many cases, the potential farmland was very fertile – a major attraction before petrochemical-subsidised agriculture. However, access to this resource was only available following reclamation. The fens and marshes that lay beyond arable farmland were often described as 'waste' but this was far from a true or fair label. As described later, the resources were indeed rich and, reflecting this affluence, they were subject to complex rights and practices that governed their use.

The products of marsh and fen included: fish (especially eels); fowl; rushes and sedge for thatching; peat for fuel and building; and withies and other wood for fuel, basket making, hurdles, and for light construction. These areas were also hugely important for grazing, even if the management of stock in a wet landscape posed some serious problems. Many of these uses changed the original, native landscape, and some, such as peat cutting, were capable of generating entirely new and distinctive landscapes over time. Large-scale reclamation and then enclosure of these wet fens and marshes was encouraged by the potential value of the land released. Over the centuries, we witness repeatedly the imperative of financial gain that has driven the inexorable process of reclamation. This often led to conflicts over resource use between local peasants and others who subsisted on the fen, and farmers and bigger landowners looking for economic benefit. These were often contested resources, bringing actors from different societies, communities and classes into direct conflict. However, other factors also influenced the interest in drying the wet landscape.

As we see in medieval times and more recently, the alleviation of floods and the protection from drastic and unpredictable inundation was a powerful driver to control water and to dry the land. Again, there may have been a difference in perspective and attitude between those used to living on the edge, the interface between land and water, and those looking to invest in farms and machinery or other resources. The latter may be desperate to control the water and avoid the flood; the former often learn to live with water and its unpredictability, and to reap from it its own unique harvests. In some parts of northern Europe, settlers in coastal wetlands built on artificial raised mounds and then sat out the flood when it inevitably came. With the floods came fish and fowl, and free fertiliser for summer pastures and hay meadows. The eventual land use varied from region to region, and over much of the Humber Levels of Yorkshire and north Lincolnshire (the Northern Fen) and the Cambridgeshire and Lincolnshire fenland (the Southern Fen) the ultimate farming use has been as intensive arable. In other regions, such as the Somerset Levels, the land has generally ended up as pasture and hay meadow, with varying degrees of intensification.

As land was taken from fen and marsh, or in coastal zones from salt marsh and mudflat, there emerged a landscape of ditches, drains, dykes, embankments and sea banks. In the early stages this was inevitably piecemeal as work was undertaken by groups of freeholders or small communities, with progression sometimes and at other times abandonment as the waters took the land back. The pattern of landscape this created had a mix of fields of different sizes and shapes, often based on opportunistic colonisation and then sometimes necessary retrenchment and even retreat. More organised reclamation was probably undertaken in some areas by the Romans or at least the Romano-British, and then from late Anglo-Saxon times by ecclesiastical foundations. In the post-Conquest period, work was organised by the larger landowners, especially the abbeys and monasteries, though progress at all times was helped or hindered by climate change beyond the influence of the communities. Any large-scale reclamation was a massive undertaking and therefore required effective social and political organisation, and an economic system to provide the necessary support and indeed the incentive to carry out the works. Where successful, the reclamation process generally resulted in a distinctive local economy and population increase. Sometimes the latter was through the indigenous population multiplying, but other times it was through inward migration of skilled labour. As often is the case, this frequently met resistance from the native people.

The impacts of the stages of reclamation, even from the earliest times, are often locked in the present-day landscape – although modern intensive farming has erased much of the evidence. Even here though, there may still be place names, lane names, and field names that tell of an earlier time and the process of progress. The early works on reclaiming the Fens to farming helped generate wealth that left a legacy of great ecclesiastical houses, though Henry VIII did much to remove that evidence. However, the magnificent churches and even cathedrals that dot the contemporary landscapes of both the Northern and Southern Fens are a reminder of the productivity of the 'improved' fenland. Today the agricultural regions of these areas and of similar landscapes in Norfolk and Suffolk are amongst the most productive in the world.

Another incentive to 'improve' these lands was to control often independently minded and non-conforming communities. Wetlands were regarded by governments and by land-owners as areas to which ne'er-do-wells, troublemakers and outlaws retreated from the long arm of authority. Indeed, these environments generated religions such as Methodism and Quakerism. In many ways, they were responsible for the uprisings that led to the English Civil War (*see* p. 129-130). By reclaiming the land from the waters, the communities themselves were 'reclaimed' to centralised authority.

Something to bear in mind from the outset of this discussion is that most, though not all, writers through time have regarded the process of reclamation and improvement for agriculture as an inherently 'good thing'. During periods of intensive drainage, and of major enclosure and improvement, there were dissenting voices, but many of these were illiterate.

There were a few individuals, such as John Clare, who wrote with passion about the impacts of improvements, but these are the exceptions and not the rule. Indeed, there is good reason, generally, why this should be so, since the spectre of famine and starvation hung in the air over the heads of our ancestors like the ague in the swamp itself. This was a strong reason and incentive to 'improve'; at least in theory. This does mean that the information and accounts that we receive are biased to a degree by the viewpoint of the beholder. When reading these today, it is important to bear this in mind. However, the inherent view that drainage is good pervades even modern writing. Coones and Patten, writing in 1986, for example, state that:

> … It is all the more depressing therefore to record the retreat which took place in the wetlands after the early fourteenth century, when many hard-won areas suffered from neglect and a lack of maintenance of their drainage works. But a start had been made, not only in the two principal regions but also in other coastal marshlands of southern and eastern England.

There is also a whole subject of enclosure and land improvement more generally, that is beyond this particular story. However, an understanding of the nature of the transformations in landscape and the agricultural economy, especially during the period from 1700 to 1950, is hugely important to any vision of these lost fens. The time from 1750 to 1850 is generally regarded as the age of the 'improver', and this agricultural revolution is mostly attached to the process of 'Parliamentary Enclosure', where common open fields and common grazing lands such as heath, meadow, waste and fen were enclosed as privately owned and managed fields. The reality is more complex and there are numerous regional variations on this general theme. Many innovations that characterised the process of improvement were in place and adopted well before Parliamentary Enclosure. However, the process of individual Acts of Parliament to facilitate the process applied a massive steamroller to the impetus of change. Some areas were already in part enclosed and to a degree improved, and others had not and could not be, because of the difficult terrain or conditions such as the wetness of the Fens.

Agricultural developments in the seventeenth and eighteenth centuries included the introduction of new crops and new technologies to facilitate cultivation and improvement. Advances in farming practice brought new lands into cultivation and the spread of root crops with sown grasses and clover made it possible to keep large numbers of sheep. This was particularly important in sandy heaths and other areas of lighter soils where the animals produced valuable manure that helped the structure and fertility of the soil. Sheep were 'folded' on lands being improved to raise the nutrient status and the organic matter content. Carefully managed rotations of these crops enabled programmes of improvement and enhanced productivity. There were major additions to both arable and pasturelands through the enclosing and improvement of heaths and other commons; and the processes described above, together with liming or marling, brought much of this about. On clay lands, the soils were under-drained using improved technologies developed over a period of around two centuries. In the marshes and fens, as described later, a process of piecemeal drainage and reclamation was undertaken. Low-lying areas were targeted by occasionally ambitious (and sometimes over-ambitious) schemes for their drainage and to bring them into cultivation. The most spectacular successes were in eastern England, across East Anglia and northwards into Yorkshire. In the fens, the lands were drained and enclosed for the production of 'all sorts of corne and grasses'. It was the great drainage schemes of Cornelius Vermuyden that brought about the most obvious changes; though, as we shall see, others both before and after him also played major roles. Nevertheless, Vermuyden was able to declare in 1652 that 'the area now known as the Bedford Level had been well and truly drained'. However, again as we note later on, the celebrations were often premature and reclamation was followed by disastrous floods and sometimes by other consequences too.

Indeed, the transformation of these wetlands generated unexpected consequences, and at the time, the available technology and knowledge were generally not able to counter these. The most obvious effects were the silting up of major rivers and other minor watercourses, with the result that water, instead of draining to the sea, began to be impounded and ponded back onto the land. At the same time, the consequence of the drainage that had taken place was the shrinkage of the peat and therefore a lowering of the land surface across large areas of the fens. Combined with the effects on the rivers described earlier, and in coastal zones with sea level changes and bad storms, this was a recipe for potential disaster.

Along with further programmes of drainage and embanking, the solution at the time was the construction of hundreds of windmills across the fenlands, with the objective of removing water into the rivers and drains. The mills were able to pump water from the lower fens and marshes up and into the drainage channels and rivers that now stood considerably higher than the surrounding lands. However, the draining and drying of the peat produced a positive feedback loop with a lowering of the ground surface, which ultimately made the problems worse and the lands more vulnerable to catastrophic flooding. Not only this, but the windmills were also dependent on suitable weather conditions in order to operate. In many ways this meant that, with available technologies, the pre-industrial drainage of the fenlands had reached the limits of its capability. The development of steam-powered pumps in the eighteenth and nineteenth centuries moved the drainage and reclamation towards the ultimate removal of the wetlands from the landscape.

The process of improvement affected the whole community as well as the environment in which people lived and worked. Often we see this 'improved' landscape in the fenland regions today, with any hint of the earlier period wiped from view. The independent commoners who eked a living from the fens often lived in poor and very basic accommodation. With improvement, they and their dwellings were swept aside and replaced with planned farms and neat estate cottages. The poor peasants generally lived in cottages that were neither built to last, nor constructed by craftsmen, but put together with materials easily and freely available by the people themselves. Sanitation, needless to say, was absent. Their squalid shelters were constructed with walls of earth, clay or turf and hazel or willow rods, some stone and perhaps timber supports. The roof was thatched with reed and turf, and the heating would be with local peat or perhaps small wood. There was generally no chimney, just a hole in the roof, and smoke went out of the door and any windows. The acrid peat smoke had the added benefit in the summer of keeping out biting insects, especially midges and mosquitoes.

From the Middle Ages up to the early 1800s, poverty was endemic in these primitive rural societies, and the impact of improvement was mixed. For some it might mean the provision of better housing annexed to a larger farm, and for others there would be paid employment, but often seasonal or part-time. For others it spelt even worse poverty as the 'free' commons were lost to a new generation of improving landowners and newly rich farmers. Very often, topographers and other writers of the time ignored and overlooked the condition and even the existence of these poor people. Sometimes the evidence remains in the landscape today in place names and field names such as Poor's Piece, Poor Lands, etc. Often though, the march of progress has swept aside most of the physical connections to the past and its people. The poor themselves, displaced from their lands, drifted to regional market towns and then to the great cities that grew out of the Industrial Revolution. In the words of a long-forgotten fenland ballad-monger:

> In Holland, in the fenny lands,
> Be sure you mark where Croyland stands.
> Croyland wine is but so-so,
> Sedge instead of hay doth grow,
> A bed like stone whereon to lie,
> And so begone, without 'Goodbye'.

THE NORTHERN FEN OF YORKSHIRE AND NORTH LINCOLNSHIRE

In the early 1960s, Alice Garnett, a geographer at Sheffield University, was one of the first authors to write of the 'Humber Fen' and the 'Humber Levels'. She described how the landscape to the east of the exposed coalfield of South Yorkshire changed markedly at the point where the River Don runs through the Don Gorge for around 4 miles (6.4km), cutting through the dramatic 300-400ft (90-120km) Magnesian Limestone Ridge that runs north / south. At the western end is the great Norman Conisbrough Castle, guarding the strategically important point of the river and route ways north to south, and east to west. This is the land of Sir Walter Scott and of *Ivanhoe*. Our wetlands lie east of here, where the river opens out into a low, broad plain of the Humberhead Levels that remain from the once great proglacial Lake Humber. The land surface is covered by postglacial deposits of drift or mud (boulder clay) and alluvium from early watercourses that meandered across this vast featureless plain in prehistory. The consequences for the landscape which evolved over time until recently, was an expansive, waterlogged or wet area with few obvious features to stand out. Most of the land is or was around 25ft (7.5km) or less above sea level; and much is at or around the contemporary modern sea level.

Garnett goes on to describe the remains of ancient peat bogs, now mostly drained, around Thorne and Hatfield Moors. She notes how, over long periods of prehistoric and historic times, much of the region was lake or fen, with just a few islands on the Keuper and Bunter Sandstones rising above the fenland around Thorne. The only other dry surfaces were on out-wash delta deposits of sands and gravels. It was on these rare zones of dry, or at least drier, land that human settlement was possible. The Roman road north from London diverted to follow these stepping-stones across the fen and marsh, resulting in the Roman station at Doncaster being on the lowest solid ground where it was possible to construct a crossing over river and wetland. The fenland itself was valued by fishermen and fowlers, and by those seeking respite from persecution and sanctuary from the law. In its later periods, from Saxon times onwards, much of the region was preserved as a royal hunting chase. This process, and the more detailed account of settlement patterns and uses, are described later.

The great wetland extended beyond the region called the Humberhead Levels today and beyond that used by Garnett in the 1960s. In the north, the fenland extended along the Derwent and Ouse to York and up the Hull Valley into Holderness, and in the south, it sent fingers of wetland and marsh along the Trent Valley and the Ancholme in north Lincolnshire. Taken together with the Vale of Pickering, these made up what I call the Northern Fens, and it was not until the drainage schemes of the early seventeenth century that the region's wetland landscape was significantly changed. The works of Vermuyden and his 'Adventurers' (as they were sneeringly called by the seventeenth-century fenmen who smashed their sluices and pulled down their dykes) and then of those who followed, changed the landscape from a wetland, with the Rivers Don, Torne, and Idle meandering over a vast flatland between the great Rivers Ouse and Trent, to one of productive farmland. The Don was diverted north along the new Dutch River to the Ouse confluence at Goole. The Idle and the Torne were taken into new channels to the Trent north of Axholme. Then, with pumping by windmills and the practice of warping (described on p. 142), the land was transformed into productive farmland and dispersed settlements and farmsteads. Through the 1800s and 1900s there followed further and more effective drainage of the remaining fens and marshes, and the improvement and under-drainage of much of the farmland. This process, as we shall see towards the end of our story, continued largely unabated until the 1990s. By the late twentieth century, even the memories of this once great wetland were erased from the corporate mental maps of the region.

THE SOUTHERN FEN OF CAMBRIDGESHIRE AND LINCOLNSHIRE

In 1961, A.T. Grove of the University of Cambridge described the characteristic landscape of the Southern Fenland as over 1,200 square miles (1920km) of land below the water level when the spring tides flood into the Wash and then run up the Rivers Nene, Witham, Welland, and Great Ouse. Running down the coastline along the eastern shore of the Wash is a belt of farmland about 2 miles (3.2km) across that has been reclaimed from the sea. This is overlooked by the old cliff from the low sandy hills of Sandringham and Snettisham to beyond King's Lynn as far as Denver. Cross over the Wash, and extensive marshes and mudflats flank the Lincolnshire coastline of Lindsey. These Lincolnshire coastal marshes merge into the now largely drained Fen running from the East Coast along the broad valley of the River Witham close to Lincoln. At the Steeping River, this wetland was around 7 miles across and grew to nearly 10 miles (16km) by the time it reached Boston. Moving further south, beyond the River Witham, were the former wetland areas of Holland, the lands around the Isle of Ely, and the once extensive wetlands in Huntingdonshire, across Cambridgeshire, and parts of western Norfolk, even into Suffolk. Much of this was former wetland, and extensive areas are today below sea level. Though now drained, this landscape remains one of the most regionally distinct areas in Britain. There is relatively little obvious variation across much of the area; the major changes being from the coastal siltlands nearer the Wash, to the peat fens further inland. Nowadays much of the peat has disappeared anyway.

In the times just after the most recent Ice Age, the sea was about 100ft (30m) lower than it is today. The fenland basin and the surrounding lands were drained by a number of rivers that ran across a broad, shallow valley which ran north-east between the chalk uplands of Lincolnshire and north Norfolk. It then flowed out into a tiny proto-North Sea. As noted later, various rocks and geological formations outcropped above the valley-bottom sediments and around the periphery of what is now the fenland. River and marine gravels and sands mark out this early landscape in the Fens of today. Some of the higher ground, such as in the Northern Fen, would have been covered with a forest of oak and pine. This was lost at an early stage as sea level and the water-table rose, and perhaps through human influence too. In both the Northern and Southern Fens 'bog oaks' have long been a feature of the reclaimed fens. As peat developed and grew above the surrounding land, the surface was colonised by trees and shrubs such as alder, willow and birch. On drier ground, oak and hazel became established. Inundation by the sea, such as in Neolithic times, caused dieback of the woodland and whole areas were left under thick deposits of marine clays and silts. Sedge peats then began to grow again over this clay layer and over the earlier peats, and often had relatively high alkali content due to their feeder streams coming off the chalk uplands. South of Whittlesea, the conditions suited the development of acidic peats and a massive raised bog developed, similar to the features that dominated the pre-drainage landscape of Thorne and Hatfield Moors in the Northern Fens. The southerly parts of the Southern Fens also retained large areas of open water and the conditions led to the formation of deposits known as 'shelly marls'. It seems that by the Bronze Age, much of the Southern Fen was relatively dry, and archaeological finds indicate settlement on the higher and drier zones. However, changes in climate, sea level and drainage conditions caused deterioration and the landscape became wetter into the Iron Age. By the Roman period, the coastline was some 10 miles (16km) or so inland from where it is today. Topographic and archaeological evidence suggest colonisation at this time and some reclamation of coastal marshes. However, it is also clear that at the same time there were significant depositions and accumulations of alluvium along the rivers and down the artificially created channels. This process produced an accretion of materials as the watercourses entered the Wash, and one consequence was a ponding up and a backing up of water flowing downstream from inland.

These general trends in deposition and drainage influenced subsequent human colonisation as communities moved into the region to eke out a living in this environment between land and water. The early Saxon settlements, for example, were along the coastline of the Wash, located on a chain of low sandy islands mostly only a couple of miles across. In the north-western part, these ran to Boston, and south to Wisbech and on to King's Lynn. From these coastal settlements expansion occurred in two directions. One was a coastal pathway made by the embanking and reclamation of salt marsh from the sea, and the other was inland into the fens, which involved localised drainage and embanking to prevent flooding by freshwater. The marine alluvium of the silt fens is now about 10ft (3km) or so above sea level. However, following drainage and drying, the peat fens have shrunk and now lie at or below mean sea level.

As discussed later, the drainage of the Southern Fens was very complex, involving many centuries of piecemeal works, and efforts both small-scale and large-scale, to overcome the difficulties presented by the vast flatland. Several problems complicated the whole process of drainage and reclamation, and then of colonisation and settlement of the land. The latter included the independence and stubbornness of the native fenlanders and the need for political control and economic resources in order to achieve effective drainage. The former included the fundamental difficulties of the expansive flat landscape, the rivers silting up at their outfalls, the potential risks of marine inundation, and the high flood levels of the rivers that ran across the fenland but which drained huge catchments inland as far as Lincoln, Luton, and Leicester. One consequence is that almost every river has been modified, straightened and canalised into raised embankments.

The Car Dyke running westwards from Waterbeach on the Granta towards the early line of the Ouse, then went from Peterborough to Lincoln, along the western boundary of the great fenland. This was a Roman construction, perhaps in part for drainage but probably with a principal role of military transport, boats being facilitated to move from Cambridge to Lincoln, and then via the Foss Dyke and the River Trent, northwards to the major settlement of York. The old path of the River Nene is followed by the Cat's Water and the county boundary from the Isle of Ely to Holland in Lincolnshire. The medieval river was 'cut' through the Isle of March with an artificial channel to join the old course of the Granta and Ouse at Upwell. The so-called 'roddons' are low silty ridges that mark out the paths of the ancient watercourses across the Southern Fenland. Here, meandering across the ancient black peat fens, the river system converged on an estuary outfall to the Wash at Wisbech or Ousebeach. When the Bedford Ouse diverted south of the Isle of Ely this was changed and then altered dramatically by the late medieval work to take the combined flow of the Granta and Ouse, and the Nene, along the Well Creek and then into the Wash at King's Lynn. The south-eastern boundary between Norfolk and Suffolk and the Isle of Ely follows the line of a roddon that was the bed of the River Little Ouse back in the medieval period.

Until the later medieval times, the landscapes of the Southern Fens were 'improved' piecemeal. River diversions, embankments, and new channels were constructed, and lands were drained. Nevertheless, reclamation was only partially successful and there remained the ever-present threats of both coastal and inland flooding. With problems inherent in any attempt at a wholesale approach to the task, and only limited co-ordination, large tracts of the fens lay out of the grasp of would-be reclaimers. The most comprehensive attempts at drainage and improvement had been by the Romans and then by the monasteries. With rivers silting up, storm damage and surges, and the collapse of poorly maintained banks, the situation remained problematic until the seventeenth century. Henry VIII dissolved the monasteries and their assets were dispersed to a new generation of landowners. These landowners, combined with opportunist businessmen in London and investors from overseas, saw the potential opportunities to be gained by the wresting of the fenlands from the waters.

The Duke of Bedford's proposals to drain the Great Level were supported by other 'gentlemen Adventurers', and were to be implemented by the Dutch engineer Cornelius Vermuyden. The solution was considered to lie in the straightening of the old meandering watercourses and the facilitation of their discharge swiftly to the Wash. So the Old Bedford River was excavated in 1637 and took water from the River Ouse, north-east from Earith to Salter's Lode. This was effective at freeing much of the land from summer flooding and allowing its use for grazing, though often not in winter. Fourteen years after this, the New Bedford River was also cut and ran parallel to the old one, leaving the land in-between as a holding reservoir for excess water at times of flood. This is the Ouse Washes and remains today as a series of major nature reserves. Tong's Drain was cut, and St John's Eau was cut to shorten the Ouse from Denver to Stowbridge. Popham's Eau led water from the Nene to the Ouse below Denver and the Forty Foot Drain joined the Bedford River. By this stage, the major changes in the main arterial drainage channels had been made, and they can still be seen today across the now agricultural fenland. The waters had not yet been altogether subdued, but with a new order imposed, landscape and much else from earlier millennia were changed forever.

With problems of silting river-mouths and shrinking peat in the Southern Fens of Cambridgeshire and south Lincolnshire, the general wetness of the landscape and occasional catastrophic floods remained. Gradually, however, individual landowners supplemented the bigger projects with their own pumping schemes, often through independent Commissions of Drainage. The River Boards had the task of ensuring that the water then got away to the sea, in this case the Wash. Thus, through this period, there was a gradual improvement in the drainage of the Southern Fens but, until the eighteenth century, large areas around Ely, lands between Whittlesea and March, and peatlands north of the Rivers Glen and Witham, were still often drowned in winter and thus problematic for agriculture. In 1773, Kinderley's Cut, and from Wisbech the River Nene, effectively took water off the North Level. This had the effect of lowering water levels in the drains in the south and west. North of the Wash, the extensive East and West Wildmore Fens were still very wet. Here and elsewhere, the high prices of grain stimulated by the Napoleonic Wars were the financial incentive for active reclamation.

The Southern Fen's largest remaining stretch of open water was Whittlesey or Whittlesea Mere, which survived until 1853 (regarded by many as the date of the completion of the drainage of the Southern Fenland). However, the process of drainage and land improvement continued literally to mop up the remaining sites, as we shall see later, and to drain more effectively the wider landscape. During the middle and late twentieth century, both the Southern and Northern Fens were further drained and improved as intensive farming grew, with petrochemical-dependent agriculture based on artificial fertilisers subsidised by UK government funds and then EU grants. By the 1960s and 1970s, almost no real fenland remained in the Southern Fens. The few exceptions were the patches of habitat such as the nature reserves at Wicken Fen, Holme Fen, and Woodwalton Fen, but of these, only Wicken really represents how the old fens might have looked.

One problem for the remaining sites, which are small in comparison with the original extent of fenland, but quite large compared to many nature reserves, is that the traditional activities that helped shape the fens have generally ceased. For centuries, these were cultural landscapes where nature and people interacted, generally in a long-term sustainable way, but the traditions have been lost and the old communities dissipated. The result is that the character of the fenland has been irrevocably changed and much biodiversity has been lost forever. Wicken shows some signs of the ancient wilderness but the lack of cultural traditional management means that ecological change known as succession takes place. Attempts to maintain some of the traditions help, but these are mostly at the level of being demonstrations rather than having the complexity and intensity of the subsistence management of earlier centuries. There is still a feel of wild nature across much of the fenland, often due to the 'big sky' of the open flat landscape. In addition, if you go to the mudflats and marshes of the Wash beyond the sea walls, albeit artificially created, there is a feel of real wilderness and wild nature. Across the bulk of the fenland itself the ghost of the primeval fen has faded, much peat has wasted and more is lost each year. The sites of now dry meres with their shell marl stand out across the landscape. In much of the fenland with the peat lost, the agriculture cultivates the clays and the lower sands, and, over time, further distinctiveness is eroded. The perched rivers and straight drains bear testimony to the processes of reclamation, and the grand churches and their villages to the affluence of the post-reclamation farming.

With the introduction of steam pumps in the early nineteenth century, the technological difficulties in achieving a drained landscape were largely overcome. Over time, diesel oil, and then electricity, replaced steam. Yet there have still been catastrophic floods during the twentieth century, with the obvious examples of 1947 and then 1953. The latter was due to a storm surge which caused the River Ouse to break its banks and overflow between Denver and the Wash. The more general threat is from spring floods hitting higher levels further south. Whilst the North Level was significantly protected from floods by the cut made in 1832, and the problems of the Middle Level were largely resolved by a major pumping station constructed at Wiggenhall St Germans in 1934, the South Level remained vulnerable until well into the twentieth century. Despite it being the most distant from the sea, it flooded badly in 1937 and 1939, and then again in 1947. The latter was one of the most catastrophic floods in history, when rapid snow thaw after heavy snow and then rain resulted in swollen rivers, which could not discharge into the sea due to extreme high tides. The waters backed up and the rivers burst their banks to spectacular effect. The consequence was a flood extending over 37,000 acres (14,973 hectares) to the east of Earith. Detailed assessments in the aftermath of the disaster suggested that a recurrence could easily occur unless drastic action was taken to improve the rate of discharge of the Rivers Ouse / Granta at Denver. With this in mind, a scheme began in 1956 with a straight channel cut from just above the Denver Sluice to an outfall to the tidal river above King's Lynn. Interestingly, this action was rather similar to part of the solution that Cornelius Vermuyden had proposed centuries earlier, but finance did not permit the works to be undertaken. By the time the project was commissioned in the late 1950s, the costs were around £12 million, but the works dramatically reduced the risks of major floods in the future. Over the whole area of the Fens, the process of reclamation and of drainage continued, along with protection against flooding. Between the mid-1940s and the late 1950s, a further 5 square miles (8km²) of tidal lands around the Wash were reclaimed as part of the post-war rush towards self-sufficiency. In A.T. Grove's account in the early 1960s, the possible reclamation of the entire Wash was discussed, perhaps to include a whole new town or even a speedway racing track. Interestingly, in terms of perceptions, the final comment is that whilst this might not happen because of the technical difficulties, it would 'bring the evolution of the fenland region to a fitting conclusion'.

THE PROCESS OF PEAT WASTING AND THE EVIDENCE OF THE HOLME POST

It is suggested that prior to the draining the peat was around 10ft (3m) above mean sea level. After the peat fens were drained, the surface shrank and wasted with a rate of approximately

2ft (0.6m) every ten years. The initial loss of volume and hence elevation was due to shrinkage as a direct result of the removal of water. After this early phase there is further loss due to wasting of peat by bacterial breakdown, and then by physical blowing away of the desiccated material. Just south of the former Whittlesea Mere is the Holme Post, driven into the peat surface in 1851 (or according to some authors 1850 or 1852), just two years before the drainage of the mere by William Wells, the local squire who was one of the architects of the drainage and who wanted to gauge the impact of shrinkage. The iron post was taken from Crystal Palace and sunk to its top in the deep peat. The impact of the Whittlesea drainage was immediately obvious and by 1860 the top of the post was a good 5ft (1.5m) above the ground surface. By 1892, there was 10ft (3m) protruding, though after this time the wastage appeared to slow. This may have been because the more easily dried and eroded upper peats had been exhausted, but additionally because of changes in land use close to the post. Land nearby, abandoned from cultivation, was colonised by birch wood, and then became the Holme Fen Nature Reserve.

Across the wider fenland, however, the peat erosion has continued unabated, to expose clays and sands lying beneath it. The fastest and most drastic erosion, for the reasons already given, often occurred soon after initial drainage. Another reason for this was that early reclamation often included the process of 'paring and burning' prior to cultivation. In this, the upper surface of materials was cut or pared and then piled up to be burnt, the resulting ashes acting as fertiliser. The general rate of loss has been around an inch each year. In the south of the Holland district, the thin peats were mostly lost by the mid to late 1800s, leaving heavy clays exposed at the surface.

In the early 1800s, it was realised that the turning up of marly clays by the plough had a beneficial impact on soil texture and structure. Because of these observations, there was a move to add clay marl to the peat soils deliberately. This was achieved by digging parallel trenches to spread the marly clay over the peat, with around 100 tons of clay per acre of land. The impacts were found to last for at least a few decades, and importantly they included the reduction of wind erosion. However, and of greater long-term importance, the insidious loss of peat by bacterial oxidation remained unchecked. By 1974, the Holme Post stood proud about 12 to 13ft (3.6 to 3.9m) above the surrounding lands.

After reclamation, the deepest peats to be found were around the southern edges of the Fens, though even these areas are several feet less than their original depths. The impact can be seen in some areas, where the chalky beds of former meres stand proud above the surrounding fields of former peatlands. Roads, embankments and even railway lines have long been subject to severe problems of subsidence and require specially designed construction. Houses too have suffered. Where once there were flimsy owner-constructed shacks, hovels and cottages, there are now more robust structures. However, the early construction of these new dwellings did not always allow for the dramatic movement in land surface, especially where peat shrinkage has been uneven. Buildings designed for stable dry land toppled and cracked. As noted earlier, the most obvious manifestation of land shrinkage is in the rivers, drains and roads perched high above the surrounding fields. The complication for land management and agriculture is that the more the land sinks, the higher the water must be pumped to get it off the surface and into the main drains.

THE STORY OF THE DRAINAGE

This account tries to set down some of the key events, and to tease out some idea of what the great fens looked like pre-drainage. We set out to find out who was responsible and why these wetlands were destroyed. It also looks ahead and attempts to draw together some of the unexpected consequences of these 'improvements'. In the context of the twenty-first century, I consider the current initiatives to re-construct areas of functioning wetland ecosystems. This cannot be comprehensive, since there is simply too much ground to cover; but it aims at a new approach and a new awareness of both loss and of future potential. In particular, I have linked the two main fenland regions of eastern England, as the Northern Fens and the Southern Fens, to show how their histories and their environments are inextricably linked. I have written a description of how the great fens and other wetlands were seen by people, both local residents and those who visited. These perceptions, and the associated great fears of diseases such as the ague – not to mention the fears of those in political power, of dissention, unorthodoxy and unrest – helped drive the moves to destroy the wetlands and to assert human control over nature.

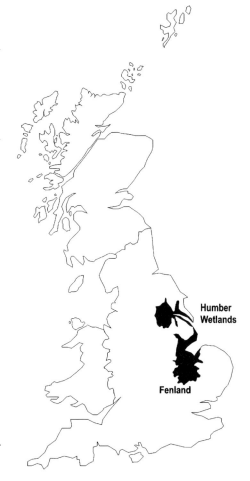

The east England fens.

The consequences of the changes wrought over three centuries probably constitute the greatest single loss of wildlife habitat in Britain and maybe in Europe. This was an ecological catastrophe almost beyond comprehension. At the end of the process, it is difficult to give any accurate figures for the scale of loss. For the reasons I explain in the book, there was the drainage of the great fens themselves, but also much wider peripheral and progressive drainage of surrounding lands too. For many of these areas we often have no perception now that they were indeed ever wet. However, a very rough estimate might be that in the Southern Fens of Lincolnshire, Huntingdonshire, and Cambridgeshire we have lost around 2,500 square miles (4,000km²). In the Northern Fens, the figure is perhaps slightly less, with around 1,900 square miles (3,000km²). This is just a very rough calculation but to put it into perspective, in the Southern Fen alone, it would amount to nearly half a million large football pitches' worth. When you read, at the end of the book, the work being done by bodies such as the National Trust to reinstate what are by today's standards large areas of wetland, it is worth bearing in mind how much we have lost.

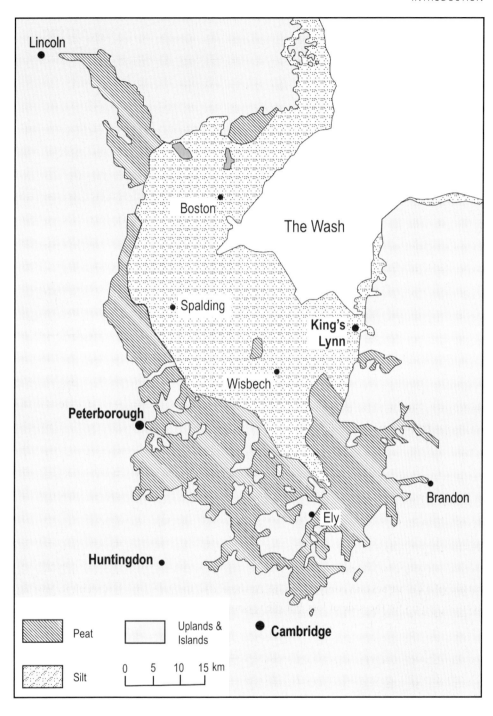

The Southern Fens.

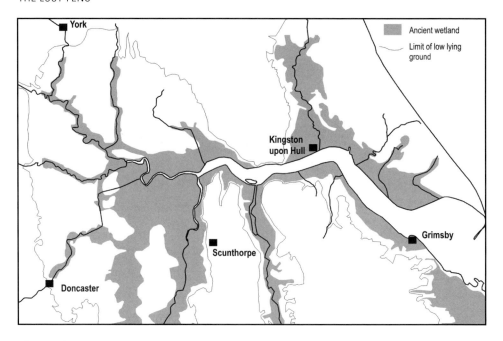

The Northern Fens.

Finally, and before we go on, it is important to realise that whilst the fens were being drained through the period from the 1630s to the 1980s, the wider landscape was also being 'improved' and desiccated. This is largely beyond the scope of this book, but if we turn our gaze fleetingly from the fen and marsh to the extensive farmlands of pasture and arable, the lowlands, heaths and commons, and the great upland moors and blanket bogs, all these lands have been intensively drained and mostly improved. Even to step inside an ancient woodland is often to pass over complex and intensive drainage networks. Through recent history, vast areas of land in countryside areas – and especially uplands – across Britain were desiccated deliberately and actively, and consequences include massive carbon release, catastrophic loss of biodiversity, and hugely increased flood-risk. This is a wider context for the fenland story. Turning back the drainage of the east England fens, this is the story of loss, but it must also be a vision for restoration where possible, and a salutary tale for the wetlands of the planet still to come under the eager and often pernicious gaze of the drainage engineer.

1

CHANGING PERCEPTIONS
OF THE FENS

Wetlands are not always, and for some not ever, the most pleasant of places. In fact, they have often been seen as horrific places. In the patriarchal western cultural tradition, wetlands have been associated with death and disease, the monstrous and the melancholic, if not, the downright mad. Wetlands are 'black waters'. They have even been seen as a threat to health and sanity, to the clean and proper body, and mind. The typical response to the horrors and threats posed by wetlands has been simple and decisive: dredge, drain or fill and so 'reclaim' them. Yet the idea of reclaiming wetlands begs the questions of reclaimed from what? For what? For whom? A critical history of wetlands' drainage could quite easily be entitled 'Discipline and Drain'.

Rod Giblett (1996)

In early modern Europe, fear and loathing of wetlands were major reasons for their loss. Especially for outsiders, these were places to avoid; and if you had to travel into or through them, then you had to do so with the utmost care and precaution. For landowners, these 'fenscapes' – neither of land nor water – were regions that needed to be tamed to generate wealth and to assert control. In 1629, one tract by William Lambarde urged the draining of the East Anglian Fens, describing them as sunk in 'water putred and muddy, yea full of loathsome vermin; the earth, spuing, unfast and boggie'. William Shakespeare set the scene in *King Lear* by describing these places shrouded in 'fen-sucked fogs drawn by the powerful sun'. They were unsafe, evil wastes, where drowning was common, corrupted waters or foul air could poison you, or travellers might be lost in their featureless expanses.

Contracting the 'ague' or marsh malaria was, until the late nineteenth century, believed to originate with the bad air (*mal-aria*) of these stagnant wetlands. Perceptions of the Fens influenced how we treated them in the past and they continue to do so today. Yet our basic perceptions and visions of fens are probably far from the truth. For us in the twenty-first century, these are truly lost landscapes and at the very least, they are David Lowenthal's 'foreign country', a description that applies to the Fens more perhaps than to anywhere else.

The landscape, once vast and intractable for hundreds of kilometres, has been entirely removed, its peoples displaced and dispossessed. Modern expectations of a 'fen' are based more on a visit to a nature reserve than anything approaching the reality of medieval fen. Open water and reed beds joined by networks of footpaths, boardwalks and conveniently placed hides give a very false impression. Only the biting, tormenting flies, the midges, mosquitoes and clegs, provide clues to the nature of the real wild fen.

Science and philosophy influence perceptions of landscapes such as fens and other peatlands, as do the need for, and the capability of, exploitation. Subsistence peoples such as those in medieval England relied on their local environment for sustenance; a relationship at the core of their very being. Local fenland communities were, in every sense, immersed in their fens. This bonding of people and nature ties with the economic and political systems that may enable or prevent co-ordinated use or organised preservation. In Judaeo-Christian societies too, there is a strong religious imperative of a moral duty for landowners and farmers to 'improve' their lands. In the fens, this is traceable to the 'improvements' of the later 1600s, but in truth it extends back to the era of monastic land management, even before Domesday.

Other drivers to improve and exploit included personal financial problems, often following political unrest (such as the English Civil War), and corporate need to feed an expanding urbanised and industrial population during the 1700s and 1800s. In other cases, a wish to remove and expose political or religious dissidents impelled the desire to improve and drain. For fenlands and associated wildlife habitats such as bogs, carrs, and heaths, these perceptions have been hugely important. They influenced the views of visitors, landowners, and politicians, and so affected attitudes to the use and exploitation of these areas. Deeply ingrained attitudes and perceptions also affected the perceptions of, and attitudes towards, the local people, who were often viewed as wild and indolent savages. The unkempt appearance, the ravages of the ague, and the resort to laudanum as a cure for this in the eighteenth and nineteenth centuries, all did little to sway such opinions. Strange peoples speaking unintelligible dialects populated these wild places; a foreign country indeed.

A fear of wilderness and especially of wetlands ran deep in the medieval human psyche. In the absence of organised, modern science, there was only limited pseudo-science, magic, myth and folklore to inform people. Most knowledge was from much-altered Greek and Roman philosophers. With the dawning of 'The Enlightenment', there were further problems for wetland environments as the French intellectual, Buffon, and others concluded that deforestation and other land improvements had and would bring benefits to Europe's climate. This disadvantaged wetlands since 'waste' lands were considered to result from over-exploitation and tree removal, and supposedly needed to be brought back into civilisation. Buffon promoted the idea of 'civilised' landscapes; in North America, this involved transforming aboriginal landscapes through clearance, drainage, and farming. Through these ideas, Buffon's philosophy was part of a long-term shift in human attitudes to wilderness and wetlands, and this ultimately led to the ideas of 'improvement' which ran so deeply through the 1700s, 1800s and 1900s. Fenlands and their component ecosystems of meres, bogs, carrs, heaths, and fens were 'waste' lands. As such, it was a human and indeed Christian duty to draw them into civilisation, to subject them to the plough, and to bring them under cultivation. Landowners with an eye on their pockets and potential profits enthusiastically received such a view. Furthermore, for landowners, orthodox religion, and central government, the removal of wetlands allowed wild and culturally remote landscapes and people to be brought into a condition of control, accessibility and accountability.

Local people often had other ideas. The fenlands had long been sanctuaries for the independently minded and the resourceful. Living by the water's edge can provide rich pickings if you are prepared to work with nature and adapt to her vagaries. The people here may have been poor in the view of outsiders, but they were rarely hungry. The fen provided fowl, fish, grazing and hay for livestock, and plentiful supplies of fuels and building materials. These were all free for the taking. By medieval times, the areas were carefully divided up between communities organised in discrete villages, each with jealously guarded common rights. Therefore, by then, anyone coming into the land without existing common rights would struggle and meet resentment. Those such as landowners who might wish to change land-use and therefore diminish the common benefits for personal gain would also get a very frosty reception. Thus by the time of the would-be improvers, these extensive lands of apparent wilderness, but in reality managed cultural landscapes, were set to be disputed spaces of the first order. The loss or even diminishment of common rights spelt the extinction of established communities, and these dour but resourceful and independent people could be counted on to resist all imposed change.

Contemporary observers of bogs and fen often linked the abhorrent nature of the physical environment to the moral character of its inhabitants. Hence, Arthur Young, a prolific writer and commentator on agriculture writing in 1799, explained the depredations of sheep thieves in Lincolnshire by stating that 'so wild a country nurses up a race of people as wild as the fen'. Certainly, in the second half of the eighteenth century, Romney Marsh, for instance, swarmed with armed smugglers. Politically too, wetlands provided a refuge for outlaws and for violent resistance to government, a breeding ground for the anti-drainage violence of the seventeenth-century 'fen tigers'. However, in England, the main source of social and political conflict in the wetlands of the seventeenth and eighteenth centuries was land rights. This habitually manifested in peasants challenging attempts to appropriate, clear or drain areas traditionally considered common land. This 'wasteland' provided grazing for small numbers of livestock but was also a source of water, fuel (often as peat), or bedding in the form of rushes or reeds.

Dugdale, in the 1700s, described the Fen country as: 'For the space of many years until of late years, a vast and deep Fen affording little benefit to the realm other than Fish and Fowl, with over much harbour to a rude and beggarly people.' A further issue for these great landscapes of waterscapes is that they are flat and expansive. They are truly 'big sky' landscapes, and this appeals to some but frightens or bores others. For some, they can impress beyond words and for others can depress beyond description. When Harry Godwin (later Sir Harry Godwin), Cambridge botanist and pioneer of palaeobotanical approaches in ecology, began his twentieth-century studies, this issue was raised. His remark to a local fenman that he considered the Cambridgeshire area 'singularly flat' promoted the reply: 'any fool can appreciate mountain scenery, it takes a man of discernment to appreciate the Fens.' This too affects how this area, its landscape, wildlife, and wilderness have been considered and viewed over the centuries.

In the sixteenth century, William Camden noted that the country between Lincoln and Cambridge was 'a vast morass, inhabited by fenmen, a kind of people, according to the nature of the place where they do dwell, who, walking high upon stilts, apply their minds to grazing, fishing, or fowling.' The stilts, like those used in the Low Countries, were essential to traverse the wetlands and importantly to scan for a distance around. In the Low Countries, they were watching for their flocks of sheep; in the Fens at this time it was generally their geese, the 'fenman's treasure'.

How we view, appreciate and even fear these great 'black waters' has influenced their fate over millennia; for some they provide sanctuary, for others unrest. For some they are a magnificent wet and wild landscape, and for others they are miserable wastes; they evoke strong views with little in-between. William Dugdale, writing in 1662, asked:

> … And what expectation of health can there be to the bodies of men, where there is no element good? The air being for the most part cloudy, gross, and full of rotten harrs; the water putrid and muddy, yea, full of loathsome vermin; the earth spungy and boggy, and the fire noisome by the stink of smoky hassocks.

THE AGUE – WHAT THE ROMANS DID FOR US

Malaria was a major contribution to the decline and fall of the Roman Empire, brought back to the Mediterranean heartland by troops who made incursions into Africa and the Middle East. Probably first Greek troops and then the Romans contracted malaria in the swamps around Egypt and North Africa. It was brought back and thrived in swampy lands such as the Pontine Marshes around Rome and other Italian cities. Then, via this route, the Roman legionnaires brought the disease to Britain and so to the Fens, and here it wreaked havoc for over 1,000 years. The same legionnaires also brought a piece of novel technology that was to help change the fenland landscape: the metal spade. This was a standard part of Roman military equipment and was ultimately the key tool in the great drainage.

The ague was a fever (such as from malaria) that is marked by paroxysms of chills, fever, and sweating recurring at regular intervals. It was also used to describe a fit of shivering, a chill; and so can mean either a chill or a fever. It was pronounced 'A-(") gyü, with the accent solidly on the 'A'. The word 'ague' is an example of how medical terminology changes with time. Not only are new terms introduced (with great speed these days) but old terms such as 'ague' may decline in usage (become archaic) and eventually may be dropped entirely (be obsolete). 'Aigue' entered English usage in the fourteenth century, having crossed the Channel from the Middle French 'aguë'. The word actually shares the same origin as 'acute' and is from the Latin 'acutus', meaning 'sharp or pointed'. A 'fievre aigue' in French, for example, was a sharp or pointed (or acute) fever. Even in the late 1900s, Julie Smith, then a health visitor, recalled mothers around Mansfield in Nottinghamshire describing their children having 'aguey fits', i.e. shivering and a temperature. In Sheffield, when at school in the 1960s and '70s, we described a boy who had uncontrollable laughter as a having an 'eccy fit', i.e. uncontrolled shaking.

'Ague cake' was an enlargement of the spleen produced by ague. Ague drop, a solution of the arsenite of 'potassa' (the salt of potassium oxide, or caustic potash with arsenious acid), was used as a treatment for ague. An ague fit was a fit of the ague with temperature, chills and shivering. An ague spell was a spell or charm against the ague. The sassafras (an American tree of the laurel family) was sometimes called the ague tree, due to the former use of its roots in cases of ague.

Strange folklore and medicines were employed in the fen areas to combat the ague and to treat its morbid effects. It was said that there was scarcely an old woman in the fens who did not have an infallible cure for the ague. Superstition directed the sufferer to cut a number of rods according to the hour at which the ague struck, so five o'clock, five rods, etc. These were burnt individually and as this was done, the patient and the healer chanted 'as the rods burn, so let the ague burn too'. Other treatments included attaching a lock of the patient's hair to a tree and then pulling it with a sudden wrench to leave it attached to the tree and not to the scalp. If that failed you could eat a common spider wrapped in a raisin, either during the cold fit, or else on three successive mornings. The spider was supposed to be gently bruised or what contemporary chefs now describe as 'distressed'. So first, distress your spider, gently wrap it in a raisin and swallow. You could hang distressed spiders around your neck or place them in a nutshell as a box so 'they drew into themselves the contagious air that would otherwise infect a person'. You might also try five grains of cobwebs mixed with crumbs of bread taken twice a day, or a bean containing small stinking worms and bedbugs. Failing all these, then half a pint of the patient's urine, taken three times, should do the trick.

In the fenland areas, ague was a persistent problem and it called for desperate cures. The Revd James Woodforde combined shock and alcohol to cure a child of the ague. This was a shot of gin followed by being thrown headlong into the pond. Whether it worked is not recorded. A soldier was tried for murder when he accidentally shot a fenland child in the head. He was trying to frighten away the ague by letting off his gun close to the child's head, but was too close and blew the patient's brains out. No doubt it cured the ague.

A more pragmatic response to the persistent illness was opium. The East Anglian Fens had some of the highest opium use in the country. The people of the marshlands used laudanum, a mixture of opium and alcohol. Opium was reputed to cure fits and ague shiverings if 'given in due time and quantity'. Children were given 'poppy-head tea' as a cure for the ague.

THE WIDER CONTEXT TO THE ENGLISH FENS: EUROPEAN WETLANDS AND THEIR PEOPLE

Formerly widespread, fens and bogs provided refuge and sustenance for indigenous communities and individuals escaping the law or persecution. Across all the coastal wetlands in north-western Europe, from Roman times to the medieval, there was a history of cultural transformation of these wild areas. There were close spatial and cultural relationships between, for example, the northern French peatlands and the Low Countries. Peat grew from around 1800 BC in Dutch Rijnland and these areas were considered 'wilderness beyond the realm of normal human affairs, where the imprint of culture, if it existed at all, was fleeting and inconsequential'. This description would have applied to all extensive wetlands across Western Europe, and the only serious, coordinated attempts at drainage came with the Romans and ended with the fall of the Roman Empire. Thereafter, until the medieval period, there were only local and half-hearted schemes of land improvement and drainage.

By the 1300s, this altered dramatically, with reclamation and settlement unseen since Roman times and exceeding earlier attempts. Pristine wilderness was altered and nature controlled and integrated into mainstream human affairs. The processes and impacts relating to these changes generated huge social and ecological consequences, with tensions running deep within the landscape and its people. The necessary skills were scarce commodities to be exported between countries such as Holland and England, and social tensions followed. This occurred along the North Sea coasts in particular, and further south in France too. Then, following problems such as bubonic plague when abandonment of farmland followed depopulation, and marginal environments were re-wilded. However, after 1500 there was recovery and population growth, and once again the 'wastes' were encroached upon. In some regions, particularly around the Mediterranean, market forces led to abandonment of former cultivation. Locally, such as in central southern Italy for example, arable land reduced and extensive wetlands re-established. These soon became abandoned lands, unhealthy swamps and malaria-infested floodplains.

A problem of bog or fen is that it is neither land nor water: it is both. There are deep tensions over ownership, resources and perceptions. In 1927, Alphonse de Châteaubriant provided a passionate account of the forces and conflicts in the saturated landscape when change threatens ancient rights. Although set in France, it could be England, Scotland, the Netherlands or elsewhere; the issues and emotions transgress regional and national boundaries. The attempted drainage of England's fens suppressing long-held common rights was significant in precipitating the English Civil War. In the Humberhead Fens of north Lincolnshire and South Yorkshire, antagonism between local commoners and Dutch 'engineers' ran deep for decades.

We see these attitudes and issues in the writings of the various ages. For example, Arthur Young, who was one of the driving forces behind the ideas and practicalities of 'agricultural improvement', in his *Political Essays* (1772), set down views on agriculture and issues such as the improvement of wastes, breaking up of wastes, and draining of fens and bogs. The latter he linked to wider issues of draining of 'common wet land both pasture and arable'. Developing the themes in detail, he highlighted the public benefits of such acts, and the potential for enhanced social status and private income of enlightened landowners. He addressed the benefits of enclosures and of land improvements through: 'Breaking up Wastes etc.', 'Breaking up uncultivated lands' (on p. 118 picking faults with a French commentator), and then on 'Inclosing of open lands', 'Marling', 'Chalking', 'Liming', 'Burning', and 'Draining Fens etc.'. He travelled extensively in Europe and entertained European visitors at his home in Suffolk, from where they set out on travels across Britain to survey the land and its management. Spurred on by writers like Young, ideas and approaches were widely exchanged during the eighteenth and nineteenth centuries as emerging science and technology helped drive on the forces of 'improvement'. Arthur Young states:

There can be little doubt but the converting of waste tracts of land into profitable farms ought to be one of the first undertakings in the great business of improvement; for from thence results the increase of food, population, and riches.

This goes further, as he suggests that:

The royal forests, and other wastes, should be immediately inclosed in such divisions, that those parts which are covered with grown timber may be preserved to that use, and others, in which young trees are growing, divided off for the same purpose, the open parts would then remain which should be struck into inclosed farms, and let to the best advantage.

This is the view that Young took with him on his tours, and which influenced his interaction, for example, with his French friends. One can imagine how, in his home area of Suffolk, he passed on his views of the landscape to his visitors. François de La Rochefoucauld described Brandon in Suffolk:

I think the most driving, barren, and desolate tracts of land I ever met with, are crossed by the roads leading between Barton Mills and Brandon, and Bury and Brandon in Suffolk; but these are terribly loose and dry in their present state, and in a windy day fill the air with clouds of them. I instance these particularly, because I am fully persuaded that inclosing them and planting a certain quantity, would so far change the nature of the worst of them, as to make them fertile enough to yield good crops of corn, turnips, and grasses. Every one who is acquainted with those tracts of country, will be sensible what a prodigious improvement this would be.

Drainage was a key agricultural problem that was only partly solved during Young's lifetime. Approaches to water management and farming had exercised farmers' minds and ingenuity for centuries, and consequently these issues assumed an importance in politics and the economy hard to imagine today. In 1797, when Young was active on the Board of Agriculture, one particular authority on drainage, Joseph Elkington, was awarded £1,000 (then a fortune) for his 'Mode of Draining' in order to promote the knowledge to others. Writing in 1811, Young in his essay 'On the Husbandry of Three Celebrated British Farmers: Messrs Bakewell, Arbuthnot, and Ducket', described the processes of comparison and evaluation between Flanders, the Netherlands, and England, and their transfer, implementation and monitoring in Essex. He noted the problems in draining farmland, the observations of Arbuthnot, and subsequent implementation of the Flemish system in Essex, and its success. Young comments on his journeys to inspect farming approaches in 1784:

Returned home, finishing a little journey, instructive from a variety of intelligence I received and pleasing from the conversation and politeness of my companions, who, I have no doubt, are convinced of the real importance of attending to the agriculture of the countries through which they may have occasion to travel.

His companion François de La Rochefoucauld described the uncultivated lands of the Norfolk Brecks as 'twenty miles or so of wretched land we drove through that day', expressing surprise at the amount of unenclosed common lands still present 'even at the gates of the capital'. He continued, 'These lands are for the most part enormously extensive and are no use for anything but the sheep of those parishioners who have a right to send them there [i.e. common rights]: worse, they are sometimes so overgrown with bracken that they are good for absolutely nothing.' François identifies reasons why land remained unenclosed, including multiple ownership and local public opinion, 'the last and most persuasive reason is that the prime mover can always be sure of making himself unpopular, because the poor have, from time immemorial, the right to cut the bracken and brushwood for firewood. People in this country fear unpopularity more than anything else.' Nevertheless, he goes on, 'It is widely reckoned that, each year, in England, seventy parishes are cleared and enclosed. In a few years from now all will be in proper cultivation: everyone is agreed about this.'

DESCRIPTIONS OF THE FENS

Charles Kingsley was a prolific and influential writer in Victorian England. In his *Prose Idylls*, quoted in the *Leisure Hour* of 26 May 1877, we have a different view of the Victorian Fens:

> Little thinks the Scotsman, whirled down by the Great Northern railway from Peterborough to Huntingdon, what a grand place, even twenty years ago, was that Holme and Whittlesea, which is now but a black unsightly steaming flat, from which the meres and reed-beds of the old world are gone, while the corn and roots of the new world have not as yet taken their place. But grand enough it was, that black ugly place, when backed by Caistor Hanglands and Holme Wood and the patches of primeval forest; while dark green alders, and pale green reeds, stretched for miles round the broad lagoon, where the coot clanked, and the bittern boomed, and the sedge-bird, not content with its own sweet song, mocked the notes of all the birds around; while high overhead hung motionless, hawk beyond hawk, buzzard beyond buzzard, kite beyond kite, as far as an eye could see. Far off, upon the silver mere, would rise a puff of smoke from a punt, invisible from its flatness and white paint. Then down the wind came the boom of the great stanchion gun; and after that sound, another sound, louder as it neared; a cry as of all the bells of Cambridge and all the hounds of Cottismore, and overhead rushed and whirled the skein of terrified wild-fowl, screaming, piping, clacking, croaking – filling the air with the hoarse rattle of their wings, while clear above all sounded the whistle of the curlew and the trumpet-note of the great wild swan. They are all gone now. No longer do the ruffs trample the sedge into a hard floor in their fighting rings, while the sober reeves stand round, admiring the tournament of their lovers, gay with ruffs and tippets, no two of them alike. Gone are ruffs and reeves, spoonbills, bitterns, avocets; the very snipe, one hears, disdains to breed. Gone too, not only from the Fens, but from the whole world, is that most exquisite of butterflies – Lycaena dispar – the great copper; and many a curious insect more.

An opinion of the Fens was presented in verse by Monk Lewis in the *Three Revellers; or Impiety Punished*:

In the bleak, noxious Fens which to Lincoln pertain,
Where agues exert their fell sway,
Where the bittern hoarse moans, and the se-mew complains
As she flits o'er the watery way;

While in strains thus discordant the natives of air
With shrieks and with screams the ear strike,
The toad and the frog, croaking notes of despair,
Join the din from the bog and the dyke.

… From fogs pestilential that hover around, fraught with gloom and with pain and disease,
The juice of the grape best repellent was found,
Source of comfort, of joy, and of ease.

The poem runs for twenty verses and all ends in tears as the three drunken, card-playing revellers are dragged into the night and to their tombs by three spectres. Some of the terrifying ordeals described by early visitors to the Fens may well be due to the effects of malarial fever. Dugdale, writing in the 1700s, quotes an earlier writer on the visit of St Gurlach to Crowland:

In the middle part of Britain there is a hideous fen of huge bigness, which extends in a very long track even to the sea, oftimes clouded with moist and dark vapours, having within it divers islands and woods, as crooked and winding rivers. When, therefore, that a man of blessed memory, Gurlach, had found out the desert places of this vast wilderness, he inquired of the borderers what they knew thereof. One amongst them, called Tatwaine, stood up amongst them, who affirmed that he knew a certain island in the more remote and secret parts thereof, which many had attempted to inhabit, but could not for the strange and uncouth monsters and several terrors wherewith they were affrighted, wherewith Gurlach earnestly entreated that he would show him that place. Tatwaine, therefore, yielding to the request of that holy man, taking a fishing-boat, led thereunto; it being called Crowland, and in respect to its desertness known to very few, by reason that apparitions of devils were so frequently seen there.

During the night, Gurlach became aware of his cell being:

… full of black troops of unclean spirits, which crept under the door, as also at chinks and holes, and coming both out of the sky and from the earth, filling the air, as it were, with dark clouds. In their looks they were cruel, and of form terrible – having great heads, ill-favoured beards, rough ears, wrinkled foreheads, fierce eyes, teeth like horses, swollen ankles, preposterous feet, and hoarse cries …

Worse was to come:

… who with such mighty shrieks were heard to roar, and by-and-by, rushing into the house, first bound the holy man, then drew him out of his cell, and cast him over head and ears into the dirty fen; and, having so done, carried him through the most rough and troublesome parts thereof, drawing him among brambles and briars for the tearing of his limbs.

Perhaps Gurlach had succumbed to an attack of the ague and was hallucinating. On the other hand, maybe he was being mugged by the locals. Or perhaps it was both.

Even the dwellings of the fenlanders were primitive. Heathcote (1876), quoting an early source, noted that the early settlements were:

> … small, rustical and wild; the fashion of their houses had changed little since the days of the ancient Britons. The houses or huts, were of round shape, and not unlike the forms of bee-hives. They had a door in front, and an opening at the top to let out the smoke, but window to let in the light there was none.

These houses had walls made of wattle and daub, and roofs of rushes or willow branches cut from the fens. Some of the better dwellings had stone foundations, rough stone pillars, and door 'traves'. Inside, the houses were adorned with hides of cattle, fleeces of sheep, skins of deer, and abounding feathers of 'fen-fowl'; all providing insulation and warmth. Furthermore, it was noted by writers that the area never lacked turf or wood. This was an important consideration during the so-called 'Little Ice Age', when cities like London suffered serious shortages of fuel.

Travel was challenging and the locals had their own methods, one of which was carrying a 'fen-pole', which had a heavy iron 'ferrule' at the end with long steel nails and spikes. This could be used to test boggy ground and to leapfrog over ditches. The causeways were generally good in summer but reduced to a 'morass' in winter. Miller and Skertchly (1878) described the view of the great, undrained fenland from Camden in their *Britannia*, noting the area around Crowland which:

> … lies amongst the deepest fennes and waters stagnating off muddy lands, so shut in and environn'd as to be inaccessible on all sides, except the north and east, and that by narrow causeys. In situation, we may compare small things with great, it is not unlike Venice, consisting of three streets, divided by canals of water, planted with willows, and built on piles driven into the bottom of the fen, and joined by a triangular bridge of admirable workmanship, under which, the inhabitants report, is a pit of immense depth dug to receive the confluence of waters.

Beyond the bridge on more solid ground stood the former Crowland monastery, but all around the town the ground was 'so moory' that a pole could be pushed in to a depth of 30ft or more and all that could be seen on all sides was rushes and a few alders. The account goes on to give an insight into the lives of the fenland people:

> It is notwithstanding, full of inhabitants, who keep their cattle at a good distance from the town, and go to milk them in little boats (called skerries) which will hold but two persons. But their chief profit arises from the catching of fish and wild fowle, which they do in such

quantities in the month of August they drive 3,000 ducks into one net, and call their pools their fields – no corn grows within five miles of them. On account of this fishery and catching of fowls they paid formerly to the abbot and now to the King 300l. sterling a year.

In the 1700s, Dugdale described the same region and noted how around Crowland:

> … By the inundation and overflowing of rivers the waters, standing upon the level ground, maketh a deep lake, and so rendereth it uninhabitable, excepting in high places, where the monks of Ramsey, Thorney, and Crowland reside; to which there is no access but by navigable vessels, except into Ramsey by a causey raised on the one side thereof. Within the same precincts also Ely is placed, being an island seven miles in length and the same in breadth, containing twenty-two towns, encompassed on every side by Fens and waters, and approachable only by three causeys.

Dr Adam Mercer (1505) described the Fens as 'one of the most brute and beastly of the whole realm, a land of marshy ague and unwholesome swamps'. Macaulay, in his *History of England*, suggested that the area between Cambridge and the Wash was:

> … a vast and desolate fen, saturated with all the moisture of thirteen counties, and overhung during the greater part of the year by a low grey mist, above which rose, visible many miles, the magnificent tower of Ely. In that dreary region, covered by vast flights of wild-fowl, a half-savage population, known by the name of breedlings, there led an amphibious life, sometimes wading, sometimes rowing, from one islet of firm ground to the other. The roads were amongst the worst in the island.

Crowland in winter. (Victorian print)

THE AGUE AND ENGLISH HISTORY

The problems of the ague clearly had a massive impact on perceptions of wetlands such as the Fens, and had a real effect on local people, causing misery and sometimes death. However, they had an even more drastic and direct impact through the death of key people in history. In particular, the deaths of both James I and Charles II were attributed at least in part to the ague. By early 1625, James I was nearing sixty years old. Feeling slightly unwell, he 'retired for fresh air and quietness to his country to his manor at Theobald's'. This was his main country retreat, having been built by Elizabeth I's chief minister William Cecil. In March 1625 he became ill with tertian fever, the ague; a disease that he had suffered from previously. His retinue of courtiers plus servants, and the physicians or medical men of the time, attended James. Confined to his sick room – known later as his 'Chamber of Sorrows' – the work of State went on with hurried processions of men of significance, notes and messages, plus bed linen, bedpans, and the rest.

There was a whole host of expert medical opinion from both England and from Scotland, and one can only sympathise with the sufferings of the man who was supposedly the most powerful figure in the country. However, at this point it seemed there was no immediate threat to life; it was just another episode of marsh fever. He had had these before and had always won through. A note from the Venetian ambassador stated that:

> His majesty's tertian fever continues but as the last attack diminished the mischief the physicians consider that he will soon be completely recovered. His impatience and irregularities do him more harm than the sickness.

As Benjamin Woolley notes in his wonderful book *The Herbalist*, this was a reference to James being a notoriously difficult patient. However, James must have one's deepest sympathies, bearing in mind what was to follow. Despite the prognosis of the ambassador, James' condition worsened considerably and, feeling 'heaviness in the heart', he had a poultice applied to his abdomen, but this appeared to cause a series of fits, and later he began panting, raving and had an irregular pulse. Further treatment made him complain that he was burning and roasting, and his medical team clearly began to fear the worst. The decline continued, and following bloodletting and further poultices, James I of England, VI of Scotland, died on 27 March 1625.

There were rumours of poisoning by James' younger son, Charles. The dead king's body was subjected to a post-mortem, being disembowelled and considered in detail. His skull, because it was so strong, was broken open with a chisel and a saw. When it finally burst open, it was 'so full of brains as they could not, upon the opening, keep them from spilling, a great mark of his infinite judgement'. This must have provided some comfort to his subjects, if they needed reassurance of the intelligence of their recently demised monarch. And so James was laid to rest and, Charles I, King of England, came to the throne.

> There are various forms of malaria and these differ in severity and the frequency of attacks. Along with possible confusions over descriptions of other diseases, it can make diagnosis of which illness was involved in any one incident quite difficult. However, the main forms of malaria were described according to the periods of recurrence. 'Tertian' was every three days, with number one being the first day of fever, and 'quartan' was every four days. These probably relate to tertian malaria, the benign (or non-fatal) form caused by *Plasmodium vivax*, and quartan malaria, caused by *Plasmodium malariae*. The so-called 'quotidian' was probably the manifestation of multiple infections by tertian malaria.

Marginal notes in the *Bible of John Brown of Chatteris* observed that:

> … In the winter time, when the ice is strong enough to hinder the passage of boats and yet not able to bear a man, the inhabitants upon the lands and banks within the Fens can have no help of food nor comfort for body or soul, no woman an aid in her travail, or partake of the Communion, or supply of any necessity, saving what those poor desolate places do afford, where there is no element of good …

I think we can assume that John Brown was not that keen on the Fens! Certainly, a traveller would find his journey difficult. According to Wheeler (1897), the road that ran from the high country to Boston via the West Fen was called the Nordyke and Hilldyke Causeway. Here the track was only distinguishable from the surrounding fen by rows of willows emerging from the water, and for strangers it was a perilous journey. Local guides on stilts, knowing the way through the dangerous swamps, were employed to take people across. The agricultural improver and writer Arthur Young, writing in 1793, was equally unimpressed by the condition of the great fens, or the character of the local people:

> … numbers of sheep die of the rot when depasturing in the drier parts of the Fen during the summer months. The number stolen is incredible; they are taken off by whole flocks; whole acres of ground are covered with thistles or nettles four or five feet high, nursing up a race of people as wild as the Fen.

He goes on to say:

> … The few wretched inhabitants who live in the neighbourhood for the most part sheltered themselves in huts of rushes and lived in boats. They were constantly liable to be driven out of their cabins by the waters in winter, if they contrived to survive the attacks of ague, to which they were perennially subject. The East Fen was the worst of all; 2,000 acres were constantly under water in summer. One part of it was called Mossberry and Cranberry, from the immense quantities of cranberries thereon.

In the winter of 1785, Young's European visitors, Alexandre de La Rochefoucauld and Maximilien de Lazowski, prepared for their final visit; this time they travelled north through England to Scotland. Scarfe (2001) describes their journey and impressions. Alexandre wrote: 'So, we left Bury on the 14th. Mr Young, whom I often mentioned last year, made us several notes for our tour, and our plan was to go to Ely and on to Peterborough.' Poor weather forced a change of plan and he noted that 'Mr Lazowski seemed very fed up because we would not now be going through what in England are called the Fens, and in French marais'. (Morass is the nearest English word.)

However, a new itinerary was devised which 'would enable us after all to see the fen, which was so interesting both in its natural state and in its methods of cultivation'. From Brandon they were unimpressed:

> … there is nowhere fine in these 3 miles of flat lands to Brandon: only sheep and scrub. You go through a warren; I've never seen so many rabbits. The proprietor claims to make more profit from the sale of them than he would if the land were properly cultivable.

This touches on issues of perceived profit for the improver or the traditional user. In the English fens, Alexandre describes ditching and draining with dozens of small drains leading into larger dykes, and the use of wind-powered pumps:

> Here we are in what was a drowned countryside; a lost land, barren and nowhere culti-vated, until this drainage by means of windmills was undertaken … the land yields a good harvest … it's a magnificent feat of engineering, doing honour to its designers. These great embankments, together with a great number of drainage-mills, have succeeded in drain-ing these thousands of acres that were not very long ago water-logged, or underwater … Before the invention of these mills, the Fens were being lost again to the waters and impossible to cultivate. The area is perhaps as much as a hundred miles round as you can see from the map, and is crossed by the rivers Ouse and Nene; and many of the canals dug to drain the land are navigable.

He acknowledges the benefits to locals of abundant wildfowl and fish, but potential loss of these through improvement and impacts on common rights are not considered. Perhaps Young's influence comes through in the assumption that improvement will 'be an inherently good thing'.

In South Yorkshire and Nottinghamshire, Alexandre de La Rochefoucauld and Maximilien de Lazowski were admiring land improvement and observing areas still needing attention. They noted parts of the Royal Forest of Sherwood in Nottinghamshire, sold off by Parliament for cultivation and improvement (a government fund-raising exercise). Near Doncaster, they diverted to Potteric Carr, Alexandre noting:

> In these very low-lying lands of the poorest quality, we came to a swamp [marais]; at present it scarcely merits any other name. However, they do manage to harvest some grain. The ground is a peaty turf, apparently bottomless, for you could drive a pole down without

meeting any obstruction. These lands you leave in meadow for as long as possible, but the wetness of the soil involves a great deal of work … You need to have a good understanding of these poor lands, which scarcely repay outgoings.

Wetlands generate negative responses, an effect sealing the fate of many areas of rich wild-life habitat and cultural importance. William Gilpin, writing in 1809, summed this up nicely when referring to the Cambridgeshire and Lincolnshire Fens some years earlier. He stated: 'It is such a country as a man would wish to see once for curiosity; but would never desire to visit a second time. One view sufficiently imprints the idea. Indeed where there is but one idea, there can arise no confusion in the recollection.'

Indeed, Gilpin pioneered the 'Picturesque Movement' and triggered the idea that regions such as the hilly Peak District and the mountainous Cumbrian Lake District were beautiful places to visit and spiritually uplifting. In many ways, writing by Gilpin kick-started the Romantic Movement, the Lakeland poets, and the colossal growth of tourism that followed. Prior to this, such upland areas were believed to be the works of the Devil and to be avoided at all costs. The flipside of this was that many would-be visitors then avoided low-lying wetlands as malarial swamps, and they were certainly not sufficiently picturesque for the refined visitor. The exceptions to this trend of avoidance, as we will see later, were the Victorian naturalists, particularly entomologists who visited from Cambridge for rare Lepidoptera. Other visitors were fowlers and sportsmen; for them the picturesque was not a priority. Indeed, it is only now, in the late twentieth and early twenty-first centuries, that the tourist is once again returning to these big sky landscapes, and mostly thanks to the RSPB, the National Trust, and others with their nature reserves.

THE NORTHERN FENS: A FORMER WETLAND LOST FROM MEMORY

The majority of the views described would relate to any large tract of perceived wilderness and waste. Generally, this might be a lowland fen, raised bog, upland moor or blanket mire. Most of the accounts are specific to what I describe as the Southern Fens, i.e. those of East Anglia. There are fewer accounts of the Northern Fens of Yorkshire and north Lincolnshire and most for this region are by local naturalists and antiquaries rather than touristic visitors. Furthermore, most of the northern descriptions are about the vast peat bogs, heaths and fens of Thorne and Hatfield, and not about the wider landscape. Interestingly, the area is depicted on one of England's oldest maps, drawn up between 1410 and 1420, and relating to a survey of Inclesmore in 1331. This was in part an exercise by the controlling monks to map out their peat-cutting rights.

One of the earliest descriptions of the Northern Fens is an account by John Leland, who died in 1552. He was Keeper of Libraries to Henry VIII, and was commissioned to visit the far-flung corners of the kingdom to research history and topography in the great librar-ies of monasteries and colleges. These topographical descriptions are often the first we have for many parts of the country. His writings about Thorne and Hatfield probably date from around 1540. He calls Hatfield 'Heatfeld' (i.e. a heathy clearing or open area) and Thorne is Thurne (probably the place of the thorn tree). Leland states that 'The quarters about Heatfeld be forest ground, and though wood be scars there yet there is great plenty of red deere, that haunt the fennes and the great mores thereabouts as to Axholm warde and Thurne village'. He proceeded by boat from Hatfield to Thorne, given as a distance of 2 miles (3.2km); although, as Martin Taylor (1987) points out, this may not equate to our modern sense of a specific distance between places. Leland would have used the old English Mile, which might be up to 6,600ft (10 furlongs). (It is an often forgotten fact that the mile was only fixed at 5,280ft (8 furlongs), by a Statute of 1592 in the reign of Elizabeth I.) Apparently at Thorne there was a castle, well dyked and used 'for a prison for offenders in the forestes', presumably taking the King's deer and other such heinous crimes. Around Axholme, he found wetlands with bog myrtle: 'The fenny part of Axholm berith much galle, a low frutex swete in burning'.

A modern history providing a fascinating and informative read on this relatively poorly known region is Taylor's account of *Thorne Mere and the Old River Don*, published in 1987. Again, Taylor's interpretation of the topographic and historic evidence is interesting as he suggests that Thorne Mere was tidal and therefore in part brackish. He also points out that there was more than one water-body, and that the main 'Thorne Mere' was probably 'Bradmere'. This might well be the site referred to in a charter of 1138-1147 concerning Haines or Haynes, a local place name:

> Be it known that I have granted and given for the safety of my soul, and of the souls of all my friends, to the Holy Abbey of Saint Mary at York and to the monks who serve God there Haines with the moor and marsh which surround it for their beneficial use likewise in the moor as in the profitable ground and the marsh, and Munkeflet with all its fisheries; and over above that at the feast of the assumption of saint Mary three good pike in Bradmere and twelve bream.

In a document of 1215-1240, according to Taylor, there is a note from William Count Warenne (the Lord of the Manor) to his water bailiffs, in which he refers to an order to cause the monks of Roche to have a tithe of the residue of his eels from all his fisheries in the parishes of Hatfield and Thorne, and Fishlake. From a detailed sifting of the evidence, Taylor decided that Leland travelled by boat to Thorne not on the main Thorne Mere or Bradmere, but across one of the lesser lakes, Thurmere. This type of interpretation involves considerable speculation and there is no absolute certainty, but Taylor's arguments are convincing. Leland proceeded on his way from Thorne to Axholme:

> From Thurne, by water, to the great lake caulled the Mere, almost a mile over, a mile or more. This mere is full of good fisch and fowle. From the Mere by water to Wrangton cote a 3 miles in a small gut or lode. All this way from the Mere to Wrangton the water berith the name of the Brier. The ground there is very fenni on both sides. From Wrangton to … where I came on land in the Isle of Axholme about a mile; so that from Wrangton thither the water is called Idille; yet it is the very same water that Bryer ys and of certente Idille is the ancient name.

The seventeenth-century Yorkshire antiquary, Abraham De La Pryme, wrote that at the time of Leland's visit people used to go in boats over the carrs between Lammas and

Michaelmas in order to look after their swans. Transport by boat was not only for day-to-day matters of work, but as noted in *The History and Antiquities of Thorne* (1829), for getting to the parish church too. He gives a very early account of a tragedy when a boat carrying a corpse and mourners was caught in a storm and people drowned. This was presumably on the mere, or at any rate journeying from Thorne to Hatfield in the early 1300s. The church at Thorne was a capella, a chapel subsidiary to Hatfield church, so the latter took priority in matters of marriages and funerals. Consequently, the inhabitants of Thorne petitioned the Archbishop of York:

> … in the reign of Edward II, the inhabitants attempted to obtain the extension of parochial rights to it. They directed a petition to the Archbishop and Abbot of St. Mary, in which they set forth the great inconvenience that was sustained in consequence of their distance from the Parish Church and the difficulty of access to it. They stated that a little time before some of the people of Thorne were conveying a corpse for interment at Hatfield, when a storm arose and many persons were drowned and their bodies not found for several days. They beg that their chapel being old and decayed, might be new built: that their town might be made a distinct parish, and their chapel a capella parochialis free for the administration of the sacrament and the sepulchre of the dead.

It is clear that this was a vast and remote area dominated by wetland and water for much of the year; both a productive landscape but also an inconvenient and even dangerous one too. As recorded by De La Pryme in late 1687, it was vulnerable to sudden inundations:

> Towards the end of this year [1687] there happened a great inundation on the levels, by means of much rains that fell, and the high tides; which increased the waters so, that they broke the banks and drowned the country for a vast many miles about. My father, and every one in general that dwelt there, lost very considerably in their winter corn, besides the great expense they were put to by boating their cattle to the hills, and firm lands, with the trouble of keeping them the two or three months. I have been several times upon these banks (which are about three yards in height), when the water has been full to the very tops, and nothing appeared on that side but a terrible tempestuous sea. The water remains about half a week, and sometimes a week, at its full height, whose motions some hundreds of people are watching night and day. But if it chance to be so strong, as to drive away, as it often does, any quantity of any of the banks, then it drowns all before it, and makes a noise by its fall which is heard many miles before they perceive the water; and in the places where it precipitates itself down, makes a huge pond or pit, sometimes one hundred yards about, and a vast depth, so that in that place, it being impossible for the bank to be built again, they always build it half round, many of which pits and banks may be seen beyond Thorne.

Then again, but even worse, on 17 December 1697:

> … we had a very great snow, which was on the level ground about two foot and a half thick. After a pretty hard frost, which froze over again for several days. On 20th it thawed

exceedingly fast, upon which there came down a great flood that the like was never known; about forty one years since there was the greatest flood that was ever remembered, but that was much less than this; for this came roaring all of a sudden, about eleven o'clock at night, on Bramwith, Fishlake, Thorne, and other towns, upon which all the people rung all their bells backwards (as they commonly do in case of a great fire), but though this frightened all to the banks, and bid them all look about them, yet, nevertheless, the loss was very great. The people of Sykehouse, and Fishlake, they had banks to save them, yet it overtopt all; drowned the beasts in their folds and destroyed their sheep; several men lost their lives; the houses in Sykehouse and Fishlake being drowned up to the very eaves; so that they reckon no less than £3,000 damage was done by the same in the parish of Fishlake. It came with such force against all the banks about Thorne, which kept the waters off the Levels, that everybody gave them over, there being no hopes to save them, and ran over them all along, and the ground being so hard they could not strike down stakes upon the tops of their banks, to hinder the water from running over. At last, it being impossible that such vast waters should be contained in such short small bounds, it burst a huge gime close by Gore Style. Near Thorne, where there had been a vast gime formerly, and so drowned the whole levels to an exceeding great depth, so that many people were kept so long in the upper part of their houses that they were almost pined, whilst all their beasts were drowned about them. It was indeed a very sad thing to hear the oxen bellowing and the sheep bleating, and the people crying out for help round about as they did, all over Bramwith, Sykehouse, Stainford, and fishlake, and undoubtedly in other places, yet no one could get to save or help them, it being about midnight; and so many poor people were forced to remain, for several days together, some upon the tops of their houses, others in the highest rooms, without meat or fire, until they were almost starved.

This was not the end of the floods, with at least two or three equally destructive inundations described for the area over the century after De La Pryme. In 1747, G. Stovin esq. wrote a description of Hatfield Chase from his visit, when he was accompanied by the Revd Samuel Wesley: 'the water of the morass is of the colour of coffee. There is plenty of furze bushes, etc. and variety of game, such as hares, foxes, kites, eagles, curlews, ducks, and geese.' The peat bogs were probably dominated by at least two great 'raised mires', and, even after extensive drainage, it was suggested in *The History and Antiquities of Thorne* in 1829 that 'the depth of the morass near Thorne, in some places is 20 feet thick'. In the heart of the bog, it could well have been much more. The two notes that follow give an idea of how the region was perceived and we shall return to other accounts later. Thomas Bunker, the Goole naturalist, wrote of a visit in 1876 to Thorne Moors:

We had now reached the moor, and at once walked a short distance through the heather to a spot where we could see clearly what plants were growing on this wild spot. On looking around I found myself near the edge of a large waste in many places white with bog cotton, and probably 10,000 acres in extent; a few clusters of bushes at distances of half a mile or more showed where the ground was firmer.

Then in 1878, Davis and Lees described the area:

… the Waste covers even now an area of some ten square miles, and formerly it was much larger. This tract, very nearly at sea level, presents to the eye a dreary expanse of level peat moss, intersected by numerous dykes of almost stagnant water, diversified by a few pools or 'wells', and relieved in a few places only by oases of soil, a foot or two higher than the plain, on which grow a few Firs, or a thicket of Birch and Alder, or a few bushes of Bog-myrtle and Sallow.

IMPACTS OF THE AGUE ON HISTORY AND THE FENS

The relevance of this disease to English history and the fenlands in particular is worth careful investigation but space here does not allow this. The risk of ague was a factor which influenced perceptions of, and attitudes to, fens and wetlands more widely. The disease affected the great alongside the lesser people. So for example, in 1633, whilst the Lord High Treasurer was on a journey with Charles I (who was to be crowned in Scotland), he stopped at Doncaster and had a fit of the 'stone' (a common and rather unpleasant complaint), and some 'aguish distemper': the marsh fever.

In 1685, the disease also took Charles II. The King awoke feeling unwell and took a treatment that had been prescribed by one of his medical men. This clearly did not work and when Lord Thomas Ailesbury, the Gentleman of the Bedchamber, found him, he was a deathly pale colour. For Charles II things were about to get a lot worse. His barber arrived to give him his morning shave and the King suddenly suffered a series of convulsions. The barber was so alarmed that he performed an emergency phlebotomy or blood-letting. He 'let' 16oz of blood from a vein in the royal right arm.

The King's medical advisors then prescribed various medicines in order to draw out impurities from his stomach and rid his whole nervous system of anything harmful to it. He was given an antimonial emetic to promote vomiting, and a series of enemas to cause evacuation of the bowel. One of these alone was a pint of fluid injected into the rectum. As if that was not enough, his team cut off his hair so that a blistering agent could be applied directly to his scalp. This treatment was followed by a red-hot cauterising tool applied to his skin to make it blister. The monarch then suffered two hours of convulsions and absolute agony before drifting into semi-consciousness. That same evening, the medical staff applied 'noxious plasters' to his feet in order to draw down the 'humours' from his brain. Charles was then given a light broth and a laxative to 'keep his bowels active'; liquorice was also given in case his own over-heated urine scalded him because of all the blistering agents that had been administered. Apart from a powder of white hellebore to make him sneeze, he was then left to rest for the night.

However, despite the 'excellent' medical attention, the King continued to decline. Apparently, the final throw of the medical dice was to give him one of the most rare and sought-after medicines – the powdered skull of a man that had died but never been buried – but for Charles it had no great effect. Now, however, the physicians came to a new conclusion, which one has to say was a little late in the day. The King was suffering from the ague, then still very common in London. The clue they felt was in the repeated and recurring attacks of fever. They now prescribed 'Peruvian bark', which as a source of quinine would probably have helped if it had not been for the quack treatments and excruciating pain that had already been meted out. Close to death, they now gave him crushed 'bezoars' or stones from the intestine of the wild Persian bezoar goat. Charles II died of the ague on 6 February 1685, soon after noon. He was fifty-four years old.

Together these descriptions help us form an idea of what the region was like before drainage, and of course prior to modern recording of wildlife. There is a wealth of anecdotal evidence to suggest that the area teemed with wild fauna, with birds in their hundreds of thousands. Human predation, on a huge scale, peaked in the eighteenth and nineteenth centuries – and then declined, presumably because of the almost total loss of wild stock, massive loss of habitat, and improved availability of imported food. With changing habitat and increased human pressures, by the nineteenth century the wild harvest was uneconomical. However, although the culling declined, the birds could not recover because of landscape change, with around 98 per cent or more of the historic wetland destroyed.

Cornish, writing in 1895, described the carrs south-west of Doncaster, stating that they were an outlier of the great fen that originally extended north to the River Humber, east to the Trent lowlands, and south to Nottinghamshire, with the Isle of Axholme, Thorne Waste, Marshland and Hatfield Chase fen. Eagle Clarke, in 1887, wrote of Potteric Carr before Smeaton's drainage in the late 1700s, stating that it had vast numbers of duck, bittern, ruff and reeve, black-tailed godwit, marsh harrier, great crested grebe and water rail, breeding commonly. Dutchman Cornelius Vermuyden's drainage of Thorne Moor and Hatfield Chase in the 1600s is well documented and there is anecdotal evidence of a huge wetland resource prior to that. Taylor, in 1987, suggested that the pre-Vermuyden landscape in the east would have rivalled the present-day Coto Doñana in its wealth of birdlife. Chris Firth, in 1997, remarked that 'the destruction of the wetland habitats [here] would, by today's standards, be regarded as an ecological disaster of enormous proportions … [that] could be argued as equal in proportion to the present day destruction of rainforests'.

Yet the drainage of Hatfield Chase only directly affected a part of the wetland scene of the Northern Fens, though it was a massive area. In Yorkshire, south of the confluence of the Ouse and the Trent, 70,000 acres (28,328 hectares) of Hatfield Chase were constantly inundated before Vermuyden and his fellow Dutch undertakers commenced to drain it in 1626. At its heart was Thorne Mere, almost a mile across. Close by was Potteric Carr near Doncaster with 4,000 acres (1,619 hectares), which succumbed to Smeaton and his engineers after a private Act of Parliament in 1764. This was one of many outliers known as the Yorkshire Carrs.

We gain a feel for this long-vanished landscape from the status of some of the wildlife species. The bittern was sufficiently common to have its own vernacular name and to feature in local folk rhymes: 'When on Potteric Carr the Butter Bumps cry, The women of Bulby say summer is nigh.' Even in the early 1900s, older people around Beverley could still recall hearing the local bitterns. Now, in the early twenty-first century, they are returning after an absence of a century or more.

John Smeaton, the engineer who drained Potteric Carr.

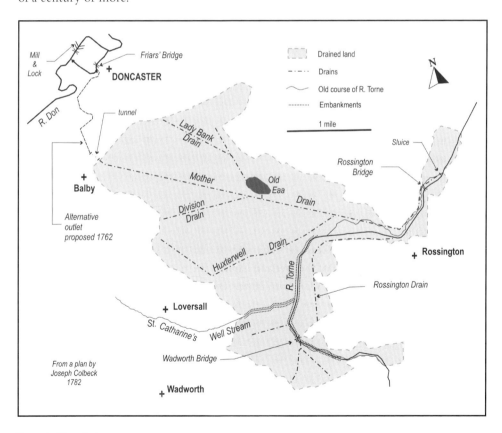

Potteric Carr drainage.

THE EYE OF THE BEHOLDER

One of the most striking observations about the local communities in both the Southern and Northern Fens is that, despite the huge difficulties in literally living on the edge, the locals were passionately possessive of their landscape. For the most part, they were absolutely opposed to change.

The perceptions and opinions of their drainage are closely interwoven. A pamphlet, published in 1701 about Vermuyden and the Northern Fens, described 'The state of that part of Yorkshire, adjoining the level of Hatfield Chase'. In this, Vermuyden is 'a monster of a man whose natural qualities no one English epithet can answer'. Yet Abraham De La Pryme, writing in the late 1600s, stated that:

> This Hatfield Chase Sir Cornelius Vermuyden purchases of Charles I in order to dischase, drain, and reduce it to constant arable and pasture grounds. This, to the wonderful surprise of the whole nation, and the vast advantage of the whole country round about, which before was but barbarously and thinly inhabited, poor and beggarly, and at the incredible labour and charges of above £400,000, he at length bravely and effectually performed; whose name deserves a thousand times more to be honourably mentioned and received in all our histories, than Scauru's was in those of Rome, for draining a great lake in Italy, not quarter as big as this.

Therefore, it really does depend on your perspective. On the one hand, these areas were seen as vast and rich lands to provide fish, fowl and the hunt, but on the other, they were desolate wastes ripe for improvement. As regions of sanctuary and independence for some, they were the sources of dissent and unrest for others. From the viewpoint of the locals, whose independence and livelihoods depended on the fenscape, these were rich environments. For the agriculturalists and landowners, they were wastelands over which human power and influence should be applied and nature made to yield. In many ways, the conflict continues today. Are these to be simply agricultural lands for intensive and petrochemically-driven farming, or do they have wider social, economic and environmental values? If it is the latter, then who will pay and how can farming be effectively drawn into the equation of sustainable development?

Even today, arguments go on about whether or not 'improvement' is sustainable and should be funded out of the public purse. The last major drainage in the Northern Fen was of the Bawtry and Idle Washlands on the north Nottinghamshire and South Yorkshire border in the 1970s. From a conservation viewpoint, this was a disaster funded by the taxpayer, yet today the farmer John Dickinson is complaining that the Environment Agency will no longer fund the necessary drainage (Benfield, 2012). The land is returning to wetland and the delivery of wider ecosystem services, and the context is the EU-subsidised food over-production of the 1980s and '90s, and consequent exacerbation of locally disastrous flooding in the 2000s. Farmers, encouraged by public policy-makers and supported from the public purse, expanded into the fen, but that support has now been withdrawn. Despite an apparent refusal to understand and face the environmental truths and consequences of the unsustainable actions, their complaints have legitimacy in as much as they

A flood in the fens. (Victorian print)

have followed what the government directed. Of course, their efforts were also encouraged by the public demand for cheap food and the farmers' desire to make money regardless of environmental costs. Should the public now pay the farmers to manage the floodwaters? Interestingly too, in terms of perceptions, the newspaper article (Benfield, 2012), made no reference to public subsidies, environmental damage, or even to increased flood risk.

Finally, not everyone likes the fenscape and the wetland, and indeed, not everyone feels comfortable in the big sky landscape of the modern Fens. Nevertheless, stand in the lowlands of Cambridgeshire or Lincolnshire on a sunny summer evening, with intensive farming shrouded by the half-light, and you step back into a primeval world of ancient fen.

2

THE FENLANDS OF EASTERN ENGLAND

THE SOUTHERN FENS: THE ANCIENT FENLANDS OF CAMBRIDGESHIRE AND SOUTH LINCOLNSHIRE

In 1904, Samuel Smiles described the East Anglian fenland as around 2,000 square miles (3,200km²) abandoned to the waters and an immense estuary of the Wash. The rivers Witham, Welland, Glen, Nene, and Ouse discharged the rainfall of the central counties of England into this vast area. In winter it was a vast sea, and in summer a noxious swamp. The waters expanded in many areas into settled seas or meres, teeming with fish and screaming with wildfowl. The more elevated parts were overgrown with reeds and from a distance these looked like fields of waving corn, and were haunted by vast flocks of starlings, which, when disturbed, would rise in such numbers as to almost darken the air. Into this great dismal swamp spewed the floods descending from the interior, their waters mingling and winding by many devious channels before they reached the sea. They were laden with silt, which deposited into the basins of the Fens. Riverbeds had a tendency to choke and block, and this forced new channels through the ooze. These meandered across the levels, until at length they discharged their surplus waters, through many openings, into the Wash. The beds of the old Rivers Nene, Ouse and Welland were still visible in the Great Level of the Fens in 1904. The Ouse, which formerly entered the Wash at Wisbech, by this time discharged at King's Lynn. This gives a rich and evocative feel for the landscape, people and wildlife now banished.

These fens, excluding the Wash itself, covered around 1,300 square miles (2,080km²), running north to south, Lincoln to Cambridge, around 75 miles (120km), and east to west, Brandon to Peterborough, about 36 miles (57.6km). Prior to the Quaternary Ice Age, the chalk upland ran continuously across from Norfolk to Lincolnshire. The predecessors of today's rivers ran north to join the proto-Rhine and south to join the proto-Thames. They reached a northern sea somewhere beyond what is now the Dogger Bank. The chalk barrier was eventually lost to forces of erosion through the rivers and the action of the sea, and the land was submerged. In this way, the sea entered an area of easily eroded soft Jurassic clay, and the fenland was the flooded plain. Its limits to the east were the more resistant chalk and to the west the Jurassic limestone. The slightly undulating clay plain had high points that later formed islands such as Ely. These acquired a 'cap' of boulder clay from the later stages of the last Ice Age, and, from about 9,000 years ago, after the retreat of ice sheets northwards and the general warming of the climate, the basin filled with deposits of varying character and origin.

The present-day Wash is the remnant of a former far larger incursion of the sea inland. However, the process has not been simple because the levels of the land and sea have each varied throughout the period, with an ebbing back and forth of the land / sea boundary. When sea level has risen relative to the land, there have been inundations with depositions of sands, silts and muds. During periods when the land was higher, the area reverted to marsh and mire. The final, complicating factor has been the meandering paths of the great and lesser rivers and streams, also carrying their sediment load and mixing, eroding and re-depositing the various sediments. A major human-induced consequence of this river-borne sedimentation happened when early settlers began to clear vegetation, particularly forests from higher ground inland. This led to sometimes massive soil-erosion episodes and a huge amount of silt and mud deposition along the ancient river-courses. More recently, how people utilised this landscape, and the way natural vegetation developed, was influenced by these varying depositions across the ancient basin. This, in essence, was the basic stage upon which all the future scenarios of the East Anglian fenland were acted out. To the early visitor it was an expansive and frightening area, more a waterscape than a landscape.

The East Anglian Fens were part of the great Royal Forest of Kesteven. This was a 'forest' in the sense of a royal hunting preserve throughout which the Forest Laws applied, and not necessarily an area of woodland or trees. According to Ingulph's *History of Croyland*, the area was 'de-afforested' by the Kings Henry I, Stephen, Henry II, and Richard. The latter granted to the inhabitants of the neighbouring towns 'permission to build upon the said marshes'. The various terms have caused confusion for early historians, who assumed the forest meant trees and that this meant a drier landscape.

The 'Forest of Kesteven' was described in 1230 as covering an extensive area with boundaries running from Swaton along the Car Dyke to Market Deeping, then on to Spalding, Bicker, and back to Swaton. Bourne Wood at Bourne, 400 acres (162 hectares) of ancient woodland, is today called 'Kesteven Forest'. Whilst not the medieval 'forest' as such, it is probably a remnant of the once extensive hunting area. The name Kesteven has two elements; one is British for 'a wood' and the second is Scandinavian for 'a common meeting place for the district'. It was formerly a part of Middle Anglia, and with the creation of the English shires might have gained an independent identity by the eleventh century.

The Isle of Ely was an inland island surrounded on all sides by lakes and meres. The rivers were broad and became more so during rainy seasons. There were few artificial embankments to contain the waters and few or no drains to carry excess water to the sea. The name Ely derived from *Helig*, a British name for willow. The latter grew in abundance with alder across much of the area, forming what were described as 'low but impenetrable forests with marshes and quagmires under them and within them'. The whole isle was described as almost dead flat, with here and there an inconsiderable eminence standing up from it. These higher areas were often surrounded by water, and when the autumn and spring rains swelled the rivers, they were cut off as so many individual islands.

Eels and eelpouts were taken in abundance from the Ouse and the Cam, which ran close by the abbey walls. The number of eels was remarkable for a fish that now verges on extinction. The monks of Ramsey paid annually to the monks of Peterborough, a rent of 3,000 eels in exchange for the use of a stone quarry. However, it was suggested that they could have paid ten-times this amount and not have noticed it. This was a rich and productive waterscape with pike abounding, and the meres and stagnant waters swarming with tench and carp. Wildfowl were abundant and 'for a single halfpenny men can have enough for a full meal'. Scores of fish came up the rivers to spawn. Wild buck was described as less abundant than in drier areas, and for some reason 'of wild boars of the forest in the Fen the head only was served up'. Heathcote wrote in 1876 that the trapping or snaring of 'the crane, the heron, the wild-duck, teal, and the eccentric and most savoury snipe, the swallow-kite, the swarth raven, the hoary vulture, the swift eagle, the greedy goshawk, and that grey beast, the wolf of the weald' was all relatively easy!

Grey heron, early 1900s.

On the other hand, some writers assumed the opposite – that the Fens consisted of a vast and unproductive peat bog. Early authors, including the monks, were prone to exaggeration. So when Ingulph described the building of Crowland Abbey, he stated that: 'Croyland consisting of fenny lands … it was not able to support a foundation of stone; wherefore the king [Ethelbald, AD 716] ordered huge piles of Oak and Beech in countless numbers to be driven into the ground.' This is a nice story but false. The abbey was not built on 'fenny ground' but on a solid gravel base, with no need for any additional foundations. Some of the accounts are truthful, however, and the charters (probably made by Prior Upton to support the claims of the abbey) list turbaries, marshes, pastures, and salt-pits. This is clearly a productive landscape.

As early as 1549, during the reign of Edward VI, a code of 'fen laws' was enacted to define the rights and privileges of the commoners and to resolve disputes and prevent robbery; this addressed the general management of the Fens. The Council of the Duchy of Lancaster, at the Great Inquest of the Soke of Bolingbroke held in 1548, drew up the code, which was

Crowland Abbey. (Victorian print)

confirmed by Elizabeth I in 1573. The rules covered important issues such as the branding or marking of livestock, with each village having a separate and distinctive mark. Nobody was allowed to put their cattle out on the common until they had been marked with the parish brand. No foreigner or person without common rights was allowed to put cattle on the common fen; and there was a penalty of 40 shillings for transgressions. People were not allowed to gather fish or fowl at any time, or to gather any turbary or fodder in the East Fen without a licence from the approver (the fen reeve). There were also penalties for putting diseased cattle on the fens, for disturbing the cattle by baiting with savage dogs, for leaving any dead animal unburied for more than three days, or for putting swine on the fen unrung. It was also prohibited to have on the common geese that were not pinioned and foot-marked, to take or leave dogs there after sunset, or to bring up crane birds out of the East Fen. Rams were not allowed to be kept on the fen between St Luke's Day (18 October) and Lammas (1 August). No person older than twelve years, except impotent persons, was allowed to gather wool. No cattle were to be driven out of the Fens except between sunrise and sunset, or during divine service upon the Sabbath or other holy days. All cattle were to be 'roided' or 'voided' out of the East Fen before St Barnaby's Day each year. No reed thatch, reed star, or bolt was to be mown before it was of two years' growth; each sheaf of thatch gathered or bound up was to be a yard in compass. Wythes (withies) were only to be cut between Michaelmas and May Day. No man was allowed to 'rate' any hemp or flax in the common sewers or drains.

During the reign of Elizabeth I, an order was passed that every township in the parts of Holland claiming common in the West Fen should show to the Queen's steward at the next court-day, its charter or title to such common right. No swans', cranes', or bitterns' eggs, or any eggs excepting those of ducks and geese, were allowed to be brought out of the Fens. No fodder was to be mown in the East or West Fen before Midsummer Day each year. No person was allowed to use any sort of net or other engine to take or kill any fowl, commonly called moulted ducks, in any of the fens, before Midsummer Day each year. (This is the time when ducks go into 'eclipse' plumage and moult their wing feathers. It means that they are flightless and vulnerable for several weeks.) A code of seventeen articles relating to fish and fishing in the Fens was devised by the fishermen's jury. The main fish referred to were pike, eels, roach, and perch, and the laws related to the types of nets allowed and how they might be used.

The sheer scale of the fenland region, and the expansive water and abundant wildlife, impressed writers up to the nineteenth century. Heathcote wrote in 1876 that:

> The great level of the Fens comprehends in round numbers as already stated, 750,000 acres. In the time of Charles II it was placed in the hands of a Corporation for purposes of reclamation and drainage. It was subdivided into the Middle, North, and South; and one of the important objects of the exertions of the present century has been to obtain a separation of these levels. Another great object was the drainage of Whittlesea Mere and the lands adjoining.

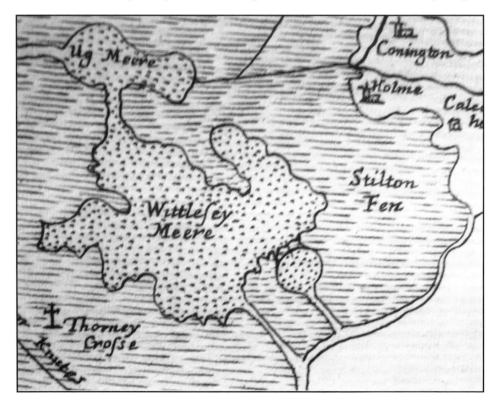

Dugdale's map of Whittlesea Mere.

Like in the Northern Fen, the larger lakes or meres proved a great fascination. Whittlesea was by far the largest of the meres and, according to Miller and Skertchly, varied from 1,000 to 1,600 acres (405 to 647 hectares), depending on the season. Bodger surveyed it in 1786 and its waters were estimated to cover 1,870 acres (757 hectares). It was around 3.5 miles (5.6km) long east to west, and 2.5 miles (4km) across north to south, with a depth from 2 to 7ft (0.6 to 2.1m). Rennie's survey in 1835 suggested it had already shrunk and by then was smaller and shallower. This shrinkage was put down to improved drainage and outfall, a process that continued up to the survey of Walker in 1844, which indicated further diminution. A branch of the River Nene flowed through the mere via Arnold's Mouth and exited in the south-east of the lake. The mere was actually larger than these estimates since it was surrounded by a 'reed-shoal' that extended over a further 200 acres (81 hectares). By the 1800s, it was pro-ducing a harvest of around 1,000 bundles of reeds per year. The land around the fringe was suggested to be 'a dank and deep peat bog with myriads of insects'; these included two special butterflies, the majestic swallowtail and the brilliant large copper. Indeed, it was these insects in particular, which attracted the Cambridge University entomologists.

According to Wheeler in the late 1800s, the Great Level of the Fens comprised a tract of land on England's East Coast, extending southwards from the highlands in Lincolnshire for

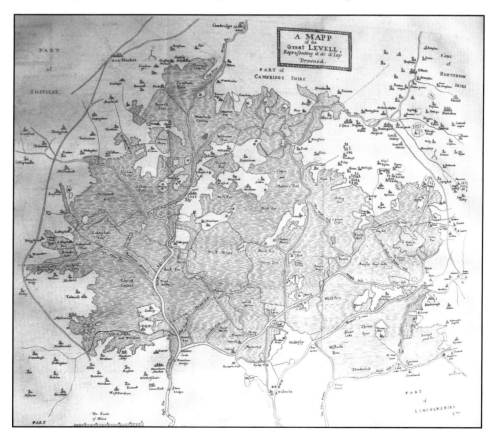

Dugdale map of the Great Level drowned, to show the core area of the Southern Fen.

a distance of about 60 miles (96km) across six counties. The Steeping River, the catch-water drains, and then Revesby, Tattershall, Kirkstead, Bardney and Lincoln, bounded the fenland of south Lincolnshire to the north. In the west was the Car Dyke and to the south Bourne, Market Deeping, Crowland, and the old South Holland or Shire Drain to the Nene. The northern boundary was the River Nene and the Wash coast to Wainfleet. It included the lands adjacent to the Witham known as the Six Witham Districts, including the East, West and Wildmore Fens. Also included were Black Sluice Level, Deeping Fen, lands north of the Welland, South Holland District, and the area along the coast from Foss Dyke to the Nene. The Witham District, Black Sluice Level, Deeping Fen, the South Holland Drainage District and some smaller districts were managed under special Acts of Parliament; the other lands were under the jurisdiction of the Court of Sewers. Wheeler, who was by training a drainage engineer, noted that the Fens had a worldwide notoriety. Furthermore, he felt there was a general though very erroneous impression, which prevailed among those who did not know the county, that it was a dull and dreary land to be avoided by all except those whom through necessity or business were compelled to visit its unattractive scenery. This harks back to the negative image portrayed by Gilpin. However, Wheeler goes on to state that on closer investigation, the fenland has many attractive features, with rich grazing land, and corn-land unparalleled for productiveness. (These of course are the post-draining improvement landscapes.) He describes the inhabitants as of generally good intelligence and of physique and health that compare favourably with other parts of Britain. Apparently, the Fens boasted robust, healthy, working men, and comely damsels! Whilst lacking variation of hills and dales, he suggests the area is one of clear and transparent air, with sunny skies and beautiful starlit nights, and with the most magnificent cloudscapes in England, with sunsets of surpassing grandeur and beauty. Wheeler, a drainage engineer with great faith in his profession, goes on to say that when other parts of England which lie along river valleys are affected by snowdrifts and floods, the Fens is 'free from such disasters, its drainage being thoroughly under control'. However, he was not alive to witness the floods of 1947!

THE NORTHERN FENS OF SOUTH YORKSHIRE AND NORTH LINCOLNSHIRE

> There are many thousands of hectares of what is now prime arable land, especially in northern England, that were in the 17th century, fen and mire … it is surprising how … Yorkshire … fenlands have evaporated from general memory.
>
> Smout (2000)

I describe the wider areas of the Northern Fen in my book *Yorkshire's Forgotten Fenland*, and this includes the northern and eastern outliers of Holderness, and the Vales of York and Pickering. Chris Smout in 2000 stated that England's third largest fenland, bordering north Lincolnshire, Nottinghamshire, and South Yorkshire, was lost even from memory. The Northern Fen, centred on the great Humberhead Levels, once extended north along the Vale of York and ultimately to the north-east and the one-time Lake Pickering. To the seaward, it included the vast wetlands of Holderness and to the south the wet valleys and marshes of north Lincolnshire. Tentacles of the Fen even spread westwards through the Don Gorge for

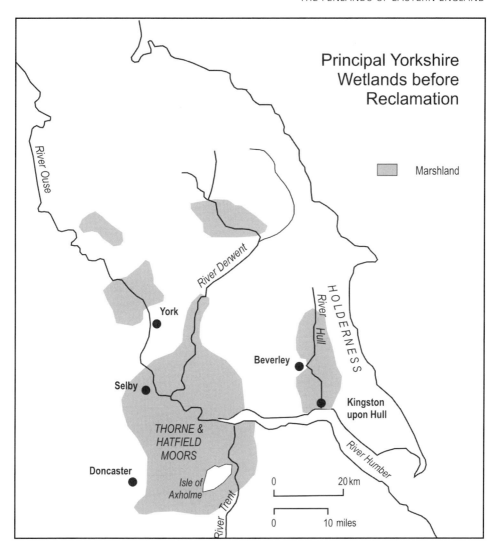

Yorkshire wetlands before reclamation.

example, to permeate into the Don, Dearne and Rother Valleys. By the early 1900s, this Fen had been virtually destroyed, the result of the long-term impact of intensive land management and the drainage efforts of the Dutch engineers and those who followed. Potential revenue was the driver for draining much of the lowland fens of England. In 1600, Parliament passed 'An Act for the recovery and inning of drowned and surrounded grounds and the draining of watery marshes, fens, bogs, moors and other grounds of like nature'. The idea was developed by King James I and his advisors, but he died before the works were begun. The project was then implemented on behalf of Charles I. The build up to, and the impact of, the drainage of Hatfield Chase have been discussed in detail by Van de Noort (2004), and by Rotherham (2010). According to De La Pryme in 1699, before the drainage of 36,420 hectares of the Humberhead Levels, the area was 'A continual lake and a rondezvous of ye waters of ye rivers'.

In 1933, Wilcox produced a map that suggested the extent of prehistoric marsh, moss and fen. This was produced at a national scale and considered only the major, lowland floodplains as the known historically wet sites. Two maps were produced, one based on geological, topographical and climatic evidence, the other on early literature. This same approach has been adopted for my own studies. Taking the historical works further, maps produced by Darby and Maxwell, in 1962, show wetlands and related features (peat and alluvium deposits, fisheries and mills for example). From this information, a picture is produced of this once extensive wetland landscape at around the time of Domesday (1086). To understand the nature of these wetlands, it is important to assess and map their extent, and to reconstruct their former ecologies. In addition, we need to get inside the landscapes and understand how people utilised them and interacted with them. However, in doing this, we face a lack of specific information, since this pre-dates any modern surveys or even classification and naming systems for the wildlife concerned. Therefore, we need to turn to other sources. Early accounts, itineraries and other sources such as feast menus and game books provide insight into ecology and use.

Human intervention for a period of nearly 2,000 years has changed and altered the landscape and its waters. For example, the now confluent Rivers Don and Went, before the Roman Turnbridge Dyke, were formerly parts of different river systems. Thorne Mere and two satellite meres were also present and are seen on Vermuyden's map of the 1600s; though Taylor's study of the Old River Don suggested different locations. The extensive wetlands suggested by alluvial deposits, particularly peat, can be imposed onto maps of the rivers to give an impression of the extensive wet landscape. The Turnbridge Dyke is believed to be Roman and the first major anthropogenic change to the watercourses in the region, and it captured the River Went and diverted part of the River Don into the River Aire. The dyke may have been for the transport of Romano-British goods, livestock, and perhaps troops, as an extension from the Fens to Lincoln.

The Dutch Drainage then obliterated Thorne Mere and the original course of the River Don and diverted several major channels in the area. Agriculture, or generation of capital from sales of land for agriculture, was the driver. The Turnbridge Dyke north of the Dutch River had disappeared by 1800, and the drainage of Potteric Carr, south of Doncaster, took place in the late eighteenth century. Finally, nineteenth-century drainage in the area west of the River Don, north of Doncaster, almost totally obliterated wetlands, apart from remnants of peat on Thorne and Hatfield Moors.

THE DEVELOPMENT OF THE WETLANDS OF THE HUMBERHEAD LEVELS

The development of the great wetlands around the Humber was described in detail by Robert Van de Noort (2004), based on the results of a long-term survey on the archaeology of the region. The development of the great expanse of fen, bog and carr began around 7,000 years ago as a direct result of sea level change. This was affected by climate change and especially by the earlier retreat of extensive ice sheets during the warming after the last Ice Age.

The underlying geology greatly influences the whole landscape. The bedrock beneath the Levels is made up of a series of layers or strata that lie one on another and dip down under the area and then under the North Sea. The result is a series of higher ridges and scarps such as the Magnesian Limestone immediately to the west and visible in the dramatic gorge where the

River Don cuts through the higher rocks. Jurassic marls with sandstones and clays form raised areas east of the sandstones and mudstones of the lower land around Doncaster to Scunthorpe, and the Yorkshire Wolds and Lincolnshire Wolds lie on the higher and more easterly Cretaceous chalk. The latter forms a distinctive west-facing scarp and to the east dips under the glacial deposits of 'till' covering the lower ground. However, there is an important and influential complication in this wetland landscape. Across all the low-lying areas, there is a covering of superficial deposits from post-glacial melt-waters, boulder clay or 'till', and sands and gravels. There are also peats from later wetlands. Riverine muds and other deposits occur in lands prone to flooding or in former river channels. During the last Ice Age, the higher Wolds remained ice-free, but the lower areas of Holderness, the Hull Valley, the Lincolnshire Marsh, the Humber Gap and the Ancholme Valley to the south, were all covered by ice-sheets, which left a legacy of boulder clays. The ice extended south to beyond Hatfield Moors, leaving an extensive end-moraine of post-glacial material dumped in the landscape. In the north, just south of York, is evidence of a later phase of deposition as the ice retreated: the Escrick Moraine, with a ridge of till, sand and gravel. The melt-water from the retreating glaciers left lakes in and around the Humberhead Levels and water backed up behind the ice that still blocked the Humber Gap to the east. The result was the extensive 'Lake Humber', which persisted until perhaps 13,000 to 15,000 years ago. By that time, it had mostly silted up. During the following period the pattern of rivers and streams was established in the valleys of the Derwent, Ouse, Aire, Went, Don, Torne, Idle, and Trent. This ultimately led to the modern riverine landscape. These rivers flowed east-wards to the Humber Gap into a sea around 64ft (20m) below that of today. They meandered and formed braided networks of sluggish channels through sands, gravels and muds, the natural banks formed by erosion and movement being re-formed by the wind to create extensive sand dunes and areas of coversands. By around 12,000 years ago, the climate was warming and sea level rising. In Holderness, of perhaps seventy or more meres that existed at this date in the humps and hollows of the post-glacial landscape, only one, Hornsea Mere, remains today.

Over the period since the landscape structure was set out, the other key factor that influ-enced the wetlands was the relative level of the land and sea. The former is influenced by the rising and falling of the Earth's surface and especially what is called 'isostatic rebound'. This is following the melting of huge quantities of ice at the end of the most recent Ice Age, and there-fore the loss of the great weight from northern and western parts of Britain. The eastern areas, such as the Humberhead Levels and the Cambridgeshire and Lincolnshire Fens, have tended to sink over time as, like a giant geological seesaw, the western and northern parts of Britain slowly rise up. Sea level on the other hand varies with climate change, and until around 8,000 years ago, the whole area was connected by a low-lying land bridge to the Low Countries of continental Europe. Rising sea level, as the waters warmed, submerged the extensive lowlands of the North Sea basin and England became an island, severed from Europe. A consequence of this rapid sea level rise was the development of extensive wetlands across the great expanse of the Humber Levels and up the composite river valleys of the region.

Robert Van de Noort acknowledges the technical difficulties in producing precise maps of the wetlands of the region because of lack of evidence. There is the complexity of overlaying the different periods of incursion and retreat by the sea. However, for the purposes of this account the general story is important, rather than the precise technical detail. There were periods of sea level fall, for example during the early Roman period and later in the first millennium AD. However, the overall trend has been for sea level to rise and to impede the drainage of the rivers eastwards. This has led to flooding outside the main river channel into the floodplains, and periods of inundation from the sea.

The development of the earliest peatlands and of fens and carrs began around 5,000 years ago. With fluctuating but generally rising sea levels, the landscape across the Humberhead Levels began to take its modern shape. The zones around the Humber Estuary and the coastal areas developed extensive wetlands of salt marsh and fringing reed-swamp, with alder carrs and sedge fens, and on drier ground stands of oak wood and hazel. Along the river valleys, the wetlands occupied land between the river and higher areas. The narrowest belt of wetland, about 500m, was probably along the River Derwent to the north, while the river floodlands along the Ancholme and the Hull were up to 5,000m wide. However, where the Rivers Torne, Don, Ouse, Aire, Went, Idle, and Trent came together in the middle of this vast expansive landscape, they formed a wetland covering over 200km². With further rises in sea level, these earlier wetlands were submerged and changed from peatlands to those dominated by mineral-rich wetlands. The early water-dominated habitats were mostly what are described as 'eutrophic', meaning that they were rich in nutrients and hence productive in reed beds and carrs. However, over time the deposition of dead organic material from plants built up to raise the land levels above the surrounding water-tables. At this point, all the nutrients coming into the ecosystem were from rainfall alone and the vegetation developed into what is known as 'ombrotrophic' or 'raised mire'. The two largest areas of this vegetation type were around what are now Thorne Moor and Hatfield Moor, which evolved over time to become massive raised mires of solid and mostly acidic peat. Underlying the peat on Thorne, for example, was a forest of tall trees that had died, perhaps as the smaller bogs grew together and made the area too waterlogged for tree growth. This was from around 5,000 years ago. On Hatfield, the wooded landscape of alder and birch was overwhelmed by bog development from about 4,000 years ago.

Over the following millennia, the basic landscape evolved from these earlier conditions, with periods of growth of peat during wetter conditions and perhaps a slowing or retraction during warmer or drier times. These changes show up in detailed analysis of the peat profiles and in the insect and plant remains preserved in the bogs. Specific markers of climate change occur at 3,260 to 2,820 years ago, with a particularly wet period during the late Bronze Age and early Iron Age, then 2,820 to 2,400 years ago with a warmer and drier period in the later Iron Age. This continued through the Roman period, but between AD 640 and AD 980, and similarly from 1250 to 1410, there were wetter periods. There was again a notably wetter time at around 1450, which corresponds to the onset of the so-called 'Little Ice Age'. During this period, we begin to get historical information too and this suggests a marked period of flooding along the coast and in the valleys of Holderness and the River Hull. Across the region from around the late 1200s to the 1400s, there was widespread flooding and increased difficulty in farming lands that had in earlier times been reclaimed from fen or sea.

From the Bronze Age onwards, and especially during the Roman period, people had an increased impact on this landscape and its ecology. Higher ground, with woodlands dominated

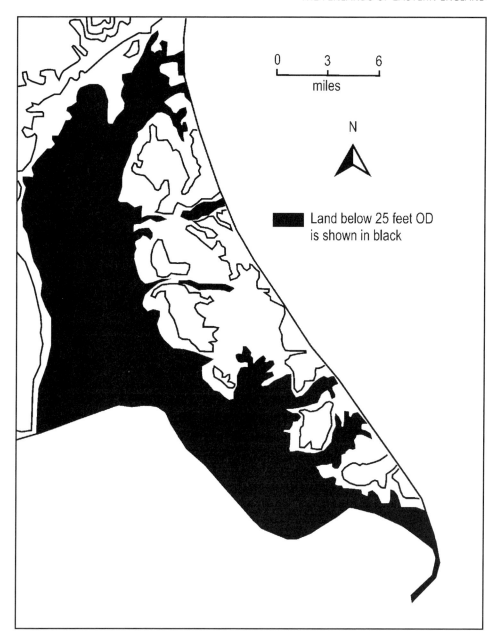

Relief map of Holderness after Sheppard, to show the main area of carrs, fens, marshes and meres.

by oak, lime, hazel, elm, pine, ash, willows and alder, had naturally occurring glades or open areas to attract large grazing herbivores. These in turn would maintain and even extend the open habitats. Indeed, in areas such as the Holderness Plain, the development of early pastoral agriculture had resulted in the clearance of woodland by around 4,500 years ago.

With an increasing human population, there was pressure on more marginal lands, including the wetlands. However, the available skills and technologies limited the impacts of people in these landscapes beyond basic exploitation. There was increasing impact through use of fire to burn and clear the forest, and to burn grass and heath areas in order to improve grazing swards. Selective hunting of herbivores, probably the indirect effect of hunting top carnivores, and the increasing influences of domesticated animals, had impacts too. Erosion and downwash of soils and other sediments resulted from the above and from limited areas of cultivation. Over the subsequent centuries, with periods of social and technical advance such as during the Roman occupation, and times of retreat and retrenchment, people gradually made incursions into the wetlands through farming improvement and drainage. At the same time, it must be remembered that whilst these were challenging environments, the expansive wetlands, with their arterial rivers and channels, were hugely important to local people. They provided a rich source of food, fuels and building materials, and they facilitated long-distance and relatively speedy travel by boat or canoe.

A RICH ENVIRONMENT FOR WILDLIFE AND PEOPLE

By perhaps 4,000 years ago, as settlers moved into this landscape, they would have encountered a vast area of mixed wetlands and other habitats with huge but relatively unproductive raised bogs, extensive wet woods of alder and willow, and areas of reed-swamp and sedge fen. Drier raised islands might have oak and pine forests. The bogs were unproductive and dominated by bog moss or sphagnum, but the other areas were rich in fish and in wildfowl. The regular inundation from rivers and from the sea in coastal zones would have created high fertility and so encouraged even greater biomass and productivity. The people in and around these wetlands hunted a diversity of mammals and birds; they gathered plants, herbs, fruits and nuts, and caught fish. To the east around the Humber Estuary and along the Holderness and Lincolnshire coasts were mudflats, tidal creeks, salt marshes and extensive sand dunes. In the coastal and estuarine areas, they fished and caught or gathered shellfish and crustaceans such as crabs and shrimps. It is also likely that the early hunter-gatherers migrated, perhaps seasonally and as conditions allowed or necessitated, between the different zones. Movement between the lower wetter grounds and the drier uplands would have been necessary as the seasonal floodwaters covered the landscape. Typical of semi-settled hunter-gatherers, they would follow herds of wild mammals that they hunted through the landscape.

Evidence from more northerly sites such as Star Carr in the Vale of Pickering suggests these people hunted and ate red deer, roe deer, elk, aurochs, pigs, and many smaller mammals too. It is likely that they also took beaver and wild boar for food, and mammals such as otter, marten, polecat and wild cat for fur. The early settlers also burnt areas of reed bed, probably to increase productivity and perhaps to open up areas of vegetation in the landscape. Though not certain, it is likely that these peoples began to domesticate animals perhaps 6,000 years ago, and were carrying out some limited agriculture by about 4,000 years ago. Therefore, during the Neolithic and the Bronze Age, the area probably had stockbreeders with cattle or sheep. These animals would, in part, have been pastured on extensive salt marshes around the estuary and on the more extensive salt marsh areas across the floodland at that time. By the later Bronze Age and early Iron Age, arable cultivation had increased across the region around the wetland fringe, and the evidence of pollen analysis suggests large-scale woodland clearance at this time. It is from the late Iron Age, and into the Roman period, that more intensive and socially organised settlements and associated field systems appear in the higher grounds of, for example, the Lincolnshire Wolds or on the Sherwood Sandstones to the south-east. Settlements also developed on the valley floodplains, marked out with double ditches and rectilinear enclosures, with associated drove-ways apparently for moving stock from summer grazing on the marshes to over-winter on higher and drier ground.

During this period, it was one thing to live around the fringes of a great wetland, but another to live within the wetland itself. However, as already noted, these landscapes are productive and facilitate relatively easy travel over distance along river channels. Wetlands also provide a degree of security through their inaccessibility, particularly for outsiders, and because they were marginal zones beyond local social and political controls. They therefore provided opportunities perhaps not available in the wider areas of drier ground.

However, even those living in the heart of the wetlands actually settled on the limited islands of higher land or on areas of deposition of more solid substrate, and not in any form of lake settlement as found elsewhere in Britain. The major archaeological site at Sutton Common, once proposed to be a prehistoric lake settlement, was most likely a Romano-British grain store. The communities that settled here were also skilled in metal smelting and working with iron from bog ore – probably smelted from locally made charcoal from coppiced hazel woodlands. There is extensive evidence of such metalworking from slag heaps and other features found in the region of Holme-on-Spalding Moor and in the Vale of York. Log boats loaded with iron, presumably for trading, have been found preserved in the sediments. Another skill used by some of the local people along the coastal and estuarine zones was salt making. This was certainly happening by the late Bronze Age, and particularly from the Iron Age into the Romano-British period. The heat of the sun was used to evaporate seawater, and then the resulting brine was heated or boiled

A boat on the lode. (Victorian print)

to produce salt crystals. The salt manufactured was used for preserving food such as fish, meat or dairy produce, and in medicines and dyes. Salt was also consumed, as today, as a food additive.

From an early time the wetlands were traversed by boat. Prehistoric log boats and sewn plank boats have been found at sites across the region. Some of these were quite sophisticated in construction, implying that the people of the wetlands, as well as travelling across the Levels, may have gone further afield too. Van de Noort notes that these craft may have represented quite significant innovation and design around the Humber Estuary. It has been estimated that some of them might have carried up to twenty-two cattle or over 100 sheep. The most commonly used boats though were dugout canoes hollowed from a single oak trunk between 8 and 16m in length. Such boats have been found in wetlands across the region from the Vale of York to the lower wetlands. One dugout canoe was even found in the sediments of 'Lake Meadowhall', close to where the M1 motorway runs today, just east of Sheffield. That specimen is now in Weston Park Museum. By late Neolithic or early Bronze Age, the people of the Humber region were trading across the North Sea and into Europe, as well as across the great estuary of the Humber and inland too.

When the Romans arrived in Britain, they brought skills, cultures, technologies and the social and political systems to change approaches to land management. This applied particularly to drainage and reclamation. Around the Humberhead Levels, they built new roads, bridges, and farms, and triggered an expansion of settlements into the wetlands. At the same time, sea level was dropping and extensive areas of coastal marsh were open to colonisation and use. However, by the latter times of the Roman occupation, the situation reversed, with the sea once more moving inland. Buckland (1979) suggested that Romano-British farming on the higher grounds around the Levels led to a downwash of soil into the wetland areas. Van de Noort, on the other hand, suggests this, and the subsequent decline in farming through environmental degradation, were only in the immediate vicinity of the lowland wetland zones. Transport systems were at the heart of the Roman success, and Ermine Street, one of the most important Roman roads, led from London to Lincoln, on to Winteringham and the Humber. By around AD 50, the Romans had built forts, and subsidiary Roman roads crossed the region. Just as earlier cultures had constructed floating wooden causeways across the marshland, so the Romans built 'floating roads' on cut timbers covered with turves.

There were Roman villas around the Humber region, and the wetland fringes of the great Northern Fen were probably exploited as a part of the organised estate system. Along with Roman forts, there were many non-military settlements across the Humberhead Levels, often on the riverbanks of the main arterial rivers. It is likely that the region was exploited for salt making and for pottery, and there was extensive rearing of sheep and cattle. The rich pastures of the riverine floodlands would be used to fatten stock, and the rivers themselves could be used to transport animals and meat. It has been suggested that Brough on the Humber Estuary was a major Roman port, and the towns of Doncaster, Lincoln, and York were all important. By the medieval period, it was from these larger settlements on the drier ground and a network of smaller villages and hamlets on the islands and other areas of drier ground, that much of the exploitation of the wetlands was undertaken.

To some extent during this time after the Romano-British period, there was a withdrawal of settlements immediately within the wetlands, probably due to social and economic changes in the post-Roman period. The other factor was probably the re-wetting of areas as sea level rose once more. However, it seems that the population decreased and its impact on the wetlands was reduced. In particular, there was re-establishment of woodland in many areas, probably with oak re-colonising abandoned farmland. The farms that remained were probably rather self-sufficient in contrast to those of the Romano-British period. They were on the higher and drier land, with seasonal use of the wetland fringe for pasture and for hunting and fishing. Gradually, a process of re-colonisation began during the Middle Ages. In the East Anglian Fens and other areas, this happened from around AD 600 to AD 700, though in the Humber, due to local conditions, it may have been later.

Some marginal settlements have been found from this period and the archaeology give clues as to the nature of the land use. There was arable cultivation but also evidence of geese, chickens, cattle, sheep, goats, pigs – all suggesting the wetland margin was very productive. The communities were fishing and hunting, including wildfowling, and there were signs of shellfish, such as oysters taken. The locals even hunted dolphin or porpoise, and whales, though obviously from further afield. Having been colonised by the Anglo-Saxons in the post-Roman period, the Vikings were the next major wave of invaders and, from the late 800s, the whole region was part of the area controlled under the Danelaw, with widespread settlement from Scandinavian countries. One of the main consequences in the modern-day landscape is the large number of settlements with Viking names. However, despite this change in the overlords, many settlements maintained strong Saxon influences.

Within the wetland areas, the Middle Ages settlements were mostly on higher or at least drier ground. These included areas of drier glacial deposits or the raised banks or levees along rivers. Essentially, there were small islands of settlements in a wider sea of wetland. Van de Noort suggested the reclamation of the marsh began before Domesday in areas such as around the Trent and the Ouse, with key settlements protected from extreme high tides by defensive banks. Settlement followed with land drained by long dykes to facilitate cultivation and/or building. A sea-bank was built along the tidal Ouse by the late 1000s, and in its lee sheltered a series of settlements. By the time of Domesday, parishes – often with multiple settlements – were recorded, as communities edged their way into the wetlands. In the coastal areas, satellite townships developed to the east, associated with the important local industry of salt manufacture. After the Norman Conquest, a number of motte and bailey castles were built across the region to secure the territory for the invaders. These fortifications, like those of the Romans before them, often controlled access to, across or along major waterways. Large areas of the Humber wetlands and associated lands, confiscated from Saxon nobles, were given to Norman overlords. It was from these castles that they controlled their new acquisitions. Owston Castle, for example, controlled the strategically important cross-Trent ferry and therefore access to the Isle of Axholme.

In the post-Domesday period, the network of towns and villages began to re-emerge. Many Roman settlements had been largely abandoned after the collapse of the Roman Empire. The new towns were sometimes on these earlier sites, and centres such as Doncaster began to grow alongside newly established towns such as Beverley, with its name, meaning 'the clearing of the Beaver', so evocative of the great fenland. With increasing populations and a number of urban centres, there were further demands on the landscape of the Levels. Many areas and communities had extensive 'commons' across the region and there was considerable potential for conflict and competition for these precious resources. Fragments of open common land, such as that which remains at Beverley to this day, are notable survivors. Further hunting forests (such as at Selby), and parks (as at Conisbrough), were also established. This process helped speed the work of reclamation and agricultural improvement, with extensive drainage schemes gradually expanding out across the wetlands. Once again, the farmers of the Yorkshire Fens were connected to the economy and society of the wider area. In some parts of this fenland, the work was encouraged by the establishment of new moated settlements in lands not yet exploited by nearby villages. Some of these moated properties were farms or monastic estate buildings, and others were the houses of nobles. This suggests that both Church and nobility were involved in the process. In this wet landscape, the moats probably helped lower the water-table immediately around the site and thus helped maintain the higher and drier land inside the moat.

By this time, the arable land on slightly higher and drier ground was worked as townfield, with open strip-fields aggregated around a nucleated settlement. These areas included the small islands such as Holme-on-Spalding Moor, Axholme, and Wroot, with cultivation on adjacent hillsides and along raised levees by the main rivers. In the lower wetter areas, there were common meadows on the mineral-rich floodplains; these were important and productive resources. They were often called 'ings', another name that persists in the modern landscape, generally indicating long-standing wetland or floodland. These lands provided summer grazing and the all-important stock of hay for the winter months. This was vital for both livestock and oxen for ploughing. Remaining beyond these areas were the true wetlands of the Yorkshire Fen, including wet woodlands or carrs, and moors and 'wastes' with high water-tables and peat formation. When water levels allowed, these areas were exploited as grazing pastures as part of a complex system for managing the entire landscape. This enabled the higher ings to be set aside for a few months to produce hay. Once harvested for the hay, the stock could go back on the ings. Winter floods then brought fresh depositions of mineral-rich sediments to these riverside fields, the whole system being maintained and sustainable. On some of the common wastes, the local villagers kept cattle, draught oxen, horses, sheep, pigs and geese.

ROYAL HUNTING IN THE WETLANDS

An important consequence of the Norman Conquest, for the region, was the imposition of Forest Law across much of the area and the establishment of hunting chases. In 1311, the Lord of Axholme, John de Mowbray, established a free chase in his manor and soke of Crowle, and retained this in a grant to Selby Abbey. Across the Chase at Hatfield, hunting, farming and woodland use were all carefully controlled. Around thirty-four parks and hunting forests are recorded across the region and it is likely there were more. The area was indeed a landscape famous for its deer and its hunting. The fact that these lands were rich hunting grounds gave them a degree of protection from agricultural improvement in the centuries to come. Conisbrough Castle Park in South Yorkshire may have originated as an Anglo-Saxon hunting area, but post-Domesday it was a Norman preserve. From shortly after the Norman Conquest to 1347, 70,000 low-lying, often inundated acres of

Hatfield Chase were the private forest of the de Warennes of Conisbrough. The place name Conisbrough derives from the Old English and means the fortified place or stronghold of the king; no doubt relating to the long-standing significance of this strategic, defensive location. According to *The History of Thorne*, the Earls of Warenne had a house close to Hatfield in the centre of the Chase where they could stop and rest when away from their seat of Conisbrough Castle. The house also had a park of 500 acres (202 hectares) which was well stocked with deer, though they were also 'to be seen roaming at large through the whole limits of the chase'.

The Chase then reverted to the Crown in 1347, and Forest Law applied to Hatfield Chase. This meant the Royal Forest Law, with the threat of punitive treatment of offenders who transgressed the strict protection for game. In practice, this was not the stuff of Hollywood myth but more often a means of raising royal revenue than punishing people. Vernon Cory, writing in 1985, described the great Chace of Hatfield as the largest deer park in England, covering 180,000 acres (72,850 hectares). Technically, it was not a park as such, but a hunting chase. The central hunting area was termed 'soft land', with 'hard land' beyond the Chase which keepers could enter in order to retrieve game. There was also hunting outside the Chase itself in districts called 'purlieus' and within which Forest Law did not apply. Apparently, Selby Abbey kept a keen interest in these areas, the clergy of the time being notable for their sporting habits. Cory estimates the deer population to have been around one deer per 62 acres (25 hectares), which is not particularly dense. There were both red and fallow deer, though the latter were perhaps restricted to Conisbrough Park.

We get some idea of the hunting potential of this landscape from the records of people visiting to pursue the game. In 1356, when Edward Balliol, the ex-King of Scotland, resided at Wheatley near Doncaster, he received a pardon for slaughtering deer. This is documented as: sixteen hinds, six does, eight stags, three calves, and six kids, all in the Chase. In the park itself, the slaughter continued further, with eight damas (fallow deer), one souram, and one sourellum (a kind of fallow deer). In the ponds, he took two pike of 3.5ft (1.05m) in length, twenty of 2.5ft (0.75m), twenty of 2ft (0.6m), fifty pickerels of 1.5ft (0.45m), six of 1ft (0.3m), 109 perch, roach, tench, and skelys, and six breams and bremettes. The bailiff of Hatfield, who was responsible for overseeing all this carnage, was Robert de Mauley; his lieutenant was John de Aldwick. The 'harvest' bears testimony to the rich wildlife of this park and chase, and to the hunting prowess (or at least perseverance) of the former Scottish king.

There was a regular and ongoing use of the area for taking fish and game, but it seems that great hunts were relatively infrequent. There was one noted by Vernon Cory as recorded in 1541, during the reign of Henry VIII, when 200 stags and does were killed in a single day. In 1607, Conisbrough and Hatfield held red and fallow deer, once as common 'as sheep upon the hills', and 'so unruly that they almost ruined the country'. The inquisitions of 1607 stated that 'the number of red deer amounts to about a thousand, and that the herd is much impaired by the depredations of the borderers'. Poaching was common and offenders might be gaoled in Thorne Castle and/or fined. The latter was a useful way of raising revenue. The management of the Chase was overseen by the 'King's Bow Bearer', a title that later became the rather less extravagant Surveyor General. Beneath him were the Master or Chief Forester, five Keepers (for the wards of Wroot, Hatfield, Broadholme, Clownes, and Wrangles), and twenty-five Regarders (to control the bounds of the Forest and attend the Forest Court). The last documented major hunt occurred in 1609, and was a remarkable affair. In the party were several people whose individual fates and actions would sway the future of the fenlands, both in the north and in the south. The royal party, in 100 boats, pursued 500 deer across Thorne Mere. Abraham De La Pryme described this tale as follows:

> When Henry Prince of Wales visited Yorkshire in 1609 he was entertained at Streethorpe on the side of the Chace towards Doncaster, the residence of Sir Robert Swift. After one day spent in plain stag hunt the chief regarder of Thorne an R. Portington esquire having promised to let the prince see such sport as he never saw in his life the prince and his retinue went with them; and being come to Tudworth, where Mr. Portington lived, they all embarked themselves in almost 100 boats that were provided there ready, and having frightened some 500 deer out of the woods grounds and closes adjoining (which had been driven there the night before) they all as they were commonly wont took to the water and this royal navy pursuing them into that lower part of the levels called Thorne Mere and there up to their necks in water their horned heads raised seem to present a little wood, and there being compassed about with the little fleet, some ventured among them, and feeling such and such as were fattest, they immediately cut their throats and threw them up into the boats or else tying a strong rope to their heads drew them to land and killed them. Having thus taken several they returned in triumph with their boats to land and the prince dined with R. Portington esquire and was very merry and well pleased at his day's work.

In 1609, Prince Henry, the Prince of Wales, was only fifteen years old; however, at that time that was considered a young adult. His story is very pertinent to the rest of this account and indeed to the future of the Fens at that time. He was the elder son of James I and was being groomed to succeed him. This was when James was only King James VI of Scotland and not yet King of England. Yet, as Martin Taylor notes, Henry was not a traditional name for a Scottish king and, it may be, that even at this early stage, he believed he was naming the future English monarch. Therefore, when James succeeded to the English throne on the death of Elizabeth I, Henry was next in line. However, in 1612, Henry died; it was perhaps one of the most significant deaths in English history. Many historians consider that the collapse into civil war would never have happened if he had not died so prematurely. It is likely that at least the relationship of tolerance with the House of Commons developed by his father King James I of England, would have continued, and maybe a more fruitful part-nership would have evolved. Roy Strong describes Henry as 'a young man of exceptional promise with a passionate interest in the arts and a commitment to revive the vanished glories of the previous reign'. This was not to be. He died of typhoid fever in 1612 at the age of nineteen. With the death of James I, on 27 March, Henry's younger brother Charles suc-ceeded to the throne; there were even rumours that Charles had his father poisoned in order to hasten the succession.

The relationship between the King and Parliament deteriorated to the point of civil war and then the trial and beheading of the King. There followed the short-lived establishment of the Commonwealth, with Oliver Cromwell as the Lord Protector. One can only wonder what the fate of both the Northern and Southern Fenlands might have been if Henry had survived. The country – and the Crown in particular – would probably not have descended into near anarchy and financial chaos, and, as a lover of the hunt, it is likely that he would have 'preserved' at least Hatfield, if not the other wetland areas. As it was, Hatfield Chase, famous for its fisheries and swans, was disforested (1629) and drained in the early 1630s. When the Chase was disforested, the deer were mostly captured and transported to other parks. However, they were not all removed immediately since, as late as 30 December 1634, John Scandaren was paid £100 for bringing forty red deer alive from Hatfield Chace to stock Burley Park, Oakham.

MONASTIC IMPACT

The other major and important consequence of the Norman takeover following 1066 was the establishment, or sometimes re-establishment, of a monastic system. This had huge implications for land reclamation and exploitation, and therefore for re-colonisation. William the Conqueror, also known as William the Bastard (due to his illegitimacy rather than his attitude), established Selby Abbey. The abbey had large land-holdings across the region and it was in these that the first large-scale co-ordinated reclamation took place. Their works included the digging of drains, such as the aptly named Bishop's Drain in Selby, during the late 1000s and early 1100s. This is shown as encircling the great Thorne Moors on the Inclesmoor Map of around 1405.

Reclamation included the building of roads, drains, and bridges, with the founding of villages and the erecting of crosses. Peat fuel was dug on a large scale from the fens, bogs and moors. The peat bog was worked into from the edges, resulting in long linear strips with a drain down each side; they were known as Moorland Allotments. These features, highlighted by Keith Miller in his 1997 book, actually survive in the landscape today, forming a major and distinctive characteristic of the area. The process of peat bog reclamation exactly mirrors that undertaken in the flatlands of Holland and Germany.

Linked to Selby Abbey, during the 1100s and 1200s a number of monasteries and priories developed across the area, and it was through these that much of the work was undertaken. At least forty ecclesiastical centres were within the Humberhead Levels, and other establishments based outside the immediate area held lands here too. This network was the foundation for the process of land reclamation and improvement in the Humberhead Levels as it was further south in the East Anglian Fens. Van de Noort suggests that this was the 'conversion' of waste to useful lands, as a parallel to the spiritual conversion of pagans to Christianity. More pragmatically, however, land improvement increased tax revenues and the value and wealth of the Church and the region. Indeed, great wealth came to the ecclesiastical centres from wetland exploitation delivered and managed through a dispersed estate of monasteries. These centres not only farmed the land but also managed fishponds and small industries.

TURBARIES AND TURVES

Some of the wetlands located close to York, such as Askham Bog and Skipworth Common, were known to be turbaries in Roman times. They supplied peat fuel to the City of York and perhaps to other Roman garrisons. By the medieval period, the use of the Yorkshire Fens for the supply of peat fuel was well established as a major commercial operation. Not only was peat turf used for fuel, but also for building. The best-known example is at Thorne Moor or Thorne Waste, where by the 1200s and 1300s a major industry was established. The famous Inclesmoor Map shows clear evidence by the 1400s of arterial drainage, roads, bridges, and peat-cutting turbaries. The ecclesiastical centres probably led this process of exploitation, as they did in Norfolk to supply the cathedral at Norwich. The fuel was for domestic heating and for cooking, and was commonly used by the great institutions and in smaller farms and cottages. However, peat turf was also used to power industries such as potteries, brick and tile making, and even salt manufacture.

Along with the peat, there was also a harvest of 'bog oak' from prehistoric timbers preserved in the peat. Heavy and durable, these black timbers, impregnated with tannins, could be either a premium fuel or used in building. Some from Hatfield Moor were even sold to be made into ships' masts.

As the turbaries were exploited, the water-table fell and the remaining land became available for cultivation. If the water-table rose, then locally the turbaries would be flooded and abandoned. The most dramatic example of this was the Norfolk Broads, which were massive medieval peat-cuttings to fuel Norwich and its ecclesiastical centre. As sea level rose, the workings flooded to become the Broads, and the turbaries were abandoned. In the Humberhead Levels, exploitation for peat continued throughout the centuries up to the present day.

THE LAKES, POOLS AND MERES

In the most low-lying areas, there was open water. This might be along the major rivers, around the estuary, or in smaller pools, meres, and lakes; some were quite large. Again, within the overall management of this complex landscape, the water-bodies were important. Along their fringes, reeds and sedges could be harvested for thatching and sometimes for fuel, and for basket making. Small willows or 'withies' would be harvested in 'osier holts' or 'willow garths', again for construction or for basketry.

Similar to the Southern Fens, these pools also supplied fish, with the fishing rights held by local towns or by the monasteries. The tidal rivers had fish weirs to facilitate the catching of eels and other migratory fish. In 1086, the *Domesday Book* noted that at Tudworth in the Humberhead Levels, there were twenty fisheries producing around 20,000 eels each year. There is documentation of payments to monasteries being in eels, and fish from the fishponds.

Across the Yorkshire Fen, wildfowling was hugely important, with birds trapped in nets and driven when flightless across the ponds and meres. The duck decoy was to follow as a later invention, but at Leconfield Castle in the Hull Valley, from the medieval period or earlier, mallards, snipes, curlews, redshanks, plovers, and swans were all caught and eaten.

A PRODUCTIVE LANDSCAPE

The Northern Fens provided fish, reed and rushes (for thatching, flooring and candles), peat fuel, brushwood from the carrs for fuel and light constructional work, and pasture for cattle. To get some understanding of the scale of this resource we have to turn to descriptions by visitors, to account books of great estates, or the documented menus of great feasts and banquets. For example, in the accounts of Leland (Henry VIII's antiquary), there is a description of the feast for the enthronement of George Neville as the Archbishop of York in 1466. This may have a degree of exaggeration, and no doubt much of the food was supplied from the Derwent Washlands, south of York. Nevertheless, it does give insight into the likely wildlife at the time in the South Yorkshire and Humber marshes and fens:

> Oxen 104; wild bull 6; muttons 1,000; veales 304; porkes 304; piggs 3,000; kidds 204; conyes 4,000; staggs, bucks and roes 504; pasties of venison cold 103; pasties of venison hot 1,500; swans 400; geese 5,000; capons 7,000; mallard and teal 4,000; plovers 400; quails 100 dozen; fowles called rayes 200 dozen; peacocks 400; cranes 204; bytternes 200; chickens 3,000; pigeons 4,000; hernshawes (young herons) 400; ruff 200; woodcock 400; curlews 100; pheasants 200; partridges 500; and egritts 1,000.

Other regional household accounts confirm cranes, herons, snipes, bitterns, quails, larks, dotterels, and bustards for the table (1526); peacocks, cranes, and bitterns (1530); and twelve spoonbills at 1s each, and ten bitterns at 13s 4d (1528). Many are wetland birds and mammals from forest or chase; these were extensive, productive landscapes. Little bittern, night heron, and purple heron probably survived in English wetlands until the 1600s. Cranes and spoonbills were extinct as breeding birds in England for around 300 years (until later reintroduction), but ruff bred at Hatfield Chase until the 1820s. Thomas Pennant in 1766 described taking ruff in nets, fattening them in captivity, and then selling them for the table at 2s each.

Again, it is difficult for us today to imagine the problems faced in catching this wildlife, even though it was so abundant. Before guns were invented and widely available, nets and traps were the order of the day. The Dutch duck-decoy technique came in the 1600s, with Dutch drainage engineers, and resulted in thousands of wildfowl captured annually from South Yorkshire's fens (*see* p. 86). Even Doncaster Corporation built a duck decoy. This was an investment and to make a contribution towards the upkeep of the poor of the town. Making the decoy and a special embankment (the 'Decoy Bank' over three-quarters of a mile in length) to reach it cost £160. The decoy pond was circular, with 6.5 acres (2.6 hectares) of water and six 'pipes' (to collect ducks!). In 1662, it was let for twenty-one years at an annual rent of £15, which fell in 1707 to only £3 per year, perhaps reflecting the impact of drainage. The lessee of 1707 specialised in trapping pochards, one of the best ducks for the table, by using nets raised by pulleys on poles after the birds settled on the water. All the duck pipes were still there in 1778, but the last decoy man died in 1794, and, by the late 1800s, the Great Northern Railway ran straight through what had been the decoy. Many readers will have passed through the decoy on trains into and out of Doncaster.

For over 200 years, the pressure has been to tame the wilderness and to 'improve' the land and its productivity, and from this time on the areas around the Humberhead Levels, Potteric Carr and the other carrs were turned increasingly to agriculture. In fact, the destruction and drainage here was earlier and more effective than in the Southern Fen, erasing both landscape and memory.

3

THE WILDLIFE AND FLORA
OF THE ANCIENT FENS

Moore, writing in 1997, gives a good account of how the vast fenlands might have looked to an observer prior to the great drainage. He describes a huge area of peatland between the uplands of Lincolnshire, Cambridgeshire, Suffolk, and Norfolk, with lower-lying silts around the Wash. This area was what we call 'topogenous mire', essentially a great big peat bog. Its presence was due to topography and the build-up of dead vegetation across the great basin in which it lay. In some parts of the landscape, the sphagnum mosses and other bog plants built them up to such an extent that they became 'ombrogenous' or 'ombrotrophic' mires. These are what we call 'raised mires' or 'raised bogs', dependent solely on rainfall for their water and nutrients. These systems become incredibly rich and diverse ecosystems because of the unique conditions. The two main raised mires of the Northern Fens were described before the drainage as rising up in front of you like a great rippling, wobbly, wet jelly (Woodruffe-Peacock and Stephen Warburton; unpublished). Skidmore, writing in 1992, notes that in early accounts there are descriptions of how the great mire rose up in front of you and 'you could shake the bog to the horizon'.

In the Southern Fen, the great complex of topogenous (fens) and ombrogenous mires (bogs) was subjected to regular and dramatic flooding from the sea in the east and from the rivers in the west. This complicated the situation as silts and muds were dumped on the peats and new peats formed on top of the silts. However, there were other aspects to these expansive landscapes often not fully appreciated, and we see some evidence in the remnant sites we still have. The area was a 'big sky' landscape and Godwin, in the Introduction to his 1978 book *Fenland: Its Ancient Past and Uncertain Future*, describes it as follows:

… vast shallow basin, several hundred square miles in extent, stretching from Lincoln in the north to Cambridge in the south, and from Peterborough and Huntingdon in the west to Boston and King's Lynn close to the coast of the Wash. The whole structure and economy of the area has been determined by the superfluity of water brought into it on the one hand by inundations of sea-water, particularly during times of a rise of sea-level relative to the land,

and on the other by fresh-water from an extremely large catchment area of surrounding upland that is concentrated within it by the flows of such considerable rivers as the Witham, Welland, Nene, Great Ouse, Little Ouse, Lark and Nar.

My question, though, is what this landscape looked like before the great drainage. Even today, on a late afternoon in winter as mists descend and the sun sets, we *can* get an impression of the primeval fen as human imprint is diffused through nature's veil. From the work of archaeologists and historians such as Godwin (1978), Birks (e.g. 1996) and others, we know that the riverine landscape across lowland England at the Mesolithic period were dominated by alder woodland. By Neolithic times, woodland clearance, especially on higher grounds, led to copious alluvial deposits in the low-lying riverine plains and food-lands. By the Iron Age there were further human impacts, with meadow and pasture present and, for example, evidence of hay cutting. Indeed, the impact of human activity across a wide hinterland affected the Fens from a time well before any human drainage schemes were dreamed up. Defoe, writing in 1724, noted that, 'in a word, all the water of the middle part of England which does not run into the Thames or Trent comes down into these Fens'. With all the water came silts and other sediments as the land extended seawards and England got a little flatter.

Along with the communities described so far, there would have been large areas of wet woodland, carrs, and riverside woods of alder, willow and other species. There would have been a vast and intimate mix of pools and meres, and of drier areas with wet heath and meadow. On the islands were drier woods, heaths and grasslands. In the raised mires and wet bogs were areas of fen and wet woodland, and in the Fens were extensive willow and alder carr. Along the coastal zones there were extensive sand dune and salt marsh systems, but again mixed with heath, grass, fen, and scrub woodland. Then around the vast wetland complex, on the higher drier grounds of the Lincolnshire Wolds in the south, the Yorkshire Wolds in the north, and the upland zones of the English midlands, there were extensive heaths, commons, woods and forests. South of the Southern Fen, was the vast expanse of bleak but ecologically wonderful Breckland and then the heaths and fens of Norfolk and Suffolk. When we try to imagine how this great wild landscape has changed and how so much has been lost, it is important to hold this image in your mind. Not only was the 'fenland' destroyed, almost in its entirety, but the lands surrounding it were changed beyond recognition too.

Celia Fiennes (1662-1741) was a contemporary of Daniel Defoe and the daughter of a colonel in Cromwell's army. Having begun her travels at the age of twenty-two 'to regain my health by variety and change of aire and exercise', she wrote of the Southern Fens following a journey to Cambridgeshire and Huntingdonshire in 1697. After a trip to Hinchingbrooke House, she went via Stilton to Whittlesea Mere, still one of lowland England's largest freshwater lakes. She found it an impressive spectacle:

> … a great water on the right hand about a mile off which looked like some Sea it being so high and of a great length … there is no coming near it in a mile or two, the ground is all wett and marshy but there are severall little channels run into it which by boats people go up to this place; when you enter the mouth of the Mer it looks formidable and is often very dangerous by reason of sudden winds that rise like Hurricanes in the Mer.

Skaters and sledges on Whittlesea Mere. (Victorian print)

John Bodger mapped Whittlesea Mere in 1786, and calculated that it covered 1,870 acres (757 hectares), measuring 3.5 miles (5.6km) from east to west, and 2.5 miles (4km) from north to south, varying in depth from 2 to 7ft (0.6 to 2.1m). Fiennes noted that 'people boat it round the Mer with pleasure' when the weather permitted. In winter, when the mere's waters froze, it was a popular place for skating and sleighing. Interestingly, Fiennes was not impressed by Ely when she visited in 1698, 'only a harbour to breed and nest vermin in'.

This chapter does not, and indeed cannot, attempt to give a full account of the wildlife and flora of the old fens. Instead, drawing on records, sightings and accounts from diverse sources, it aims to give a flavour and a glimpse of what we have lost. Sadly, we will never know much more of this lost landscape and its ecology.

The early natural history of the Fens was described in the *Liber Eliensis*, written in the eleventh century, with an account of the natural products of the Isle of Ely. The Isle was described as plentifully enriched with different herbs, and excelling the other parts of East Anglia with the fruitfulness of its soil, the charming pleasantness of its fields, and in the immense number of its flocks and herds. It was noted that its vineyards were not especially praiseworthy, but it possessed forests stored with animals of the chase and was surrounded by great waters and wide swamps. On the island itself, was an abundance of domestic animals and a multitude of wild ones. These included stags (red deer), and little roes (roe deer), goats and hares in the woods and close to the 'morass', ermines, ferrets, otters and weasels. It was suggested that in severe winters these were caught in traps and by snares and other devices.

By the floodgates of the fen were innumerable eels caught with nets, plus great pike, pickerels, perch, roach, barbel, lampreys (also known as water snakes), shad, and the royal fish, the turbot. The account then turns to the birds, mentioning vast quantities of geese, coots, cormorants, gulls, herons and ducks. The latter were described as 'a great number in winter-time; and when the birds were moulting, they were often caught by hundreds at a time. They were taken by snares, nets, and bird-lime'.

FEN RAGWORT

It might seem surprising to be concerned about a ragwort, but fen ragwort (*Senecio paludosus*) is the rarest and most impressive native British ragwort. It can grow up to 6.4ft (2m) high and has a bright yellow flower head. However, unlike the weeds with which farmers are most familiar, and the Oxford ragwort which has famously spread along railway lines and into urban heartlands, this magnificent plant is not invasive or an aggressive coloniser. For a long time it was actually believed extinct in Britain and then a solitary population was re-discovered near Ely. The site was subsequently designated as an SSSI (Site of Special Scientific Interest). This plant was once found throughout the fenland areas of eastern England; its habitat is fens, marshes and other suitable wet environments. However, as with so many fen species, its sites were drained for agriculture.

As we have seen, a few wetlands, like Wicken Fen, survived the worst of these impacts, albeit reduced and desiccated. Now, through careful management, such areas are being restored and they represent the very best of their kind that we still have. Bearing this in mind, there is now a programme to re-establish the fen ragwort at suitable sites across the area that was once its natural range. It has so far been re-introduced to two sites, including Wicken Fen. By the mid-1990s, up to twenty-two plants were thriving at Wicken and flowering profusely. Detailed ecological research has also begun to unravel the specific requirements of this beautiful plant, and it now has a much brighter future.

THE BIRDS OF THE UNDRAINED FENLAND

In the 1930s, the late Professor Darby wrote of the fenland birds in the times before drainage. He quotes from a monastic scribe called Felix, who wrote in the early eighth century of the life of St Guthlac:

> There is in Britain a fen of immense size, which begins from the river Granta not far from the city, which is named Granchester. There are immense marshes, now a black pool of water, now foul running streams, and also many islands, and reeds, and hillocks, and thickets, and with manifold windings wide and long it continues to the north sea … Guthlac … inquired of the inhabitants of the land where he might find himself a dwelling place in the wilderness. Whereupon they told him many things about the vastness of the wilderness. There was a man named Tatwine, who said he knew an island especially obscure, which oftimes many men had attempted to inhabit, but no man could do it on account of manifold horrors and fears, and the loneliness of the whole wilderness.

The island described by Tatwine was Crowland, now in Lincolnshire. The legend goes that all the birds of the wilderness, with ravens and swallows mentioned by name, came across the fen to St Guthlac. The fen provided home not just to men, but also to wild birds, and their abundance was a means of livelihood for many. The fowler was especially important in the Fens and in folklore until the late twentieth century. Monk Thomas of Ely wrote in the twelfth century that:

> There are numberless Geese, Fiscedulae, Coots, Dabchicks, Watercrows, Herons, and ducks, of which the number is indeed great. At mid-winter, or when the birds mould their quills, I have seen them caught by the hundred, and even by three hundreds, more or less. Sometimes they are taken in nets and snares as well as by bird-lime.

Camden, in his *Britannia*, described the Fens not long before serious enclosure and drainage began:

> That at certain seasons of the year, not to mention fish, amazing flights of fowl are found all over this part of the country, not the common ones which were in great esteem in other places, such as teal, quails, woodcocks, pheasants, partridges, etc, but such as have no Latin names, the delicacies of tables and the food of heroes, fit for the palates of the great – puittes, godwittes, knots, which I take to mean Canute's birds, for they are supposed to come hither from Denmark; dotterels, so called from their extravagant dotishness, which occasions these imitative birds to be caught by candle-light.

The submission by the commoners to Parliament in 1780 provides further evidence of the wildlife riches of this unique landscape:

> The fen called the West Fen is the place where the ruffs and reeves resort in greatest numbers, and many other sorts of water fowl which do not require the shelter of reeds and rushes migrate hither to breed, for this fen is bare, having been imperfectly drained by narrow canals which intersect it for many miles. Twenty parishes in the Soke of Bolingbroke have right of common on it, but an enclosure is now in agitation. The East Fen is quite in a state of nature, and exhibits a specimen of what the country was before the introduction of draining.
>
> It is a vast tract of morass, intermixed with numbers of lakes, from half a mile to two or three miles in circuit, communicating with each other by narrow reedy straits. They are very shallow, none above four or five feet deep, but abound with pike, perch, ruffs, bream, tench, dace, eels, etc. The reeds which cover the Fens are cut annually for thatching not only cottages, but many good houses. The multitude of stares that roost in these reeds in winter break down many by perching on them. A stock of reeds well harvested and stacked is worth two or three hundred pounds.
>
> The birds which inhabit the different Fens are very numerous. Besides the common wild duck, wild geese, garganies, pochards, shovellers, and teals breed here, pewit, gulls, and black terns abound; a few of the great terns or tickets are seen amongst them. The great crested grebes, called gaunts, are fond in the East fen. The lesser crested grebes, the black and dusky and the little grebe, cootes, water-hens, and spotted water-hens, water rails, ruffs, red-shanks, lapwings or wypes, red-breasted godwits, and whimbrels are inhabitants of these Fens. The godwits breed near Washingborough, three miles east of Lincoln; the whimbrels only appear for a fortnight in May and then quite the country.

THE FATE OF THE SWALLOWTAIL BUTTERFLY

One of the most exciting and characteristic insects of the old fenland was the swallowtail butterfly (*Papilio machaon britannicus*), one of the main entomological attractions of sites such as Wicken Fen. The swallowtail is now confined in Britain to the Norfolk Broads, though it was once also a classic butterfly of the geographical fenland and persisted at Wicken Fen until the 1950s. However, its distribution appears to be closely linked to that of its food plant, the milk parsley (*Peucedanum palustre*), itself a nationally scarce species. The plant is almost confined to the old fenland and the Norfolk Broads and has become extinct in most of the northern part of its range. By the 1950s, probably in 1952, the swallowtail became locally extinct at Wicken, most likely because of a decline in habitat extent and quality for its food plant the milk parsley. At this site, the carr woodland had spread to reduce milk parsley habitat from 297 acres (120 hectares) to only about 20 acres (8 hectares), a consequence of falling water-tables and abandonment of traditional management. At the time of extinction, the nearest other colony of swallowtails was 96 miles (160km) away on the Norfolk Broads.

Because of the unlikely event of natural re-colonisation, there were numerous attempts to artificially reintroduce the swallowtails from Norfolk. However, these all failed because of the poor condition of the food plant, which seemed to have problems re-establishing in the newly managed and now suitable areas of Wicken Fen. To get round this problem, teams of conservation volunteers came in during 1974 to transplant milk parsley to new areas, and over 2,000 milk parsley plants were planted around the mere on Adventurers' Fen. In 1975, a further 228 swallowtails (adults bred in captivity at Monks Wood Experimental Station from Hickling Broad stock, 124 females and 104 males), were released on the Fen. Despite 20,000 eggs being laid and 2,000 caterpillars pupating, numbers again fell steadily and, by the 1980s, the species was again locally extinct. By the 1990s, further work was done to transplant eggs from Norfolk to raise larvae in glasshouses. The larvae were then placed on the food plants in the Fen, and adults could be seen flying across the site in the summer months.

Following all this, the reserve has been carefully managed to encourage the milk parsley. However, it is not enough that the plant is present; it must also be the 'right sort of plant'. The milk parsley needs to protrude above the surrounding sedge for the female butterfly to lay her eggs on it. In order to encourage this, the milk parsley fields are cut once every four years, allowing this biennial plant to gain a foothold before it is cut back. If the fields were not cut back, the sedge community would be invaded by willow and alder buckthorn, and the conditions would become unsuitable.

One final attempt to re-introduce swallowtails was made, when captive-bred Norfolk-sourced larvae were released onto the Fen. In 1993, Jack Dempster and Marnie Hall started a reintroduction project, jointly funded by the Butterfly Conservation Society and the (then) English Nature Species Recovery Programme, and supported by the land-owner, the National Trust. A number of butterflies were released onto the Fen and good numbers of flying adults were seen in 1995. However, once again, the attempts failed and several years of summer droughts produced poor milk parsley growth; the swallowtail was extinct again by 1996. No further attempts have been carried out and none are proposed as, at the present time, significant areas of suitable habitat are still not available, and it has still not proven possible to re-establish pre-drainage water levels on the Fen.

The swallowtail story does illustrate a hugely important point about these now isolated, scattered and (relatively) small relict sites. Many of the animals and plants have limited powers of dispersal and so cannot cover huge distances to get to new areas. Therefore, if they become locally extinct, re-colonisation is very unlikely.

This paints a vivid picture of the landscape already under assault and about to be erased from the map and from memory. Writing in the mid-twentieth century, Wentworth-Day noted that the 'stares' were starlings, roosting in the reed beds in their millions. Today, the areas where these major winter roosts occur, such as in Somerset, have become major tourist attractions. These spectacular 'murmurations' are a great wildlife spectacle, especially in the open fenland scene. Gathering in late afternoon and dusk, they sweep across the area like a huge trail of smoke and the air is filled with the noise of their buzzing wings, described by Wentworth-Day as 'like the sound of a breaking sea'. Black tern was another interesting bird noted in the submission to Parliament. Known in the Fens as 'blue darrs', at that time they bred in the fenlands in hundreds, but by the 1800s they were reduced to just a few pairs, and by the 1930s to the status of an occasional visitor. Wentworth-Day (quoting Macaulay) stated that the marshes of Lincolnshire were covered during some months by immense clouds of cranes. He also noted that 'fen nightingales' (frogs) abounded.

Miller and Skertchly, writing in 1878, noted that:

… when the fen district was subject to yearly inundations, or the islets alone were the permanent abode of man – when vast tracts, which have now become corn fields, were a wilderness of sedge and reeds – wild fowl innumerable had a home on this watery plain. The waders and the swimmers found abundant retreats for nesting, unmolested and …

The living clouds on clouds arose!
Infinite wing! till all the plume-dark air
And rude resounding shore were one wild cry.

… An East Anglian writer says, 'The Norfolk Fens must in days of yore have literally swarmed with different species of birds … But Norfolk in its present state, is the last stronghold of several aquatic species.'

Yet most of the knowledge we have is anecdotal or incidental. However, as in the South Yorkshire Fens, feast menus and household accounts give an impression of some of the species that must have been abundant. In *Archaeologia*, Volume 36, there is a list of the presents received at the wedding of the daughter of Mr Moor of Losely in 1567. These were from a Mr Balam out of Mershland in Norfolk:

Crane (9), Hernshawes (i.e. Herons) (5), Curlewes (38 dozen), Ducks Mallards (44), Teeles (26), Plovers (9 dozen), Swannes (9), Larks (38 dozen), Bytters (16), Knotts (4 dozens), Styntes (7 dozen small) Godwytts (22)

Victorian writer Kingsley, commenting on the grandeur of Whittlesea's shining mere as it was in its old wilderness state, noted that, 'grand enough it was … while dark green alders, and pale green reeds, stretched for miles round the broad lagoon'. This was a landscape full of water and wetlands and wildfowl. However, as noted by Darby, there is a paucity of information on which to base any account of the fenland birds in the early days. With little knowledge of identification and a largely illiterate society, this is hardly surprising. There are lists of birds sometimes given for the different counties that make up the Fens. So Drayton's *Polyolbion* (1611) lists in verse: duck, mallard, teale, gossander, widgeon, golden eye, smeath, coot, waterhen, water-woosell, dobchick, puffin, swanne, ilke, crane, herne, snite, curlew, cormorant, and ospray [sic]. The Welsh topographer and naturalist Thomas Pennant in the early 1700s suggested that, with the exception of the crane, all these were still present in the Fens. Drayton's *Polyolbion* gives a useful insight into the avifauna of the Fens at the time, although its style is perhaps as different from a modern county bird recorder as can possibly be imagined. He describes the crane:

… There stalks the stately Crane, as though he march'd in warre,
By him that hath the Herne, which by the fishy Carre
Can fetch with their long necks, out of the Rush and Reed,
Snigs, Fry, and yellow frogs, whereon they often feed.

Then the bittern:

… Together still to be, in some small Reedy bed,
The Buzzing Bitter sits, which through his hollow Bill,
A sudden bellowing sends, which many times doth fill
The neighbouring Marsh with noyse, as though a Bull did roare:
But scarcely have I yet recited halfe my store:
And with my wondrous flocks of Wild-geese come I then,
Which looke as though alone they peopled all the Fen,

Thomas Pennant (1726-98) was a leading zoologist of his time, and wrote for a wide audience as well as corresponding with the main authorities of the era. He produced his *British Zoology*, begun in 1761, and was encouraged by leading biologist Carl Linnaeus, someone with whom he corresponded. One of his other major books was his topographic itinerary *A Tour in Scotland and a Voyage to The Hebrides*, published in 1771, which took in a good deal of England as well. Pennant describes the birds of the Fens in some detail. He notes, for example, that:

The fen called the West Fen is the place where the Ruffs and Reeves resort to in the greatest numbers; and many other sorts of water fowl, which do not require the shelter of reeds or rushes, migrate here to breed; for this fen is very bare, having been imperfectly drained by narrow canals … it is observable that once in every seven or eight years, immense shoals of Sticklebacks appear in the Welland below Spalding, and attempt coming up the river in form of a vast column. They are supposed to be the collected multitudes washed out of the Fens by the floods of several years.

Pennant goes on to discuss the damage to the valuable reed crop (for thatching), by the huge numbers of starlings which both flattened the standing reeds and spoiled them by fouling. 'I have seen a stock of reeds worth two or three hundred pounds, which was the property of a single farmer.' This was a vast amount of money at the time and Gurney observes that 'it is easy to believe that the reed owners found them an intolerable nuisance'. The fenmen did their best to minimise the damage, and around King's Lynn, for example, there was 'havoc made in their ranks by the long guns of the fen fowlers who greatly resented their depredations'. Pennant suggests that 'The birds which inhabit the different Fens are very numerous; I never met with a finer field for the zoologist to range in'. Thomas Hall was notable for killing 432 starlings with one discharge of shot, and at Whittlesea, he apparently accounted for 504 birds in such a way.

He notes wild ducks, geese, garganies, pochards, shovelers, and teals as breeding. There were also tufted ducks in the East Fen, but not breeding, and pewit gulls (black-headed gulls) and black terns abounding; the latter 'in vast flocks almost deafen one with their clamours'. Nowadays, seeing even a single black tern is a special occasion. Pennant also notes that 'A few of the great terns or tickets are seen amongst them'. He saw great crested grebes on the East Fen, lesser crested grebe (presumably great crested not in breeding plumage), black and dusky grebe (i.e. black-necked grebe), and little grebe. These were inhabitants of the fen along with 'coots, water-hens, water-rails, ruffs, redshanks, lapwings or wipes, red-breasted godwits and whimbrels. The godwits breed near Washenbrough and when fattened sell for half a crown or five shillings apiece'. He realised that whimbrels were a passing visitor, and saw them around Spalding. On the Wash at Foss Dyke he observed that 'vast numbers of avosettas [avocets], called the yelpers from their cry. They hover over the sportsman's head like a Lapwing and fly with their necks and legs extended'. In his observations, he was beginning to realise that many wading birds changed plumage inside and outside breeding season, something that had confused many early ornithologists. He also made notes on the hunting and culinary value of the birds:

> … [Knot] when fattened, are preferred by some to the Ruffs themselves. They are taken in great numbers on the coasts of Lincolnshire in nets such as employed in taking Ruffs with two or three dozen stales of wood painted like the birds placed within: fourteen dozen have been taken at once.

Pennant also recorded seeing short-eared owl, woodcock, and herons. The latter he noted in a vast heronry at Cressi Hall, 6 miles (9.6km) from Spalding. In one oak tree alone, he counted eighty nests. Although this seems incredible in one tree, local historian Pishey Thompson wrote of a very large tree at Leake, not far from Pennant's observation, absolutely covered with herons' nests. Alfred Newton also reviewed the birds of the Fens in the mid-1800s, when writing in the *Zoologist* in 1879, although he included many coastal rather than fenland birds. There is also some knowledge of the more ancient bird fauna of the region from remains found in peat deposits. These include pelican, whooper swan, wild duck, garganey, great crested grebe, bittern, and coot.

For earlier historical information, we are dependent on a few references to birds in the context of the economy and life of the region in early times. For example, in 1286, Eustace of Cotes 'and a certain goose, his fellow, were wont to enter the warren with nest and to take plover and such-like wild fowl'. Laurence Seman of Cambridge and Thomas Baker of Landbeach did the same but illegally, being caught and tried for their offences. Darby notes that the eggs of the birds were also valuable and were eagerly sought for and collected out in the marshes. Court rolls are often a good source of information on behaviour and economy in times past. The assize rolls note how a boy went into the marsh on 'lignipedes' (perhaps patterns for walking on soft ground), to look for ducks' eggs, but sadly came to a sticky end and was drowned. Miller and Skertchly (1878) provide a fascinating summary and commentary on many of the early sources of information.

Hill, in his 1948 book, gives an indication of the productivity of these landscapes in an account of the preparations for the visit of King Edward I and his Parliament to Lincoln on 20 January 1301. The King was the guest of John Dalderby, Bishop of Lincoln, at his manor house at Nettleham until 12 February, when he moved to Lincoln until 4 March. In the previous October, the Sheriff of Lincoln had received an order to provide 400 quarters of corn, 1,000 quarters of oats, hay enough for 400 horses, 100 cows and oxen, 100 pigs and 300 sheep. In November, a further order arrived for 400 quarters of corn, 100 beeves, 60 live pigs and 400 sheep for the use of the royal household. The beeves and sheep were to be well salted and placed in the larder at Lincoln. Additional to the food was drink, with 3,121 gallons of ale priced 1*d* per gallon consumed between 19 February and 1 March. A principal citizen of Lincoln, merchant Stephen de Stanham, supplied sugar, figs, and other goods to a value of £96 14*s* 5*d*, and fish to the cook's office at £54 10*s*, and herrings and stockfish to the King's son Edward for £6 16*s*. Whilst much of this food and drink was supplied from a wide area, clearly a considerable amount came from the fens and wetlands that surrounded the city.

Activities such as fowling were regulated as much as was possible in a remote and bleak landscape. In the sixteenth century, measures were adopted to try to control the fowlers. In 1534, an 'Acte agenst the Decstruccyon of Wyld-fowle' was passed. This was in response to the taking of ducks, mallards, wigeons, teals, wild geese and divers other kinds of wildfowl. The problem was that:

> … divers persons next inhabiting in the countries and places within this realm, where the substance of the same wild fowl hath been accustomed to breed, have in the summer season, at such time as the said old fowl be moulted, and not yet replenished with feathers to fly, nor the young fowl fully feathered perfectly to fly, by certain nets and other engines and policies, yearly taken great number of the same fowl, in such wise that the brood of wild-fowl is almost thereby wasted and consumed, and daily is like more and more to waste and consume, if remedy be not therefore provided.

This gives a clear picture of the pressures on the resource at that time of the year when the birds are particularly vulnerable. The Act was in two parts. The first prohibited the taking of birds between the last day of May and the last day of August; the second prohibited the taking of the eggs of certain birds – on pain of imprisonment. However, the issues were difficult to resolve and the first part of the Act was repealed in 1550, because benefit was 'thereby taken away from the poor people that were wont to live by their skill in taking of the said fowl whereby they were wont at that time to sustain themselves, with their poor households'.

Therefore, the protection only lasted a short while and the wildfowl were open to human predation on a vast scale. By the late sixteenth century, the inhabitants of Cambridgeshire were described by Camden as 'rude, and uncivil folk who applied their minds to grazing, fishing and fowling'. However, the terms 'rude' and 'uncivil' probably here mean basic, ignorant and uncivilised rather than unpleasant. Michael Drayton noted that 'the fowler is employed his lymed twigs to set', a reminder that, in the early days, actually catching birds required a degree of cunning and art. Geese were a major resource for the fenmen, both the visiting winter migrants, and the domestic tame geese. Pennant again provided some insight into the identity of these birds and suggested that the domestic stock was descended from greylag geese that bred wild in the fens. Gurney noted that the geese owned by fenmen were a key source of their wealth, with huge numbers of tame geese bred for their feathers. These were plucked five times a year, the first after Lady Day (6 April) for feathers and quills, and then for the feathers only. A single individual might keep up to 1,000 geese and each bird would rear seven or eight young. By the end of the season, they might have several thousand birds. The flocks were attended by a 'gozzard' or 'goose-herd', who, twice a day, drove them to water. This helped keep them both exercised and in good health. Once they were ready for the market, the surplus birds were driven to London to supply the poulterers.

Isaac Casaubon visited Ely in 1611 and was struck by the character of the region. He wrote that the 200 houses at Benwick were all on small islands and the inhabitants were occupied in fishing and fowling. It was here that he came across both bittern and dotterel and his description is a vivid recollection:

> In the Ely country there is a bird about as big as a hen, in colour a mixture of yellow and grey, etc., having very long legs, and called Bliterra. It is said to be in the habit of introducing its bill into one of the nearest reeds, and of thundering forth a voice so horrible that those unused to the thing, say it is that of an evil spirit, and so loud that two gentlemen assured me it could be heard for three or four miles. It is not agreeable meat.

He goes on to describe the dotterel:

> The Otus or Otis, indeed, is a bird less than a partridge, and a mimic, wont to be beguiled and caught by silly imitation. Great men and kings are keen in the chase of this bird. It furnishes very delicate meat, if my palate is sufficiently instructed. I have also seen them alive. They say that if the fowler lifts one of his feet the bird does the same, if he extends an arm the bird extends a wing, and imitates all his actions.

Fowling was growing from a local pastime and source of sustenance to a significant industry, with exports from the Fens to the towns and cities. Godwits, for example, were fattened for the London market. Casaubon continued:

> We also saw certain choice birds which are fattened for sale. Amongst the rest one called the Godwit, that is to say, Dei ingenium, which is wonderfully commended, so that at Wisbeach, where provisions are very cheap, the bird feeder said he sold these birds for five or six English halfpence (solidis) – equal to fifty or sixty French apiece but when he took them to London he brought back twenty English pence for each. The bird is of the size of a small partridge, or even less. Its colour is grey, and has a bill longer than my middle finger stretched out. I ate it at the Lord Bishop's table, and did not think highly of it: I do not see the reason why it is so greatly preferred to the Otus.

Clearly, taste and choice of wildfowl for the table varied from person to person! The quality of the dish was also an important point of discussion. Dr Muffett, writing in the late 1500s, suggested that:

> A Woodcock is a meat of good temperance. Quails and Plovers and Lapwings doth nourish but little, for they do engender melancholy humours. Young Turtle Doves do engender good blood. A young Heron is lighter of digestion than a Crane. A Bustard well killed and ordered is a nutritive meat. A Bittern is not so hard of digestion as is a Heron. A Shoveler [Spoonbill] is lighter of digestion than a Bittern. A Pheasant hen, a Moor-cock and a Moor-hen, except they be set abroad, they be nutritive …

It is generally household accounts, itineraries of visitors, and the notes of hunters and fowlers that provide the most detail on the landscape and its wildlife. By their very nature, these are at best a smattering of observations from random locations across the region. However, they can give a vivid picture of the type of birdlife found. They also provide an insight into the incredibly rich resource of the Fens, beyond anything that we can comprehend today. For example, there are accounts from the Lestrange household 1519-1578, from Hunstanton in north Norfolk, right on the edge of the fenland. These household accounts survived over the centuries and extracts were published in the early 1900s. This gives a unique insight into the species that were regarded not as sporting game but as produce of the land for the kitchen and hence the table. These birds were variously netted and snared, or were shot with crossbows or even guns. When they arrived for the kitchen, the catch was logged and recorded meticulously. Mallard were the most frequent of around forty-two species, which included swan, plover, stint, curlew, redshank, green goose (i.e. grass-fed tame geese), and 'wylde' goose (probably pink-feet and brent geese). There were also 'cockle ducks', which were presumably scoters that were common in the Wash and ate cockles and mussels. Some of the names of birds are difficult to interpret but many are obvious. There are references to dotterel, with 2s paid to 'Blogge of Walsyngham for xxiv dotterelles', and then forty-eight dotterel with godwits and stints (probably ringed plover). Great bustard was also brought to the Hall. And in 1527, on 11 July, 'A crane & a busterd kylled with ye crosbowe'. Earlier, on 23 April, it was noted that 'a bustard & iij mallards kylled with ye crosbowe'.

In 1543, there is a reference to 'Itm. Of Canseller's killing oon busterd 7 iiij cranes whereof iij cranes were given oon to Sir Roger Toownshend another to Sir Richard South and the thred to my lady Hastings'. The Lestrange accounts have numerous references to cranes, which were clearly quite common, and much sought after for the table. Indeed, as early as the reign of King John, cranes were favourite quarry to hunt with falcons, and there seems to have been little difficulty in finding them. Therefore, we can assume that such birds were not uncommon in this abundant habitat of expansive marshes and fens. If the King, based at Winchester, was not inclined to go hunting, then he would despatch fowlers under safe-conduct to 'proceed to diverse parts of the kingdom for the purpose of catching cranes and other birds'. In this way, the royal larder was kept well stocked.

In 1422, it was the coronation of King Henry VI, and the birds served included 'egrettes, curlew, cocks, plover, quails, snipe, larks, swan, heron, crane, partridge, bittern, and peacock'. Court rolls and other accounts give glimpses of information. In May 1318, several persons were fined at a Court Baron of the Bishop of Ely for collecting bitterns' eggs (*ova botorum*). Bitterns were at the time more numerous than herons in the Southern Fens, largely due to the scarcity of tall trees for heronries. Bittern was favoured for the table, mentioned in most 'dietaries' of the time. They were less fishy than herons and were recommended eaten without sauce and just with added salt.

Another bird highly regarded for food, but often overlooked in histories, is the spoonbill. This has sometimes been missed because of the peculiar names given to it, particularly 'popelere' or 'popelar', and 'shovelarde' or 'shoulard'. The Lestrange accounts detail twenty-three spoonbills and most of these were 'branchers', i.e. young birds, which suggests local breeding. Indeed, this was the prime condition for eating spoonbill, which were procured by means of a pole with a hook on the end. When Cardinal Wolsey visited King's Lynn in August 1521, he and his retinue were presented with three shovelards (spoonbills), three bitterns, ten cygnets, twelve capons, thirteen plovers, eight pike, and three tench. It is certain that spoonbill was a native breeding species at this time and Gurney, writing in 1921, asserts that other birds such as night heron would also have been present. An Act in 1564 under Elizabeth addressed the need to deliberately destroy rooks' nests, but laid down specific protection for 'herons, egrytes, paupers, swannes or shovelers'; both 'paupers' and 'shovelers' being references to spoonbills. The legislation and the household accounts make it clear that in the sixteenth and seventeenth centuries both young spoonbills and young herons were much favoured for the tables of the rich. Indeed, many birds that ate fish, or birds of freshwater, were highly esteemed. Despite breeding in Britain, the spoonbill was a summer visitor and so, for winter festivities, attention turned to cranes and bitterns. Whilst it was the young spoonbills that were generally eaten in England, the older birds could be taken too. There is a note in Gesner's *Historia Animalium* which refers to the taking of older birds on the shoreline, probably by netting: 'a schofler vel shoelard, Platea nostra … is taken on the sea-shore in England, and fed in confinement on fish and the insides of fowls, and other offal from the kitchen'. Thomas Muffett, in 1595, wrote that 'Plateae Shovelars feed most commonly upon the Sea-coast upon cockles and shell-fish; being taken home and dieted with new garbage and good meat, they are nothing inferior to fatted Gulls'. The latter were black-headed gulls; they were well fed on bullock's liver and were especially favoured.

As noted, the heron or hernshaw was another bird for the table and was also considered excellent for hawking – 'a marvellous and delectable pastime'. The high regard with which they were held for sport was reflected in the various statutes passed to protect them from unauthorised persecution. Both Scottish and English kings passed laws to protect herons. One of these stated that there must be no shooting with hail-shot or handgun within 600 yards (549m) of a heronry. Henry VII forbade all killing of herons except by means of the hawk and the longbow. In other words, the use of the more accurate and deadly crossbow was forbidden. Some ancient tenures of woods detailed the expected production of herons for the table, and it is clear that they were much favoured at Hunstanton.

Surprisingly the bittern is mentioned only once in the Lestrange accounts, on 22 April 1527: 'Item a buttour kylled with ye crosbowe'. It may simply be that the account relates specifically to the immediate estate and bittern was limited there because of the lack of extensive reed beds.

William Farren (in Lack, 1934) wrote that his father as a boy in the 1840s had seen large baskets of ruffs and reeves that had been netted in the Fens and brought to Cambridge market. The demand for exotic wildfowl at the table continued until quite late. Pennant recorded them being caught in big numbers, with one fenman taking six dozen in a single morning. By the mid-1800s, they were reduced to uncommon summer visitors. The local fowlers and fishermen regarded proposals for draining the fens with understandable suspicion and concern. Their lives and livelihoods were at stake. The argument was clear from their perspective:

> … The Fens preserved in their present property, afford great plenty and variety of fish and fowl, which here have their seminaries and nurseries; which will be destroyed on draining thereof; so that none will be had, but at excessive prices.

The counter argument was, 'a tame sheep was better than a wild duck'.

Because of the pressures for 'improvement', between 1630 and 1653, with the break for the English Civil War, the so-called Bedford Level in the Southern Fenland was drained. In 1662, in his *History of Imbanking and Draining*, Dugdale suggested that the concerns of the wildfowlers were groundless. In his words:

> As to the decay of fish and fowl, which hath been no small objection against his public work, there is not much likelihood thereof; for notwithstanding this general draying, there are so many great meres and lakes still continuing, which be indeed the principal harbours for them, that there will be no want of either; for in the vast spreading waters they seldom abide, the rivers, channels, and meers being their principal receptacles; which being now increased, will rather augment than diminish their store. And that both fish and fowl are with much more ease taken by this restraint of the waters within such bounds, as we daily see; forasmuch as all nets for fishing are better made use of in the rivers and meers, than when the waters are out of those narrower limits; and that decoys are now planted upon many drained levels, whereby greater numbers of fowl are caught, than by any other engines formerly used; which could not at all be made there, did the waters, as formerly, overspread the whole country.

THE SWALLOWTAIL STORY – A TWIST IN THE TALE

The fenland and broadland swallowtails seem very closely tied to their food plant the milk parsley, a species of rich fen which grows in sedge and litter fields and is strongly affected by site management. It depends on suitable cutting regimes of sedge and litter.

However, whilst a key problem is the drying of the site and the ecological succession to scrub and carr, there are other problems linked to the history of drainage and then isolation. The Norfolk population and probably the relict Fen population prior to extinction have become genetically different from their predecessors, and this changed genetics is at the core of their current failures. Furthermore, studies on museum specimens of swallowtail butterflies in comparison with those of the Norfolk Broads, suggests that the two populations were different. Therefore, the Wicken butterflies were genetically different from those of Hickling Broad in Norfolk, and this was probably a result of the fragmentation of the once extensive old fenland habitat. Nevertheless, there is still more to this story.

Early records of the swallowtail in Britain indicate a formerly much wider distribution in southern England. Associated with this, was possibly the use of a more extensive range of food plants. It is suggested that these included the relatively common wild carrot (*Daucus carota*). If this were the case, then the establishment and maintenance of colonies would be so much easier. Obviously the landscape was also dramatically different, with extensive commons, 'wastes' and small wetlands, and this too would have favoured the swallowtail.

The now endemic British subspecies, *Papilio machaon britannicus*, is strictly a fenland butterfly and it feeds only on milk parsley, yet the more widespread continental subspecies, *Papilio machaon bigeneratus*, has a less restricted diet. The early records could be just occasional vagrants from continental Europe. However, I suspect that this is not the case since the species was collected in some numbers in Dorset and perhaps elsewhere too. The swallowtail butterfly had been locally abundant in the fenlands of Huntingdonshire and Cambridgeshire but, by the late 1800s, with drainage and agricultural improvement, there were already concerns for its survival. Maybe as the Fens became the last refuge of this butterfly in Britain, perhaps isolation further defined our endemic subspecies?

One of the big issues for an isolated population of butterflies is the risk to survival, and the lack of breeding opportunities, for individual adults which leave their home site. In the undrained fens, this would be good; the insects moved out to breed and find new areas, and the genetic mixing required for success took place. However, in an isolated pocket of habitat, literally an island in an unfavourable sea of farmland, the results are disastrous. Here we see evolution in action. The conditions most favour individuals that do not disperse widely, but which remain in their original breeding site. This may help them survive but it also encourages inbreeding and discourages any wider dispersal to new areas. This appears to be what has happened to the swallowtail in the Fens.

Researcher Jack Dempster found that by studying museum collections of swallowtail butterflies, he could track the physical changes, as manifestations of underlying genetic transformations. Following the drainage of the wider fen landscape in the 1800s, the swallowtail population at Wicken began to develop smaller wings and a narrower thorax, both features associated with weaker flight and shorter flying distances. Interestingly, after the 1920s, the Norfolk Broads population began to show the same changes, and so in both populations the adults that fly within the site survive and breed. Those which are stronger, and fly outside the core site, perish. Within only a few decades, the populations were showing remarkable evolutionary adaptation to their changed environment. This is a remarkable case study and a serious message for conservation.

Indeed, his argument had some merit, since the fish and fowl in the drains and dykes were abundant and more easily caught. However, perhaps Dugdale did not foresee the total removal of all these 'great meres and lakes', and the impact of that scale of drainage seen today. I suspect he would have been shocked at what destruction happened in the following centuries.

Dugdale was right that the drainage would bring about a revolution in the methods of catching the wildfowl. The traditional method had been to drive large numbers of birds into a net at the end of a mere or pool by means of a large number of assistants and boats. However, as successive meres were drained, and, importantly, as firearms became more widely available and better suited to the task, the birds became less tame and less abundant. This meant that the fenman had to rely less on obvious physical means such as driving the birds, and more on trickery and intrigue. They had to entice whatever birds they could get, into the nets during the winter months. Their task became considerably easier and more efficient with the importation of a Dutch invention – the 'Dutch Decoy'. The term 'decoy' had been in use in England but only applied to tunnels or cages of netting into which the birds were driven. In 1678, the pioneering English naturalist John Ray described the decoy in his *Ornithology* as a 'new artifice but lately introduced by the Dutch'. His description is of a decoy used to entice large numbers of winter wildfowl. The Dutch Decoy was to become one of the characteristics of the fen landscape. It has been suggested that at the time of James I, Sir William Woodhouse was the first person in England to erect a decoy for taking wild ducks. The decoy pond was generally a small pool of perhaps only a few acres. On this water were set a number of tame ducks trained to swim up the pipes or channels, of which there were usually four, six, or eight arms called 'pipes'. These pipes were enclosed with netting. A screen generally made of reeds was set up alongside the tunnel to hide the decoy-man and his dog from the wild ducks. Wildfowl, attracted to the pond, followed the tame ducks up the pipes and were caught at the neck end. Oldfield's *Historical Account of Wainfleet* describes the success of ten decoys on the old East Fen just a few years before it was enclosed. The ten decoys, of which five were in Friskney parish, provided 31,200 ducks (made up of ducks such as mallard, wigeon and teal) for the London markets. The government carried on trying to regulate and control the independent-minded fowlers, with a variety of Game Preservation Acts. That of 1710 set the period from 1 July to 1 September as the season in which people might not: 'by Hayes, Tunnels, or other Nets, drive and take any wild Duck, teal, Widgeon, or any other Water Fowl in any of the Fens, Lakes, Broad Waters, or other places of Resort For Wild Fowl.'

Shooting wild duck. (Victorian print)

There were other reasons and causes for controls over hunting and game. For example, in 1765 an Act was passed for the preservation of fish in ponds and conies in warrens, with provisos for the taking of rabbits or conies. The concern was for the integrity of the flood banks and the damage that rabbits might cause. The exemption clause stated that:

> Whereas great mischief has been, and still may be, occasioned by the increase of conies upon the sea and river banks in the county of Lincoln, or upon the land or ground within a certain distance from the said banks; for remedy thereof be it enacted that nothing in this act contained shall extend to prevent any person from killing and destroying, or from taking or carrying away in the day time any conies that shall be found on any sea or river banks, erected, or to be erected, for the preservation of the adjoining lands from being overflowed by the sea or river waters, so far as the flux and reflux of the tide does extent, or upon any land within one furlong distance of such banks, but that it shall be lawful for any person to enter upon any such banks, land or ground, as aforesaid, within the County of Lincoln, and to kill, destroy, and carry away in the day time, to his or their own use, any conies so found upon any such, doing little damage as may be to the owner or tenant.

For the locals, catching conies or wildfowl was an important means of sustenance or of commerce. The older traditional way of catching wildfowl by driving them into nets on one of the larger pools continued for some time. Defoe wrote about Cambridgeshire:

> In these fenns are abundance of those admirable pieces of art call'd duckoys; that is to say, places so adapted for the harbour and shelter of wild-fowl, and then furnish'd with a breed of those they call decoy-ducks, who are taught to allure and entice their kind to the places

they belong to, that it is incredible what quantities of wild-fowl of all sorts, duck, mallard, teal, widgeon, etc. they take in those duckoys, every week, during the season; it may be indeed guess'd at a little by this, that there is a duckoy not far from Ely, which pays to the landlord, Sir Tho. Hare 500l. a year rent, besides the charge of maintaining a great number of servants for the management; and from which duckoy alone they assured me at St. Ives, (a town on the Ouse, where the fowl they took was always brought to be sent to London;) that they generally sent up three thousand couple a week.

However, Darby points out that although hosts of wildfowl frequented the area, the Cambridgeshire peat fens were not the real decoy lands because they were liable to floods, and were without trees or underwood. By the early nineteenth century, most of the Cambridgeshire fenland was 'winter grounds' – being dry in winter. By the time of Payne-Gallwey's classic *Book of Duck Decoys* (1886), there were no active decoys left in the county, though memories remained of three – at Leverington, Chatteris, and Whittlesea. Just as in South Yorkshire, the decoyman had gone, just a passing feature in the evolving landscape of the Fens. The memories followed and were lost, and the wildfowl disappeared.

In the 1950s, Wentworth-Day gave figures for the catches from selected decoys in the nine-teenth century, and the numbers are massive. Overall, the Ashby Decoy in Bottisford, 2 miles (3.2km) from the River Trent, was the most successful decoy recorded in England. Accurate records from 1833/4 until 1867/8 gave an average of 2,741 birds *per annum*. The highest recorded individual drive yielded 113 wild duck, and the most successful day produced 248, the species taken including mallard, shoveler, teal, wigeon, gadwall, and pintail. Over thirty-five seasons there were around 100,000 birds 'harvested', with around half being teal and half mallard. However, this was the end of the era as many of the decoys were lost directly or indirectly through drainage and improvement. This was the case both in the Northern Fen, such as at Potteric Carr, and in the Southern Fens, such as Fleet Decoy in Fleet Fen, which was lost with the cutting of the South Holland Drain in 1793.

The Dowsby Decoy near Falkingham took around 12,000 to 13,000 wild duck in an exceptional season. It was recorded that from 1 October 1765 to 1 April 1766 it caught over 13,000, and these were sold as follows: 13,008 birds sold to Mrs Gibbs of Langtoft at 7s a dozen: £379 8s; eleven dozen (132) birds sold at the decoy: £5 8s 10d; and twenty couples sold to Mrs Dodd: £1 10s. This gives an overall income from the decoy of £386 6s 10d, which in 1766 was a very tidy sum. Many of the birds caught were for the London markets. In one season, 1829, the Friskney Decoys sent 31,200 wildfowl to the city. This was five years before the enclosure of the fen, after which the catch fell to 5,000 birds or less.

Netting of wading birds, particularly plovers, had long been a profitable enterprise in the Fens. The birds taken were mainly waders and included dunlins, knots, ruffs and reeves, redshanks, lapwings, golden plovers, and occasionally curlews, and both bar-tailed and black-tailed godwits. Fowlers took as many as four dozen and nine lapwings at one go, and twenty-four dozen in a single day. One of the most famous or perhaps infamous hunters of all time was the Edwardian Lord Walsingham, generally considered in knowledgeable cir-cles to be one of the greatest shots that ever lived. In January 1889, he shot the biggest and most varied bag ever recorded. It included thirty-nine pheasants, six partridges, twenty-three mallards, six gadwalls, four pochards, one goldeneye, seven teal, three swans, one woodcock, three snipe, one woodpigeon, two herons, sixty-five coots, two moorhens, nine hares, sixteen rabbits, an otter, a pike, and a large rat. Again, this gives some idea of the wildlife abundance in these areas even in the late 1800s, well into the drainage era. Nature eventually had its revenge and Walsingham's obsessive hunting led to his bankruptcy.

In 1934, David Lack discussed the changes in the bird fauna of the fenland over a period of around 150 years preceding. Lack based his writing on the studies of Jenyns and Farren in the 1800s, along with more contemporary observations. Some of the typical species mentioned were bearded tit, barn owl, marsh harrier, hen harrier, red kite, greylag goose, stone curlew, ruff, black-tailed godwit, black tern, great bustard, corncrake, spotted crake, water rail, raven, marsh tit, savi's warbler, wood warbler, spotted flycatcher, stonechat, common redstart, wry-neck, and quail. By the mid-1800s, birds such as snipe, water rail, and spotted crake, all once characteristic species of the region, were reduced to a few breeding pairs just about hanging on. By the 1930s, all these species were either extinct or dramatically reduced. Overall, over 20 per cent of the Cambridgeshire breeding bird fauna present at the beginning of the nineteenth century was lost by the middle of the twentieth. David Lack acknowledges the fact that there may have been multiple and complex causes. However, he states that there was clearly one over-riding factor, which was the drainage of the fens and marshes. This destroyed many of the old breeding grounds and rendered those that remained more accessible to human disturbance and depredation. Whittlesea Mere, the last big, open water-body, was

Water rail. (Victorian print)

drained in 1851. Lack attributes the loss of bearded tit, marsh harrier, hen harrier, ruff, black-tailed godwit, black tern, spotted crake, water rail, Savi's warbler, and stonechat, directly to fenland drainage and the increased cultivation of this and of other 'waste' land. 'Improvement', enclosure, and cultivation of other areas – such as chalk downland and drier heaths – clearly affected species like great bustard, corncrake, quail and stone curlew, but they were also part of the bigger picture of the fenland avifauna destroyed by the inexorable process of agricultural intensification. This was probably further exacerbated by the availability of firearms. The latter certainly affected the species that were considered good to eat: especially ruff and great bustard. Birds of prey, believed to be harmful to poultry and to game, were also victims of the massacre, including raven, red kite and even barn owl.

According to Miller and Skertchly in 1878, the marsh harrier went first, then the hen harrier, whilst the Montagu's harrier and short-eared owl lingered on in smaller areas of breeding habitat. With birds of prey there is sometimes confusion when reading old accounts, since the term 'buzzard' was used in the Fens for harriers rather than the true buzzards. Two purple herons were shot near Ely in the winter of 1826-27, and another at an unknown date. A great white heron was shot on Thorney Fen in summer 1849, and two little egrets were shot at Whittlesea in about 1850. I think we can see a trend! The slaughter continued in later times, even when the avifauna was all but gone. Another wetland 'special', the bittern, was still recorded most years up to the 1930s, and, for example, was seen at Wicken Fen in 1926, 1928, 1929, 1933 and 1934. Nevertheless, one was shot on the Washes around 1931 and one at Manea in January 1924.

Surprisingly, the population of some birds increased with habitat change. Common snipe became more common over the period from the early 1800s onwards, and perhaps this was due to a reduction in open water but a consequent increase in wet pasture and meadows. Great crested grebe, a bird of pen water habitats, was apparently rare and just hanging on, whilst its smaller cousin the dabchick increased; again probably benefitting from the networks of smaller drains. The short-eared owl was apparently unknown in the region in the early 1800s; by the 1930s it was present in small numbers. Similarly, woodcock, tufted duck, and pochard appear to have colonised the area during the latter stages of the great drainage.

Drainage not only affected breeding birds, but visiting species too. The hooded crow was an abundant winter visitor, but by the 1930s was very scarce. Lack suggests this may also be due to land cultivation. However, it was more likely a national or international decline affected by changing climate, and has continued to the present day. Fenland drainage dramatically affected the visiting winter wildfowl. The dotterel, another formerly abundant winter visitor, was probably affected by cultivation of downland, lowland heath, and commons. The huge numbers killed for the pot were also responsible for much of the decrease.

BIRDLIFE IN THE 1930s

Whilst Darby and Lack discussed the catastrophic declines from around 1800 to 1930, little did they know that worse was to come, and that further losses of the remaining avifauna would take place in the next few decades. They also described the Cambridgeshire landscape in the 1930s: 'flat, but that is not to say that it is uninteresting, and to those who know it well, the fenland in the north of the county has an extreme attraction possessed by no other part of England.'

By the 1930s, almost the whole of the fen country was under cultivation, with few woods and almost no heaths. Wicken and the nearby fens were the only large stretches of uncultivated ground remaining. Despite Dugdale's seventeenth-century assertions, there were no longer any significant areas of permanent open water. By the 1930s, the most typical bird of the region was the wood pigeon. Skylarks were common on the open ploughed fields, but meadow pipits only on grassland. Corn bunting was described as not uncommon, and stone curlew bred on open fields. Nightjar occurred in a few areas and quail bred most years. In winter, the birdlife became what we would now regard as typical of the wide-open, lowland agricultural landscape, with flocks of lapwing, golden plover, black-headed gull and common gull. Rooks and the winter thrushes, fieldfare and redwing, joined these winter birds. With occasional areas of marsh along the river valleys, birds such as reed bunting, yellow wagtail sedge and reed warblers, mallard, lapwing, redshank, common snipe and occasional shovelers all bred. Whilst ponds and pools across the whole area were now rare, where they did occur, dabchick, moorhen, and coot all nested.

Lack goes on to describe the birds of the 1930s fenland, the landscape of which, like the rest of Cambridgeshire and East Anglia generally, was almost all under cultivation. He noted the islands that rose slightly above the flat landscape, and especially around Wisbech and Ely, and the large open fields. Any hedgerows were small and their place generally taken by ditches and small 'rains' that connected up to larger dykes and lodes. With woods and copses extremely scarce, the only trees, except in and around villages, were willows and poplars. Here, huge flocks of lapwing and golden plover, with abundant black-headed and common gulls, populated the winter fields. Herring gulls and pink-footed geese were also common. Rooks were generally common and increasing, and the most typical birds of the cultivated fen were corn bunting and sedge warbler, together with reed bunting. Dotted in amongst the wide open landscape was the occasional plantation, and this might harbour long-eared owl, sparrowhawk, and even nesting herons.

It was noted that areas of wet pasture and meadow occurred in the Fens, and especially in the strip of land between the Old and New Bedford Rivers of the Washes, near Earith and Mepal. These areas held similar species to those in the riverside marshes noted earlier. In wintertime, these 'washes' were flooded to become one of the richest water-bird sites in the country. Occasionally, there were small patches of uncultivated reed bed or tall grass. These attracted reed bunting, sedge and reed warblers. The only extensive areas of such habitat by this time were those remaining at Wicken Sedge Fen, Burwell and Reach Fens, with some also at Fulbourn Fen. Wicken Sedge Fen was notable for breeding grasshopper warbler, short-eared owl, and Montagu's harrier. Reed bunting, sedge and red warblers also bred along with mallard, shoveler, garganey, teal, common snipe, redshank, and water rail. There were also occasional stonechats.

MAMMALS OF THE ANCIENT FENS

Miller and Skertchly summarised the sources known at the time of their writing. As would be expected, the beaver was quite common in the ancient fenlands, as evidenced in the north by the place name Beverley. Utilising open pools and not necessarily constructing dams of their own, they probably behaved much as they do in mainland Europe today. In Britain, by perhaps 1200 or 1300, the beaver had been hunted into extinction, probably through hunting for its fur. Both roe deer and red deer were very common in the ancient Fens. When the great Forest of Kesteven was a royal hunting ground, the borderers often got 'into sad disgrace' for disturbing them. The people of Whittlesea, Thorney and Ramsey, in the year 1306, 'wasted all the fen of Kyngesdelfe, of the alders, hassacks, and rushes … so that the king's deer could not have harbour there'. Similarly, a 'certain wicked John Le Wode' was also damaging the deer habitat when he 'burnt a great portion of the same fen … [and] caused great loss to the king, in his harts, hinds and goats'. The situation of deer in the Northern Fen was described earlier and shows the tensions between the ordinary people subsisting in this environment and the use of land for hunting and game preservation. Throughout their long history, the fenlands have been contested landscapes.

Another once-important game animal was the wild boar; a prized beast of Saxon and Norman hunts. Wild boar survived in Britain until 1620, and must have formerly been common in the fenlands. Although they are now re-establishing across much of Britain from escapees, there is presently little suitable habitat across most of the Fen regions. Wild boar is an important species in terms of ecosystem functioning, and especially in the dispersal of certain fungi and potentially their inter-relationships with flowering plants. So in many ways, it would be an exciting moment to have them once again roaming across a re-wetted landscape of fens and carrs!

The mammal fauna of the fenlands in more recent times was better known. For the Victorian fens particularly, with the advent of modern gamekeepers and of amateur naturalists, the situation is reasonably well known. Wetland specialists such as otter had been lost, and larger mammals such as badger were generally rare, though fox was quite common and often 'preserved' for the hunt. The other smaller mustelids (the weasel family) appear to have been quite uncommon and were rigorously and routinely exterminated to conserve game. Another wetland and farmland specialist, the harvest mouse, was quite localised but frequent in some areas such as around Ely. The eminent naturalist, Gilbert White of Selbourne was the first to document the species, communicating his discovery in a letter to Thomas Pennant on 4 August 1767:

> I have had no opportunity yet of procuring any of those mice which I mentioned to you in town. The person that brought me the last says they are plenty in harvest, at which time I will take care to get more; and will endeavour to put the matter out of doubt whether it be a nondescript species or not.

'Nondescript' here means 'undiscovered or 'undescribed', showing that even some commonplace mammals and birds were not yet known to science.

Both water vole and field vole were widespread and common, the latter sometimes 'abounding in the Fens to an astonishing degree'. Brown hare and rabbit were both widespread and very abundant. Other small mammals, such as hedgehog, mole, mice and shrews were generally abundant. The water shrew, thriving along ditches and dykes, was, as might be expected, quite common in the fens. Of the bats, both noctule and pipistrelle were common but other species less so.

THE INSECTS AND OTHER INVERTEBRATES

Apart from classic and well-recorded sites such as Wicken Fen, and in the Northern Fens of Yorkshire and north Lincolnshire, Thorne and Hatfield Moors, little is known of the invertebrate faunas of the wider pre-drainage fenland. However, from the insight given by detailed studies on these remaining, and grossly affected sites, we can assume that it was incredibly rich. Wicken has long been the haunt of entomologists and lepidopterists in search of rare and exciting finds. Thorne and Hatfield have produced one of the richest lists of insects and other invertebrates of any wetland site in Britain. Indeed, some of these insects are unique to this location in Britain, and in a few cases to Europe. Peter Skidmore provided a very personal account of the insects and the entomologists involved in their study. He touched, for example, on the special butterfly of the Northern Fens (the large heath or Manchester ringlet: *Coenonympha tullia*), which is absent from the southern East Anglian sites. He also gives a very compelling account of the impacts of land-use change and especially of drainage. It is very likely then, that in the drainage and 'improvement' of the Fens, we have lost to Britain and perhaps to the world, numerous animal and plant species. The most striking losses may well be amongst the invertebrates and especially the insects. However, this is not the place to discuss the details of the entomologists' work and findings. They are described abundantly elsewhere and interested readers should turn to the accounts of years of meticulous research (e.g. Limbert *et al*, Buckland *et al*, Van de Noort). However, it is worth taking note of some of the more spectacular insects and their demise with the passing of the wet fen landscape.

The most notable, and the most sought after by Victorian entomologists, were the fenland butterflies and to a lesser extent the moths. Miller and Skertchly noted both the limited area that was searched and the paucity of resident entomologists. Apparently, they were far less numerous than might have been expected given that the region had been so famous for its insects; forty to fifty years previously, English entomological collectors had depended on the Cambridgeshire and Huntingdonshire Fens for 'many choice species'. Monkswood on the western fringe was also noteworthy for its rarities. In the early 1800s, with the huge popularity of entomology and especially butterfly collecting, the Whittlesea Fens were famous for the spectacular swallowtail, and the similarly special large copper. Both these species 'abounded' around Whittlesea. Holme Fen, adjoining Whittlesea Mere, was still relatively unaltered, as was 'a portion of Wicken Fen'. Beyond the limited sites remaining by the 1870s, the commentators stated that, 'Extensive drainage works have annihilated this once rich entomological hunting ground'. Wicken Fen, with its dense growth of water plants and its broad expanse of reeds and rushes, was described as one of the best, if not the only, remaining example of the old fens, furnishing 'a greater number of fen insects than any other equal area in the district'.

By the 1870s, the numbers of many fenland butterflies and moths had reduced dramatically or disappeared altogether. The most obvious were ones like the swallowtail, which were once spread generally over the Fens, but by then were found regularly only at Wicken Fen. Dependent mostly on its food-plant the marsh milk parsley, the decline was clearly due to 'continued drainage, together with its unstinting capture and destruction of the pupa by the annual cutting of the sedge'.

Dramatic changes occurred during the 1800s, as true fen species retreated and those of drier habitats expanded to fill the vacant niches. Most of the heathland insects had long since disappeared. The absence of detailed information on the formerly common species of the fen-land is a problem because almost all knowledge was just of the particularly rare insects of interest to the collectors. This is something that has only relatively recently been fully recognised by ecologists generally, and can still cause difficulties in evaluating sites and habitats. Despite the difficulties, there was already substantial lepidopteran (butterflies and moths) fauna recorded by the 1800s, with around 1,161 species known, including fifty-seven butterflies. It was also felt likely that there were more rare species to be added to the lists. Miller and Skertchly noted that several species new to Britain had been recorded in recent years. Yet already by the 1870s, some of the rarer species were believed extinct. Of the large copper butterfly that formerly abounded around Whittlesea Mere, Revd E.C.F. Jenkins, writing in 1859, commented that:

> … this beautiful insect, some thirty years ago, was so abundant in the unreclaimed Fens about Whittlesea, that I never expected to hear of its utter extermination. Its brilliant appearance on the wing in the sunshine I shall never forget, and to watch it sitting on the flower of the Eupatrium cannabinum and show the under side of its wings, was something ever to be remembered.

He goes on to explain how he 'took' sixteen in about half an hour in one spot on one par-ticular day. He attributed the demise of the large copper to both collectors able to find larvae on the very recently drained fens, and to the practice of burning off the vegetation during the reclamation process. Jenkins carries on:

> Thirty years ago the Fens about Whittlesea Mere were the most interesting localities for the entomologist, the botanist and the ornithologist. I lived then in that neighbourhood and those pursuits were my delight. Papilo machaon might then be had in any amount; the flight of P. hippothoe was abundant in July; the moth L. dispar was very plentiful; besides many other rare and beautiful insects. Now however, everything is totally changed. The great Northern Railroad runs through a part of the Fen where, when I was a boy, one could scarcely walk; at the spot where I used to land from my boat, on the edge of the mere stands a farm-house; my favourite locality for P. hippothoe – where bog myrtle used to grow in profusion and scent the Air with its delicious perfume – was (as I saw myself last season) converted into a field of stinking cole-seed, with a flock of sheep eating it off.

This is but one personal account of a single microcosm of the entire destruction that was occurring across the once vast fenland. Sometimes the losses were attributable directly to destruction and at other times more indirectly to loss of say a food plant, or the shrinkage of the wider habitat. The fragrant bog myrtle (*Myrica gale*) was formerly abundant in the Fens and an important food-plant for some of the special insects such as the rosy dart (*Noctua subrosea*). It was believed extinct in Cambridgeshire by around 1850. However, the plant did 'linger' near March and was still found at Holme Fen along with the associated moth.

A LOST FLORA

Early visitors to the Fens, and early writers, noted the more conspicuous plants and especially those that were used by the Fen people, such as reed, the two 'Bulrushes' *Scirpus lacustris* (the true bulrush) and *Typha latifolia* (the reedmace), along with willows and alders. Camden, in his *Britannia*, was the first to write about the plants and his source was probably John Ray, then Professor of Botany at Cambridge. He noted that:

> … all this country in the winter time, and sometimes for the greater part of the year is laid under water by the rivers Ouse, Grant, Nene, Welland, Glen, and Witham, for want of suf- ficient channels and passages, but when these keep to their proper channels, it so abounds with grass and a sort of rank hay (by them called 'Lid') which, when they have mown enough for their own use, in November they burn the rest, about which time one sees all this moorish country in a flame, to his great wonder and surprise.

Miller and Skertchly believed that this grass was *Glyceria*, the flote grass used by the locals as fodder and known to them as 'White Leed'. By the late 1800s it was still abundant, though much reduced because of drainage. They suggested that the ancient fens would have been totally covered by water in winter, but in summer would have dry places intermingled with spongy swamps, large lakes, and pools of water. This offered every condition suitable for all the varieties of marsh plants which, vigorous and in profusion, must have covered the surface during the summer season.

Professor Babington (Professor of Botany at Cambridge University) noted that the kind of vegetation that formerly occupied the Great Level of the Fens was little known to botanists. The Fens were a botanical '*terra incognita*'. He listed the most significant higher plants on Wicken Fen, one of the better-recorded sites. Lyson, in 1808, produced a list of rare plants, including *Schoenus mariscus, Selinum palustre, Cicuta virosa, Teucrium scordium, Lathyrus palustris, Ophrys loeselii, Malaxis paludosa,* and *Sparganium natans.* In 1878, they were still to be found in Wicken Sedge Fen, apart from *Ophrys loeselii*, which was believed extinct.

In *The History of the Drainage of the Great Level of the Fens* (1830), Wells described how 'the turf moors are covered with such plants as the heath, ling, and fern. The Myrica gale, plants and natural productions, and a grass with a beautiful white tuft called the Cotton Grass, are found in abundance'. Apparently, the cotton grass (*Eriophorum angustifolium*) was a conspicu- ous feature across much of the fenland in the early 1800s. By about 1870, it was in only a few places. Miller and Skertchly were sceptical about Wells' comment on heath and ling being so widespread. However, perhaps he was right and they were simply unaware of the changes in vegetation across some areas. The extensive wet, heathy moors such as were found in South Yorkshire and north Lincolnshire could have been a feature of the Southern Fenland land- scape too. Even by the Victorian time, the image of the Fens was changing from the vast tracts of wet heath, bog, fen and woodland, to that of open water and reed-fen. Miller and Skertchly suggested, quite reasonably, that the heath vegetation was typical of shallow bogs and moors found on higher ground but not typical of the deeper fens, but maybe they underestimated the former extent of deep peats and raised mires.

The type of vegetation attributed to the moors was with heaths (*Calluna vulgaris*, *Erica tetralix* and *cinerea*), sundews (*Drosera rotundifolia, intermedia*, and *anglica*), butterwort (*Pinguicula vulgaris*), cranberry (*Vaccinium oxycoccos*), bog asphodel (*Narthecium ossifragum*), and the spagnum mosses. However, it seems likely to me that these communities would have been abundant across wet heaths, bogs and more acidic areas in the Fens, and that Wells was correct in his description. That Miller and Skertchly dismissed his plant lists because they did not 'belong to the real Fen Flora', perhaps reflects the genuine loss of these communities between the early and late 1800s across much of the Cambridgeshire and South Lincolnshire Fens. They are found in Norfolk on sites such as Sheringham Common, and here they are close to 'typical' fen communities. Of course, they are also in lowland bog sites such as Thorne Moors in Yorkshire, and Fenns and Whixall Mosses in Shropshire. Certainly, by the 1930s, such vegetation had been banished from the landscape and perhaps even from memory.

Lack noted that in Cambridgeshire, there was a complete absence of 'downland vegetation', with the exception of Newmarket Heath and the golf course on the Gogs (Royston Heath being outside the county). Such species are certainly found in the Thorne and Hatfield Moors areas of the Northern Fens, with Jackson in 1882 (in Limbert, 1987) noting that the area 'affords plenty of cranberries, and an odoreferous shirb called gale; some call it sweet willow or Dutch myrtle'. The Thorne area had become famous amongst botanists in 1831, when one of the country's rarest plants, rannoch rush (*Scheuchzeria palustris*), was discovered at only its second English station. Again, another northern speciality, this is a species very intolerant of drainage, and always very rare. Land improvement has removed it from most of its few sites. George Pryme, in 1870, noted that:

> The drainage of the Fens has necessarily produced a vast destruction of the indigenous Marsh Plants and of the Insects which fed upon them, and many plants which were once common have become rare, others linger only in small patches of primitive Fen, as yet innocent of the labours of the drainers, while a few are probably extinct.

This is followed by lists of the plant species considered 'Probably extinct', 'Lingerers likely to disappear', and 'Once Common, but now Rare':

Probably extinct: *Senecio paludosa, Cineraria palustris, Sonchus palustris, Malaxis paludosa, Sturmia loeselii*

Lingerers likely to disappear: *Lathyrus palustris, Comarum palustre, Cicuta virosa, Helioscladium inundatum, Oenanthe lachenalii, Selinum palustre, Valeriana dioica, Carduus pratensis, Villarsia nymphaeoides, Menyanthes trifoliate, Pedicularis palustris, Veronica scutellaria, Teucrium scordium, Pinguicula vulgaris, Anagallis tenella, Myrica gale, Orchis latifolia, Orchis incarnata, Epipactis palustris, Luzula multiflora, Sparganium minus, Schoenus nigricans, Cladium mariscus, Eleocharis acicularis, Eriophorum angustifolium, Lastrea thelypteris, Osmunda regalis*

Once Common, but now Rare: *Ranunculus lingua, Nymphaea alba, Nuphar lutea, Nasturtium palustris, Bidena cernus, Achillea ptarmica, Carduus palustris, Utricularia vulgaris, Alisma*

Gathering leeches in Yorkshire. (*The Costume of Yorkshire*, 1885, edited by Edward Hailstone)

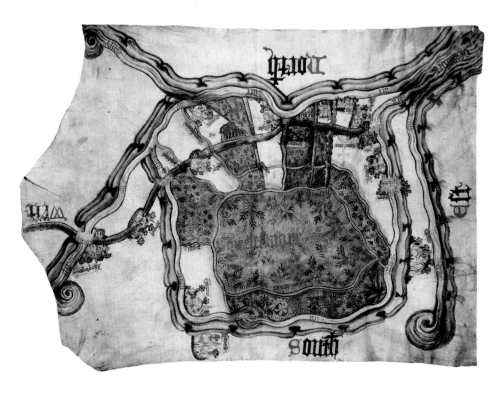

Map of Inclesmoor, *c.* 1410, based on a survey, probably in the 1320s. (© The National Archives, ref. MPC1/56)

Pike. (Victorian print)

Eels. (Victorian print)

Bittern. (Victorian print)

Grey Heron.

Marsh helleborine. (Victorian print)

Marsh marigold. (Victorian print)

Swallowtail butterfly life cycle.
(Victorian print)

Great fen ragwort.
(Victorian print)

Thorne Mere and the last royal deer hunt in 1609 – formerly in the collection of the late Robert Coulman but now apparently untraceable. It is unclear whether this was painted at the time (or at least by an eyewitness), or at a later date.

Prince Henry slaying a red deer stag, 1603.

Working the turf bank at Burwell, Cambridgeshire.

Spalding tulip fields in the early 1900s.

Watering the horses in the early 1900s.

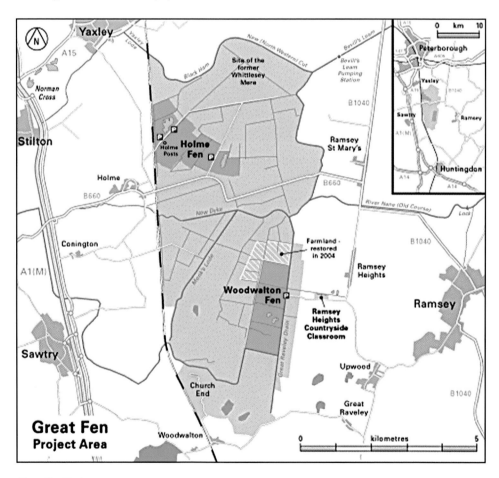

Great Fen Project map.

ranunculoides, Butomus umbellatus, Triglochin palustre, Scirpus fluitans, Carex pseudo-cyperus, Carex ampullacea, Carex vesicaria, Calamagrostis lanceolata, Calamagrostis epigejos

Miller and Skertchly said that they wrote of these lost rare plants 'With the view of preserving and handing down the remembrance of some of our lost Fen Plants', a quite fitting aspiration. Interestingly, they also noted the balance of diversity – with new species arriving with changed land-use, and the impact of invasive alien waterweeds. They cited Canadian pondweed, the 'American Weed', noting 'its present obnoxious position of an impeder of drainage and a source of considerable expenses to our Fen Districts'. Yet one could view this as nature fighting back against the drainers and blocking the ditches!

A number of early authors give hints as to the former flora of this unique landscape, but obviously these were only limited observations. With almost everything destroyed, the bulk of the information is lost forever. However, the Fens' proximity to the centre of learning at Cambridge ensured that some notable botanical lists survived to give a tantalising insight into what once was. Camden referred to 'Reeds, alders, and other water shrubs, especially willows … Besides these grow large quantities of Scordium or Water Germander upon the banks of ditches'. By the late 1800s, the latter was rare. Miller and Skertchly stated that it was not until drainage by steam replaced that by mills, and the process to improve was driven by potential increase in land value, that the final destruction came about. This made it worthwhile 'to enclose and cultivate every bit of it' and it was only then 'that any serious attack has been made upon the indigenous Marsh plants; but so long as rivers, drains, and ditches remain with water in them, most of the submerged plants will survive, although diminished in numbers.' They described those plants whose roots needed to be kept wet, such as marsh fern (*Thelyptris palustris*), and which were almost certain to disappear once the land had been made dry, even if for only a short time. They gave as an example the loss of bog pimpernel (*Anagalis tenella*), marsh violet (*Viola stagnina*), marsh fern, saw sedge (*Cladium mariscus*), and sweet gale (*Myrica gale*), from West Fen and another fen near Ely.

The specific evidence for these changes is, by its nature, patchy and localised. However, the same broad trends occurred across both the Southern and Northern Fens. Archaeological studies also help provide fascinating insights into the ecology of these landscapes in times past. Unfortunately, as the contemporary wildlife of the regions has been decimated by 'improvement', so too has the unique evidence held within the 'peat archive' been largely destroyed. Within a saturated peat bog, there are many organic acidic chemicals from the slow breakdown of vegetation and there is very little oxygen. This means that organic material trapped within the peat layers is preserved, sometimes for thousands of years. The materials may be specimens or usually fragments of insects, or the pollen and tissues of plants. Human remains, often from ceremonial killings, are occasionally found, and these 'bog bodies' are equally well preserved. However, careful and meticulous piecing together of the evidence from these remains of animals and plants can provide a unique insight into the landscape, ecology and climate prevailing across these areas in times past. This palaeo-ecological and palynological research is one of our most powerful tools in unravelling a lost ecology, and researchers such as Paul Buckland and Nikki Whitehouse have unearthed remarkable evidence at Thorne Moors, of how and why the landscape has changed over the millennia. There is too little space here to go into this work in detail, but much is published and is of global significance.

In the Northern Fen, it is the core peat bog sites of Thorne and Hatfield that have attracted most attention, whilst the wider landscape has been considered relatively much less. The reason is simply that the wider landscape was swept away so much earlier. Only the huge peat masses were so intransigent as to remain long enough to survive for contemporary research. It is worth finishing this chapter with a description of the sheer size and wetness of the great peat domes of Thorne Moors, from Woodruffe-Peacock in 1920-21. The description is of the variation in volume and hence height with seasonal conditions, attributed to the very wet core of the bog.

In rainy seasons … its central mass was feet higher when full and swollen with water than in dry summers with normal rainfall, as it lifted as it swelled on the principle of in summer the dry and in winter the wet sponge. This I have over and over again observed personally from the great central Railway line, as in wet times nothing on its northern side was visible which could be clearly distinguished in dry summer weather. In 1875 it was estimated that the winter rise and summer fall of the bog was about six feet, in an abnormally wet season in the sixties, eight feet.

4

DRAINING AND IMPROVING THE FENS:
THE BACKGOUND TO THE GREAT DRAINAGE

If you marle land, you may buy land,
If you marle moss, you shall have no loss,
But if you marle clay, you throw all away.

Anon.

SETTING THE SCENE: SCIENCE AND LANDSCAPE

The soil of the isle of Axholm, is among the finest in England; they have black sandy loams; they have warp lands; they have brown sands; and they have rich black loams, soapy and tenacious; the under stratum at Haxey, Belton etc. is, in many places, an imperfect plaster stone.

Arthur Young (1772)

I am not going to attempt a definitive account of draining, since there is enough on that to fill many volumes. Each fen, each marsh and every common has its own unique story. No, what I intend to do, is to provide a broad overview of what in many ways was a simple and straightforward sequence of events, but which was also horribly complicated. The real process amounts to a hugely complex mess of politics, history, environmental calamity and local twists and turns. There are overall general 'truths' about the process of land improvement and of drainage, which occur again and again through history. The gradual incursions of people into the great wetlands occur over a great many years, but the end, when it comes, is often quick. Nature sometimes, especially in the early days, recovers the land and drives the colonisers back – but usually succumbs eventually. However, the actual final draining is not the end of the process; for as we see in both the Northern and Southern Fens there follows a process of intensification and desiccation of the wider landscape of the drained fen. Therefore, in England's fens it is clear that the main period of drainage was from the mid-1600s to the mid-1800s, beginning perhaps with the Humberhead Levels and the Great Level, and finishing perhaps with the removal of Whittlesea Mere, and eventually the final remnants in the 1940s. Nevertheless, the process began long before that first date, and continued well beyond the second. The intention here is to raise awareness of these processes, and consider the major events and the milestones along the way. What happened and why? Who was responsible and why did some succeed and others fail?

DRAINAGE AND IMPROVEMENT AS AN INTERNATIONAL AFFAIR

Human impact on landscape through agricultural 'improvement' occurred over millennia. Those influences on wetlands increased in extent and intensity over the last thousand years, with Europe a centre for the development of the technologies and ideas of landscape transformation. In Europe, from early in the second millennium to the mid-1300s, the population doubled, though not uniformly. In Western and Central Europe, France, Germany and England, populations surged to around 300 per cent. This placed huge pressures on natural resources but made cheap labour available to facilitate change. Across Europe, internal colonisation and associated land 'clearance' or 'improvement' accompanied population increase. The High Middle Ages radically altered the cultural landscape. Pioneers moved to the mountains, clearing extensive forest; and in lowland marginal lands, marshes, bogs and fens bore the brunt of human expansion. In the coastal and riverine wetlands, this necessitated drainage dykes and ditches.

Colonists reputedly brought ideas and approaches to wetland reclamation to Britain from the lowlands of northern Europe in the period after the Romans left. The great expanse of around 60,000 acres (24,281 hectares) of Romney Marsh in south-east England, for example, was supposedly reclaimed by the Frisians. A dead level area about 14 miles (22.4km) long and 8 miles (12.8km) wide, it stretches from Hythe in Kent to Winchelsea in Sussex, and the marshmen used to say that the world was divided into Europe, Asia, Africa, America, and Romney Marsh, such was the sense of both isolation and of vastness for those who lived there. Another important but often forgotten reclamation was the embanking of the Thames; this was formerly a wide and meandering channel several miles across and with, at low tide, extensive areas of mud and ooze on either side of the river channel. Names such as Marsh and Moorfields Marsh hark back to a time before drainage.

Evidence of this expansion remains in place name suffixes such as -bourg in Normandy, -bastide in south-west France, and -berg, -rode, and -reuth in Germany, and in the physical layout of some of the planned townships. 'Improved' lowland landscapes in England are also full of wetland prefixes and suffixes: Fenny-, Fen-, Wet-, Marsh-, -mire, -mere, -moor, etc. Some clearance and cultivation was early, so there is little surviving evidence or awareness of former landscapes. Other areas were cleared late, and retain elements of earlier landscapes. Therefore, in France, in keeping with the division into the northern floodplains and the southern high plateaux, the process of internal colonisation and clearance was diverse. The Paris basin and the broad valley of the Loire were favoured areas colonised early. In the late twelfth century, there followed waves of clearance and settlement, establishing patterns of rural land use and peasants' rights over subsequent centuries.

Germanic colonisation of eastern countries was long-term and complex, but the pattern for wetlands is relevant. Settlement by peasants began in earnest in the twelfth century through systematic recruitment by landowners of colonisers, in exchange for advantageous grants of rights in the new lands. Slavic princes recruited experienced peasants from long-established areas in Germany and the Netherlands. Skilled peasants were prepared to trek long distances from densely populated Holland, Flanders and Westphalia to lands between the central Elbe, the Erzgebirge, and Lower Lusatia. Here they applied techniques of wetland drainage and forest clearance learned at home, transforming rural landscapes.

However, the booming populations were not to last. Disease, especially Black Death in the fourteenth century, and climate deterioration during the 'Little Ice Age', affected communities and halted much of the expansion. Lands reclaimed from 'wildernesses' were abandoned, and coastal areas became vulnerable to sea level rise and storms. At a European scale, population stagnated up to the fifteenth century then began to increase dramatically, affecting settlement patterns and land use. With constant threats of food shortage, there was rapid extension of cultivation and land clearance. Some of this pressure was on previously cultivated lands abandoned after the Black Death, but population increase forced further exploitation of previously virgin lands in mountains, woods, marshes, and along rivers and coasts. Moors and anciently barren and unproductive grounds were cultivated, meadows turned arable and forests destroyed. Landowners had to prohibit further forest loss to preserve vital resources, placing peasants under more pressure to exploit other areas.

There was continued drainage and exploitation of bogs and marshes along the North Sea coastline, with extensive drains and dykes. In the Netherlands, around 44,000 hectares of marsh were reclaimed from 1565 to 1615. The German coast had 40,000 hectares drained and protected during the late 1500s and early 1600s, and Eastern Europe was similar. Lithuanian peasants migrated to northern East Prussia, and Dutch Mennonites left the Netherlands for religious reasons, to colonise and drain the Vistula-Nogat Delta from about 1550. Polish manorial lords were so impressed by the increased land values that resulted, that they were keen to apply Dutch drainers wherever possible. Tensions often grew between old, established rural communities and incomers over colonisation and improvement. This was certainly the case in the English fens when European settlers arrived on their doorstep to drain their wetlands. Co-operation between the two groups occurred around the boundaries of established fields and the edge of common waste, but problems arose over important common rights. In marginal landscapes, common and traditionally held rights were hugely important. The titles of particular types of occupiers clearly showed their status. Later, when commons and wastes were under threat of enclosure and 'improvement', those without established common rights had nothing. With population increase and rigorous controls over common usage, there were issues of 'ownership' and competition between neighbouring settlements. We sense in this situation a bubbling cauldron of human endeavour, of unrest and of sheer pressure of numbers. For nature and the environment we were rapidly moving to a tipping point from which there could be no recovery.

The relationship between agriculture and its natural resources, and the progress of industrial development, is critical. Industry and urbanisation require increased agricultural productivity, allowing the primary sector to meet the rise in demand for food. Important too is the ability of farming to 'release' resources (mostly labour, capital and land) to support industry and services. To do this, agricultural revolution must go hand-in-hand with industrial evolution, and maybe political revolution. Such changes might include new techniques and equipment to cultivate the soil, new ways to drain and 'improve' land, advanced crop rotations, heavier stocking of animals and intensification of mixed husbandry.

Politics and even religion probably had as much influence on the drainage of the fenlands as did the available technologies. The drainage of the fenlands was but one part of a greater landscape change that emerged in the 1700s and 1800s with the movement towards scientific improvement. The writings of the European natural philosophers influenced agricultural improvers like Arthur Young in England. These in turn revolutionised attitudes to farming and the land in an age of enlightenment and of rational thought. Old values were set aside and new agendas imposed. In England, the English Civil War followed the drainage of fen and swamp in the 1600s. Later on, these same landscapes bred the germs of Methodism and Quakerism. Maybe the experiences of Royalists returning from exile in the Low Countries to their English estates, was a pivotal moment in the changed approach to productive landscapes. They came back often poor (relatively) but with ideas of land improvement from Holland, Flanders, and France, that they wished to implement on their own lands. An example of this was the case of Heneage Finch, Third Earl of Winchilsea in the East Riding of Yorkshire. Saddled with debts due to his part in the Royalist rising of 1655, from 1657-8 he travelled in Europe. Whilst abroad he began to formulate and draw up plans for the improvements to his estates that would be necessary on his return; the objective being improved farming and increased rents. In particular, he focused on his 'low lands'. The approach was to be the deepening of the beck and of ditches, and more draining of the extensive wet areas. His accounts demonstrate the exchange of ideas and techniques, and the pre-eminence that the Cambridgeshire Fens achieved in terms of their reputation, or at least that of their improvers. He offered to pay for a man:

> ... to see the late great drains of the Fens of Lincolnshire and the Level of Bedford, Isle of Ely and others thereabouts, and any other works you think necessary, and to take observations, and draughts of all such works and engines, as may be of use to our land, he may likewise endeavour to procure such workmen and tenants as may be most advantageous to my ... drowned lands.

The intention was to remove water by using pumps such as a portable horse-mill, and with ditching and banking to improve and drain the floodlands of his estate piece by piece. The idea of mills to pump water off the carrs came from Holland. Once drained, the land would be enclosed and farms would be built on it. These would be stocked with cattle and carts and riding horses. Trees (alders and osiers, with 10,000 willows a year) were to be planted. These would provide shade in summer, shelter in winter, and timber to burn or sell. Better pastureland held in common was to be ploughed and arable areas were to be enclosed. There was little suggestion that there might be opposition to this, or if there were that it would pose any problem. Thus, we see the ideas of European scientific farming imported into England. The ideas were not translated into immediate action and the East Riding carrs of Winchilsea's estates were not finally drained until the nineteenth century.

It is clear from itineraries and other accounts that there were extensive exchanges of ideas and of technologies between scientists and other improvers in England, France, Scotland, the Netherlands and elsewhere in Western Europe. Scarfe (2001) describes an example of such a tour, with the visit of the young French aristocrats Alexandre de La Rochefoucauld and Maximilien de Lazowski to Britain in 1786. With the manipulation and improvement of wetland of particular significance in Flanders and the Low Countries, but occurring more widely too, the importation of Dutch drainage engineers and their ideas was of huge significance.

The famous but controversial Dutchman, Cornelius Vermuyden, moved to England to take on a series of major land reclamation projects. The first big one was the draining of Hatfield Chase, south of the Humber Estuary, from 1626 to 1629. He also advanced projects for similar massive draining of the Somerset Levels, although these were never executed. Vermuyden employed skilled foreign labourers (French, Flemish and Dutch) to drain the Hatfield Level of the Humber, and their ideas and knowledge of the manipulation and improvement of wetlands from Flanders and the Low Countries were important and significant in determining the future of the English fens.

As Marc Bloch has suggested, these Dutch engineers did not undertake this work purely for the public good; their operations in the Fens and also in the French coastal marshes were proto-capitalist exercises 'directed by an association of technical experts and business men … financed by a few large business-houses, mostly Dutch'. Their objective was less public land reclamation than private wealth generation. As such, these wetland initiatives became the financial models for further eighteenth-century reclamation enterprises in Brittany and Guienne, where 'companies were founded for the express purpose of financing – or indeed speculating in – land reclamation, which now also received government patronage'. Obviously, as noted earlier, there was often deep suspicion, even open hostility, among local land workers towards these speculators and investors, these 'Adventurers'. The idea was germinating that not only were foreigners being employed to take away the English fens, but that it was paid for by foreign money. This not only caused resentment, but a deep suspicion about where it might end, especially for the fenmen when Dutch and Flemish settlers moved in 'next-door'.

Nonetheless, financial greed was not in itself a great enough incentive to drive the early modern processes of wetland draining, clearance and cultivation. Exploiting the general reputation of marshes and bogs as places of evil and infamy, religion and public morality were also invoked as reasons for their reclamation. Indeed, the very notion of 'reclamation' – as with the later eighteenth-century idea of 'improvement' – struck a strong moral chord with contemporaries, especially among the first generation of engineers and drainage experts in England, many of whom were Protestants and Huguenots fleeing religious persecution and civil strife on the Continent. Certainly, among such avid Bible-readers, the constant threat of flooding posed by the marshes and fens to surrounding agriculture and dwellings might have recalled Noah's flood, and was therefore to be checked not just on social and financial grounds, but also on religious ones. In seventeenth- and eighteenth-century Europe, the effects of regular flooding must have reinforced this impression. Florence was heavily flooded in 1740 with the loss of many lives and Avignon was swamped in 1763 when the Rhône burst its banks. In the winter of 1787, heavy rains and flooding swept away seed grain in Saxony, causing famine the following year. In the Breton forests too, a lack of draining expertise meant that heavy rains waterlogged and weakened the roots of trees, drowned all seedlings, and left the forest vulnerable to storm damage with devastating effect at least four times in the eighteenth century. In both the East Anglian Fens and the Northern Fens (as described earlier), there were regular periods of catastrophic inundation with consequent damage to property and people.

Effective draining, then, was crucial, and it involved both the removal of water from the landscape and the protection of areas by embankments. However, the situation is more complicated, as although removal of water might be by simple gravitational drainage, often there was a need to pump the water to a higher level. Here technology became a limiting factor. By 1710, the English reclaimers of the Fens had imported from Holland the technique of using windmill-powered pumps to drain the wetlands. Nevertheless, this alone was not enough to facilitate widespread cultivation of the land, because the effective drainage of field soils was also necessary, but still not fully understood. It was not until much later in the century that a further discovery and subsequent innovation in draining expanded the practice of wetland reclamation, first in Britain and then on the Continent. This took place near Leamington Spa in 1764 when a local farmer, Joseph Elkington, solved the problem of under-drainage, of clearing not just the surface waters from an area of wetland but of siphoning off low-level underground water-tables by tapping and diverting their springs. In 1795, the British Parliament awarded Elkington the handsome sum of £1,000 in recognition of his innovation, and asked him to survey the general application of his method of under-drainage in other parts of the country. Drainage, under-drainage, and irrigation too, were then important advances in land management in eighteenth-century Western Europe. Generally, the application of these new techniques was most effective where there were large local labour forces. This is understandable not only because drainage was a labour-intensive process, but also because it was in heavily populated areas that the demand was greatest for increased agricultural production and hence for more land on which to provide it. The population increase in Britain, especially after 1740, was at once the cause of wetland reclamation and a means to implement it.

Windmill from Bligh's English Improver, improved 1652.

Increased food production was also the major incentive for fenland drainage in England in the eighteenth century. Arthur Young, writing in 1772, suggested 'breaking up uncultivated lands' and 'draining Fens' as the chief means not only of enhancing productivity of these holdings but also of raising income for those who farmed them. The logic was straightforward. Reclaimed lands could be enclosed and incorporated into the new crop-rotation cycles which avoided leaving fields fallow; they could specifically be used for cultivating fodder crops which in turn would feed greater numbers of livestock which would, in their turn, produce more manure, further reducing the need for fallow and fertilising yet greater yields on the reclaimed lands. If this was the English model, it also began to be widely adopted in France in the late eighteenth century. In Normandy, for instance, a better supply of fodder crops from reclaimed lands, including marshes, encouraged animal husbandry, especially of cattle; the cattle in turn produced more milk, which reduced waterborne disease and gave local children a much-improved chance of surviving their first decade, the period in which mortality rates were highest. That the English model was dominant would appear proved by the fact that in 1800, at the height of hostilities between Britain and France, the revolutionary Directoire commissioned an eighteen-volume translation of selected agronomic works by Young, published under the title *Le Cultivateur Anglais*. Their author was suitably triumphalist in 1799, writing of the ubiquitous benefits brought to Lincolnshire by the drainage and reclamation of its fens. He claimed that by this act the local population could boast 'health improved, morals corrected and the community enriched'.

THE CHALLENGE OF DRAINING THE ENGLISH FENS

To understand the process of drainage and reclamation or 'improvement' of the fenland landscapes and waterscapes, it is necessary to bear in mind the fluctuation levels of land and sea over the time-period, and the changing human pressures, aspirations, and applications of technology. To effectively drain land in a flat, expansive landscape requires knowledge of water and land management, and suitable engineering technology to undertake and maintain the process. In part, therefore, drainage follows the evolution and availability of necessary pumping, dyking and draining technologies. However, in a flat land you also need political control and will so that everyone drains. To drain one area but not another cannot succeed. In this way, much of the lowland fen differs from wetlands on hills and higher ground, where an individual owner can, often effectively, drain a single parcel of wetland. Finally, economic or other social pressures must drive along the process. There must be capital available and a financial incentive to undertake the considerable work and often at great risk. These were not easy or certain ventures, and there was the need to maintain the system once it was in place. This all takes place over a long period, a backcloth of rising and falling sea levels, and therefore of increased and decreased risks of massive and catastrophic inundations. The position of the land-sea interface varied, with changing levels as material was dumped by the rivers converging through the Southern Fens into the Wash, and the Northern Fens into the Humber. On the one hand, local people benefitted from the unfettered use of the wetland resources and therefore resisted enclosure and drainage. On the other hand, the fenlanders lived in a waterscape at constant risk from major flooding. Therefore, they may have supported some degree of embanking and flood-risk management.

THE HISTORY OF DRAINAGE IN THE SOUTHERN FENLAND

WHAT THE ROMANS DID FOR THE FENLANDS

The Romans were responsible for the first serious attempts to drain inland marshes and fens, and to resist the incursions of the sea with sea walls. They also either invented, or at least perfected as a part of their military technology, the modern spade, the most basic requirement for undertaking such land-improvement works. Running along around 150 miles (240km) of the old sea-border of the fenland, are the so-called Roman Banks, which Skertchly estimated required around 11 million tons of material to build, presumably by slave labour. This practice continued into the final stages of drainage with the use of Scottish and Dutch prisoners of war during the 1600s. It has also been suggested that East Anglians who were deported from Boadicea's territory following her defeat by the Romans, provided labour for this early improvement. This was all part of a plan to develop the Romano-British agricultural estates on the maritime silts and clay-lands, and around the fen edges. There is evidence visible in aerial photography of farming settlements with fields surrounded by ditches. The farmsteads themselves were generally on slightly raised ground, and the products were wheat, barley and woad. At the time of the Romans, the River Witham entered the sea at Wainfleet, and the Nene and Great Ouse at Wisbech. The Little Ouse was the only river that entered the sea at present-day King's Lynn. Between the estuaries of these great rivers was a coastline of flat land, mostly covered with silts deposited from the meandering, sluggish watercourses. In winter, much of this was under water, at least periodically. In summer, it would be a vast open plain of reeds and sedge, and with occasional willow and alder holts, and abundant small meres and other pools. It was along these slightly raised edges of the harder silt-lands that the Romans built their defences against incursions of the sea, which at this time was also lower than today. There may have been a secondary purpose too in that these banks may have facilitated the relatively easy and quick deployment of troops through an unruly area. In some cases, there were additional outer banks built, presumably as an attempt to reclaim land from the sea, rather than to protect existing land from risk of inundation.

The first lands reclaimed from the Southern Fens were the eastern parts of Marshland and Holland. These were reclaimed and managed for agriculture well before any of the interior wetlands were drained. There was also the obvious problem that building embankments to keep the sea out might be contrary to hopes of remaining flood-free because they also kept the inland waters in. Along with the sea defences, the Romans were also the first to attempt any comprehensive system of internal drainage of the vast fens and marshes. According to Wentworth-Day, the Romans realised that the region was subject to flooding in two ways other than by inundation by the sea. Firstly, there were upland floods coming down into the region from the inland areas – present-day Bedfordshire, Northamptonshire, and the other Midlands counties. Secondly, they were aware of flooding directly due to rainfall in the Fens. Their response to the first threat was to try to carry away the excess water with a great 'catch-water' dyke – known as the Car Dyke. This feature, of unknown length, certainly ran from Ramsey to Lincoln, perhaps starting from as far away as Cambridge, and was around 60ft (18m) wide.

For the Romans, this was a structure of great regional importance, and probably multi-functional. As well as guiding water away, it most likely served to transport men, equipment, animals and agricultural produce quickly and easily across this vast waterscape. Reflecting its strategic and military significance, the Romans built seven forts along its banks: Northborough, Braceborough, Billingborough, Garrick, Walcot, Lynwood, and Washingborough. The old West Lode and the Hammond Beck were also of probable Roman origin. The engineering approach they took regarded the great natural rivers as the arterial watercourses into which the artificial waterways, a series of cuts and channels, drained. Wentworth-Day regards this approach as hugely significant and suggests that many of the drainers who followed much later in history got it all significantly wrong. In drain-ing fenland, there may be a balance between draining or pumping water off the flooded landscape, and ensuring that ultimately the levels are such that it can drain away to the sea, in this case the Wash. Get the levels wrong, and pump as you might, the ultimate result will be a re-inundation. The outfalls to the Wash were always problematic in the Fens because of changing land and sea levels, and the silting and deposition that was present from the sluggish sediment-laden rivers and their tidal estuaries. He suggests that the often-repeated failures of the would-be drainers were because they overlooked the basic correctness and simplicity of the Roman engineers. Indeed, he goes further, suggesting that the first person to apply the same approach successfully was Rennie in the early nineteenth century, with his drainage of the East and West Fens in south Lincolnshire.

THE 'DARK AGES' OF THE POST-ROMAN PERIOD

With the withdrawal of Roman imperialism and the abandonment of the Romano-British to their own devices, the ability, skill and perhaps the willingness to maintain the drains and embankments ebbed away. Furthermore, during the period of Roman occupation, from AD 45 to AD 400, there were increased rising tides and therefore risk of inundation. This shows up in the soil profiles as a layer of marine silt deposited over the coastal zones, and the response was to raise embankments such as around the marsh at Tydd and Wisbech. The result was drainage ditches, and only a short distance to move livestock onto raised areas at times of flood. Roman improvements to the ancient channel from Peterborough to Tydd had also provided ready access to the north fenland estates. However, Saxon raids on the more remote fenland areas had already begun by around AD 200, and this prob-ably involved the burning of farmsteads and the breaking of banks and other structures. Ultimately, combined with incursions by the sea, this probably led to the abandonment of marginal lands, and localised decreased populations. These setbacks probably continued until about the time of the collapse of the Romano-British administration and conquest by the Anglo-Saxons.

The new colonists, with a heritage of crop husbandry and knowledge of ways to break up heavy clay lands with oxen plough teams, began to realise the farming potential of the old and new silt areas. It is suggested that as the Saxons settled to a farming life in the area, they maintained at least some of the Roman embankments and they kept free of silt at least some of the main channels to the sea. There is also evidence that in the seventh century, as far west as Crowland, and north-west to Wisbech, there were modest embankments to help reclaim some additional small areas of fen. The Saxons understood that the silt-land was only fertile for a few years before being exhausted by continual cropping. To combat this they developed a system of primitive rotation farming. They embanked small areas for arable land and maintained flocks of sheep to help raise fertility levels, the only cattle being oxen to pull the ploughs.

As the Saxons took up Christianity, a further influence came to bear on the Fens: that of organised monastic estates. With monasteries at Peterborough (AD 665), Thorney (AD 662), and Crowland (AD 712), there grew an increased awareness of agricultural potential attached to the ownership of productive land. The Hundreds of Wisbech had around 70,790 acres (28,648 hectares) of cultivated land extending from Sutton St Edmund in the west to Marshland in the south. The monasteries worked hard to improve their lands and to extend their estates. They built a significant embankment along the Welland to Crowland and Brotherhouse Bar. They also raised the Car Dyke further and cut channels for waterborne transport both north and south of Thorney, linking up with Peterborough. Over the next 200 years, the monasteries carried out further reclamation and embanking, and applied crop-rotation systems with large herds of cattle and flocks of sheep. Over the period too, they gained increasing influence and wealth, and developed further aspirations and greed for enhanced productivity. They gradually claimed ownership of areas of undrained marsh and fen, and demanded tithes from local communities. These tendencies also led to boundary disputes between neighbouring estates of Thorney, Peterborough, Crowland and Ely. However, the ambitions and competition between the monastic holdings came to a rather abrupt end as another influence affected the managers and owners of the fenland estates. A further wave of invaders, pillagers, and then colonists arrived during the ninth century with the Scandinavian Vikings. This effectively halted progress on the agricultural maintenance and improvement of both the Southern and Northern Fens, and the coastal zones, until the restoration of the monasteries between AD 970 and AD 980.

Active management was required in order to maintain the fen and marsh areas through reclamation, and, without this, they could produce summer hay, but lay abandoned to the floods in winter. The Scandinavian invaders were at first only seasonal, but later became more permanent. They arrived in force to winter in the Southern Fens from around AD 870. The Vikings ransacked and pillaged prosperous and productive areas such as the North Level, the Wisbech area, the South Eau, Thorney, Peterborough, and Crowland. In AD 870, the monasteries were sacked and the flood defences were broken. The last English king of the region, St Edmund, died brutally when, in AD 869, the Viking army advanced on East Anglia. Perhaps slain by the Danes in battle, the myth goes that after refusing the Danes' demand to renounce Christ, he met his death at an unidentified place known as 'Haegelisdun'. On the orders of Ivar the Boneless and his brother Ubbe Ragnarsson, he was beaten, shot with arrows and then beheaded. According to legend, Edmund's head was thrown into the forest, but was later found by searchers following the cries of a wolf 'Hic, Hic, Hic' or 'Here, Here, Here'. This was a key point in what was to be a very troubled century or more for the whole of the east of England.

The Scandinavian settlers moved into northern England first, and then pushed south to the fenland; after war with the English under Alfred, peace and co-existence were agreed. King Canute had established a degree of stability by around AD 1016, and his successor Edgar was responsible for the restoration of the monasteries and their estates. There was some repair of embankments and drains, though not of all. Saxon sites survived in Tydd, Newton, and Leverington, but many others were abandoned. Charnley describes the imagined view of the Black Fen Morass, in about AD 1000, as having a land surface around 6 to 8ft (1.8 to 2.4m) above that of today; the Black Fen Edge and the extent of peat coverage has been established from detailed site survey and assessment. Even today, the great wetland existing around 1,000 years ago is still traceable. The next major event, in truth a seismic shift in English history, was the Norman invasion and all that followed. Once more, for the fenlands, this would be a significant era.

FROM THE TIME OF THE NORMAN CONQUEST

The Domesday Survey of 1086 provides real insight and evidence of economic and other activity at this time. This shows areas of the Southern Fenland of varying population and degrees of prosperity. Administration across the land was determined through 'Hundreds' or often within the former Scandinavian Viking areas, 'wapentakes'. The Hundred addressed an area between that of the village and the shire and dated back to the early ninth century. It covered an area of approximately one hundred 'hides'; each of the latter being the amount of land supposedly needed to support a single peasant family. The administrative unit of the Hundred was a body of freeholders overseen by a Hundreds Reeve who was in effect the representative of the Crown. Amongst their duties, the Hundreds dealt with matters of drainage. Indeed, they continued to do this until the function was taken over by the Court of Sewers in 1285. These were established specifically to deal with issues of drainage because the problems were becoming more acute. With continued sea level rise and the consequences of long-term abandonment of the earlier defences and other engineering works, lands were more threatened. There was perhaps a further complication too since the deterioration of farming and land management, and the impacts of the Scandinavian raids and then settlement, had left much of the area with a relatively low population density. This meant a limited labour force available to undertake any necessary maintenance of banks and ditches, and of course only limited revenue to fund any works. Sudden increases in high tides and associated silting up of estuaries and drains had occurred previously, especially at the end of the Romano-British period, around 500-600 years earlier. It seemed that history was repeating itself.

The response to the latest problems was to raise the sea banks to try to limit the incursions of the high tides. However, this did not always succeed, especially if a high spring tide had the backing of strong storm winds from the north-east. Charnley estimated that such conditions could raise the high water level at least 4ft (1.2m) above the otherwise expected maximum. A further impact of these conditions, particularly if there was stormy weather inland, was the risk of fluvial or river floods of fresh water backed up by the high tide. A lack of understanding of flood management issues by those trying to protect their lands compounded the problems. Furthermore, attempts to limit summer flooding by erecting riverside embankments, effectively narrowed available river channels and exacerbated winter floods. There is a major embankment from Leverington and Newton to Four Gotes, which Charnley considers part of the medieval construction around the Wash.

THE COMMON CRANE IN ENGLAND

With their loud bugling call, cranes were once a familiar sight across Britain's wetlands, giving rise to place names and family names such as Cranfield, Cranmer, Cranwell, Crane, Cranbourne and Cranbrook. An obvious and distinctive bird, they have a long cultural history in Britain, they feature on illuminated manuscripts, and appeared on the menus for major feasts, such as King Henry III's feast at York in 1251. Cranes are mainly grey all over rather like a grey heron, but with black, white and red markings on the head and neck. They feed on roots, shoots, and leaves of meadow and marshland plants as well as on small animals such as voles and frogs.

The name 'common crane' reflects the wide breeding range in Europe and across Asia, and their former relative abundance in our wetlands. They nest on the ground in marshy vegetation. With a 7ft (2m) wingspan and a loud bugling call, the common crane is a genuine wildlife spectacle.

The common crane occurs widely in Europe, where again, populations have suffered from major wetland loss. However, persecution and the large-scale drainage of the Fens for agriculture, led to its loss as a British breeding bird by about 1600. By the mid-twentieth century just small numbers have visited eastern and southern England each year on migration. A small number returned to the Norfolk Broads as early as 1979, but, perhaps because of the still precarious state of wetlands during the late twentieth century, although they have bred there successfully, the population remained isolated and vulnerable for some time. However, they have more recently colonised the newly created Lakenheath Fen and are beginning to spread into the East Anglian Fens. They have also now returned to the South Yorkshire fenlands and have even been sighted over cities like Sheffield.

This is likely to have been a response to the catastrophic flooding in 1246. The 15ft (4.5m) high construction is around 6ft (1.8m) wide at the top and includes earthen ramparts at intervals of 200 to 300 yards (183 to 274m). These ramparts point in a south-easterly direction and were to deflect waves away from the main bank. The riverbanks, described in 1616 as 'for defending of lands in the Level from the Force and rage of the sea', were raised.

The early medieval period would have been problematic for communities in the Southern Fens and around the Wash. With global temperatures rising prior to the 'Little Ice Age', there was a melting of polar ice caps and more importantly an expansion of seawater with the increased temperature. The consequence was higher sea level and a greatly increased risk of marine inundation. The response was a major engineering structure, with the bank created to protect large stretches of the vulnerable coastline.

Over recent centuries, the power and influence (and of course the wealth) of the monasteries had grown. The ancient custom was that whoever reclaimed land by embanking also took responsibility for maintenance thereafter. The system adopted by the abbots was one where their tenants paid tithes and rents, thus generating significant income to the monasteries. In addition, however, the tenants undertook to maintain the embankments fronting their land.

There was extensive reclamation around Crowland, Tydd, Leverington and Newton, much on silt-land, and on higher ground north of Thorney. Extensive parts of the Black Fens were pools and meres, and these 'vaporous areas' were fished and fowled as common land by local farmers and peasants during the winter months.

These had always been productive lands and, in Domesday (1086), it is noted that the Abbot of Ely received an annual payment of 33,260 'sticks' of eels from the area, a stick being twenty-five eels. Over time, the local farmers tried to extend their limited areas of arable land by further embanking, though maintenance of these or of earlier banks was not easy to regulate or enforce. Reclamation and maintenance were expensive undertakings and, as was often the case, a landlord might be unwilling to invest unless there was a guarantee of a quick financial return. However, in 1222, the Crown set down rules for the Laws and Customs of Drainage in Romney Marsh, and this helped more widely to establish individual responsibility to the community for drains and embankments. However, in the year 1236, there was a major tidal flood and inundation across the North Level attributed to the silting of the Great Wisbech River outfall. This caused loss of life, extensive damage to property, and the drowning of thousands of animals. Following a petition of evidence with regard to the situation, the King ordered that all banks be raised and strengthened. Despite money raised by the townsfolk of Wisbech and by local tenants, little was done to the outfall itself. The passing of the first Land Drainage Act, by Parliament, in 1258, followed the 1222 rules and importantly established the Court of Sewers. This body was to decide on matters of responsibility for drainage and reclamation. The Court provided travelling judges to receive presentations from barons, abbots and other landlords, peasants and tenants, on such matters, and to assign responsibilities. Commissioners of Sewers for each Hundred were appointed to ensure that the rulings of the court were followed through. Responsibilities included the prevention of damage to flood defence structures such as embankments by, for example, cattle. The costs of work could be considerable and sometimes tax burdens (such as on fairs and markets) might be waived in lieu of approved costs.

Dugdale, writing of the floods at this time, felt that freshwater flooding was more damaging than the transient impacts of coastal inundations. Of course, the worst situation was when coastal and fluvial (river) flooding combined, as it did in 1260 when freshwater from the upland areas coincided with high tides. This caused over-topping of embankments and flooding across around 35,000 acres (14,164 hectares) of the Southern Fen with associated great losses. The pattern was to continue for centuries as embankments deteriorated and the same vast areas of land were inundated. In 1274, a major flood broke through the bank of the Little Ouse, with consequences for the river-flow in the Nene and silting up of the River Nene outfall. This remained problematic until the nineteenth century. At about this time, Hugh de Balsham assigned land west of the outfall of the South Eau at Guyhirn to the monks of Ely. They already claimed much of the flooded land and were now tasked with reclaiming Wisbech High Fen and the other inundated areas. However, despite their efforts, the area remained vulnerable to high tides and was frequently flooded by freshwater. It was a continual battle to hold back the high tides of the sea, maintain the drains, and keep outfalls free of silt. There was a further problem of only limited understanding of some of the issues. One of these matters unknown to the drainers was that of peat shrinkage and the lowering of the land surface after reclamation and drainage. Problems continued with silt management

THE RAFT SPIDER AND THE FEN RAFT SPIDER

The raft spider or swamp spider (*Dolomedes fimbriatus*) is much more common than its relative from the Pisauridae family, the fen raft spider (*Dolomedes plantarius*). Only discovered in Britain in the late 1950s by Eric Duffey, the latter is endangered and found only in East Anglia. Both these species require swampy conditions and are large and robust, and capable of catching sizeable prey, including damselflies and small fish. The latter are attracted to the surface of the water by the spider vibrating the water with its front legs. Females can lay up to 1,000 eggs in sacs, which are carried underneath the abdomen. The young spiders can be found in shrubs or trees rather than in the water. These are two of Europe's largest, most beautiful, but least common species of spider. They are the largest native British spiders.

The fen raft spider is a wetland species that is dependent on permanent, standing or slow-moving water. It is generally associated with nutrient-poor water of near-neutral or alkaline pH. Living on the water surface of pools and ditches, and around the emergent vegetation, it typically hunts from 'perches' on stems rising out of the water. Its wide range of prey are taken on or below the surface. They also need emergent, stiff-leaved vegetation with open, sunny conditions for breeding, with nursery webs constructed for the young. There were no reliable British records of this species before its discovery in 1956, at Redgrave and Lopham Fen, on the border of Norfolk and Suffolk. However, in 1988 it was discovered at a second site, the Pevensey Levels, around 72 miles (160km) away in Sussex. Over the same period, the population at Redgrave and Lopham Fen has declined and is now restricted to two small, isolated centres. Systematic monitoring begun in 1991 showed numbers fluctuating at very low levels. The total population seems to be little over 100 adult females in most years and the species is considered highly vulnerable to extinction. The Pevensey population was estimated at 3,000 adult females in 1992. In Great Britain, this species is classified as Endangered and is given full protection under Schedule 5 of the Wildlife and Countryside Act 1981.

The common name of raft spider comes from the mistaken belief that the beast forms a raft of detritus and threads and so is able to drift across the fen waterscape in search of prey. It doesn't do this, but it will readily go under water after prey or down a plant stem and out of harm's way if disturbed. Most historical records of the very rare *D. plantarius* are difficult or impossible to verify because of the frequent taxonomic confusion with the congeneric species *Dolomedes fimbriatus*. In addition, the camouflaged nature of *D. plantarius*, and the difficulty of locating it amongst tangles of emergent aquatic vegetation, make recording and assessing it very difficult.

SPECIES THAT MAY CAUSE CONFUSION

The main source of confusion in the UK is with the semi-aquatic *Pirata* and *Pisaura* species of wolf spiders. Several have more or less distinct white lateral lines on the carapace, and are very active and quite large, though not in the *Dolomedes* range. Mature *Pirata* can be a similar size to young, perhaps ²/₃ grown, *Dolomedes*. They often inhabit rough and marshy grassland and will retreat down plant stems and under water.

and river flows and, in 1301, a dam was built to divert the River Ouse back towards Wisbech. After ongoing complications and problems, in 1438 the King instructed that the structure be removed 'under Pain of Death'.

In 1290, the Commissioners of Sewers instructed tenants in Tydd, Newton, and Leverington to raise the embankments to stop freshwater pouring into the Fen. This received agreement from Adam de Tydd with the provision that the high lands along the Shire Drain were not 'charged', i.e. flooded. By 1314, King Edward II was instructing Geoffrey de Colville to inspect the embankments and to issue orders for their repair. In 1297, Geoffrey de Sandiacre was directed to investigate the banks at both Newton and Wish St Mary. They were found to be 'in decay' and again orders were given for their repair. After a further twenty-one years, in 1335, following another major flood, a similar directive for inspection and repair was issued.

During the thirteenth and fourteenth centuries, there was a continuation of small-scale reclamation in silt and clay areas north of Crowland, and north and south of Gorefield. These were mainly localised initiatives with private banks to enclose small areas to prevent freshwater flooding, dealt with separately from the main drains and banks under the authority of the Commissioner of Sewers and the Dyke Reeves. The obligation to maintain these minor banks may have been resented by the tenants unless these directly affected their land and interests. An example of the state of affairs is given by the petition in 1395 at Fleet, which maintained 'that the portion of land in Sutton and Tydd is so low that … they are yearly drowned'. The result of the petition was work to replace the Lady Nunn Eau with a new straight channel, the Straightreach. Further representations were made in 1395 to make up the Welland Bank, the Southeau Bank, and Dowesdale Bank. Since the Crown owned these structures, the works were carried out immediately. There was a continuous process of petitions to the Commissioners of Sewers to resolve problems and disputes. With increasing small private embankments, there were consequent problems of uncoordinated reclamation since the floodwaters had to go somewhere. In 1438, after further excessive flooding and breaches in the Fen Dyke or Murrow Bank, orders were given to 'cleanse' the South Eau to Throckenholt and Cloughs Cross to Guyhirn. There followed numerous other Drainage Acts through the fifteenth century, but with continuing difficulties in enforcement. This situation was compounded by many Commissioners also being landowners and therefore having serious conflicts of interest.

In the North Level, the first major land drainage works were undertaken by Bishop Morton of Peterborough. Under his direction, a new cut was taken from Stanground to Guyhirn and the Great Wisbech River was straightened to Rummers Mill. This took the bulk of the River Nene flow and slightly reduced the risk of embankment failure down the South Eau and the Shire Drain. However, in the Land Drainage Act of 1531, there was recognition at last of the need for statutory powers if the Commissioners were to be able to achieve the objectives set. Interestingly, it also became a felony to maliciously damage the flood banks, and this was a crime punishable by death. The 'Acre-Shot levy' was introduced by the Act to raise funds for maintenance of banks and drains based on the holding of the individual landowner. It gave the Commissioners the power to use a by-law in the event of 'great need', i.e. a breach and a flood. The necessary levy was raised on lands protected by the drains and banks. However, throughout the bulk of the fourteenth and fifteenth centuries, there was little co-ordinated effort to reclaim lands from the waters. Any significant works undertaken targeted the coastal marshes. These included projects at Tydd and along the Wisbech estuary in 1490. The Great Level of the Fens remained in a relatively unreclaimed state down to the late 1500s, with constant threats of inundations and damage to areas that had been improved and to property and settlements. Smiles (1904) stated that:

> … it would be difficult to imagine anything more dismal than the aspect which the Great level then presented. In winter, a sea without waves; in summer, a dreary mud-swamp. The atmosphere was heavy with pestilential vapours, and swarmed with insects. The meres and pools were, however, rich in fish and wildfowl. The Welland was noted for sticklebacks, a little fish about two inches long, which appeared in dense shoals near Spalding every seventh or eighth year, and used to be sold during the season at a halfpenny a bushel, for field manure.

5

THE GREAT DRAINAGE BEGINS

In 1603 or 1607 (depending on the source but certainly shortly after James I came to the throne), there was a series of destructive floods that burst over the embankments along the English East Coast. These floods swept over farms, cottages, houses and villages, killing many people and their cattle and other livestock. Informed of the disaster that had stuck his people in the Fens, and being told that this was due to the decay and neglect of the embankments, James reportedly stated that:

> For the honour of his kingdom, he would not any longer suffer these countries to be abandoned to the will of the waters, nor to let them lie waste and unprofitable; and that if no one else would undertake their drainage, he himself would become their undertaker.
>
> Wentworth-Day (1954)

One suspects that while the welfare of his people was a consideration, the potential for lost revenue on the one hand, or increased tax revenue and profits on the other, was the major factor. The nail was now firmly set in the coffin of these great waters. All it needed now was a large and heavy hammer to drive it home. A Commission was appointed to investigate the situation and the scale of the problem. They reported that over 317,242 acres (128,383 hectares) of land lay outside the dykes and rains, and this area required drainage and protection. A bill was brought before Parliament to enable rates to be levied for the drainage of the land, but the proposal was rejected. However, two years later, a more modest 'little bill' for draining 6,000 acres (2,428 hectares) of Waldersea County was passed, being the first Act for Fen Drainage to receive the support of Parliament.

The King directed Chief Justice Popham to go to the Fens to undertake the necessary work. He also persuaded a company of Londoners to undertake another portion of the task, for which the 'Adventurers' were to receive two-thirds of the reclaimed land for their efforts. Their operations were marked by Popham's Lode and The Londoners' Lode', but overall they had only limited success. They lacked the skills and knowledge to take on major drainage schemes and had no overall plan of action. At the time, there were no 'engineers' as such, and the people responsible for this sort of work were described as 'undertakers'. At some point in the early 1600s, a large tract of marshland in South Holland, between the Roman Bank and South Holland Embankment, was enclosed by a new bank. This new construction extended from the River Welland to the River Nene at Tydd. Then, in 1615, a grant was made to Adventurers on behalf of the Duke of Argyle, of marshes by the sea in Wigtoft, Moulton, Holbeach, and Tydd St Mary, these to be reclaimed by the Duke with a fifth reserved for the King and a rent of £75 5s *per annum* to be paid to the Crown.

However, it was now apparent that there was nobody in England who was experienced enough to be capable of such a major task as the drainage of the wider areas of the fenland. So the Dutch engineer, Cornelius Vermuyden, known to have been successful in ditching, draining and embanking in the Low Countries, was invited to put forward his plans. Holland and Flanders had previously supplied both the expertise and often the skilled labour necessary to reclaim many other parts of the Fens. A Flemish engineer called Freeston reclaimed the extensive marshes near Wells in Norfolk. Joas Croppenburg, a Dutchman skilled in the making of dykes, reclaimed and embanked Canvey Island along with a workforce of Dutch labourers. Another Dutchman, Cornelius Vanderwelt, was responsible for the enclosure and drainage of Wapping Marsh. Skills were also imported from other European countries with a history of land drainage, for example two Italians, Acontius and Castiglione, reclaimed Combe Marsh and East Greenwich Marsh, both on the south bank of the Thames.

Between 1621 and 1625 (according to Wheeler), there was a very high tide, described as being the highest ever known in the Thames, and the sea walls in Kent, Essex and Lincolnshire were overwhelmed. The lands close to the East Coast were very badly affected and Cornelius Vermuyden arrived in England specifically to address the problems of a major breach in the Thames flood embankments near Dagenham. From this successful operation, he went on to drain the Royal Park at Windsor, and it was in this context that he came to the attention of King James. The King was anxious to drain and so reclaim the Crown estates at Hatfield Chase in Yorkshire, and commissioned Vermuyden to undertake the job. When Leland, Henry VIII's antiquary, visited the area in 1607, he travelled between Thorne and Hatfield by boat, over what was about to become very fertile but dry farmland.

DRAINING THE YORKSHIRE AND NORTH LINCOLNSHIRE FENS

As in the East Anglian Fens, the first attempts at co-ordinated drainage of the Yorkshire Fens began with the Romans. Constructing causeways and canals sought to both control and to utilise the extensive wetland landscapes. Although many canals and drains undoubtedly had a land-improvement function, they were also very important for transportation of produce and animals, soldiers and military equipment. There is still some debate as to the origin of the Turnbridge Dyke, the River Don's northward channel in the Humberhead Levels, and one of the major channels suggested as originating as a Roman military canal. Van de Noort argues that this may have been a pre-existing river channel present certainly in the late Neolithic and early Bronze Age, perhaps straightened and improved by the Romans. The Bycarrs Dike that links the Rivers Idle and the Trent in the south, and the lower parts of the River Derwent in the north, may have been Roman modifications. Along with the major works were extensive areas of coastal reclamation and innumerable small-scale drainage and restoration schemes around the fringes of the great Northern Fenland.

By the Middle Ages, with post-Roman abandonment and the impacts of fluctuating sea levels, the main drainage works were undertaken by the ecclesiastical centres with their extensive agricultural estates. These may have begun under Christian Saxon influences but were interrupted by the Viking settlements. They were resurrected once more after the Norman Conquest. As already discussed, the abbey at Selby led the way in the north with major drainage schemes around Thorne Moors. The abbots may have also undertaken some modifications to the Turnbridge Dyke, though this is uncertain. Both ecclesiastical centres and nobility were involved in drainage schemes. Hugh de Pudsey was both Lord of Howdenshire and Bishop of Durham, and was responsible for the re-colonisation of wetlands in the Vale of York. The Knights Templar at Faxfleet were involved in major water management works with the 'Temple Dam', and the Canons Thornton at Thornton Land with the 'Thornton Dam', and Gilbert Hansard at Blacktoft with the 'Hansardam'. Around the 1160s, the Abbot at Meaux Abbey commissioned the construction of the Ashdyke in the lower Hull Valley. Primarily for transportation, this had a second function of drainage, with probably a network of lesser dykes across the area. North of Hull there was the construction of the Foredyke and possibly a complex of fishponds and a fish-house: all part of the Meaux Abbey estate. In the 1200s, there were the first co-ordinated attempts to resolve issues of flooding in the Ancholme Valley with the straightening of the river between Bishopsbridge and the Humber. As in other parts of the region, the silting of the river channels was always a problem here and dredging was being undertaken from the 1300s onwards. *The History of Thorne* states that 'As early as the first of Edward III (1327), the inhabitants commenced the drainage, to improve the land and general face of the country'.

Colonising and reclaiming the fenlands was always potentially problematic and many attempts failed. This was especially so when climate and sea level were changing to make life more difficult with poor crops and rising water-tables. There were further complications such as population decline due to the Black Death in the 1300s, and changing economic and social circumstances. Much arable land was converted to sheep farming for the flourishing wool trade, but then labour shortages also made this difficult and people began a move into the urban areas. With cooler and wetter weather in the period from around 1250 to the late 1400s, and significant sea level rise, water was becoming even more of a problem. The Chronicle of Meaux Abbey reported extensive flooding in the Hull Valley during 1253 and 1265. Commissioners were appointed to assess the riverbanks and the sea defences in 1285 and there were continuing difficulties during the 1300s and 1400s. Some areas had new walls or banks built to provide defence in times of flood, and in other areas, special ledges were constructed for cattle to retreat to if the floods rose too high. One of the major risks with floods was the loss of livestock and subsequent starvation. It is clear that in these times of changing water levels, the difficulties for those living in or around the Yorkshire Fens were enormous. In some cases, lands were enclosed and defended, but in many situations, there was abandonment and the farmers moved into the local towns. One consequence of particular importance for the future drainage of much of the area was the social, economic and political power over these lands ending up being vested in just a few large estates. Following the Dissolution of the Monasteries, lands were distributed to large aristocratic estates and the Crown.

THE FIRST LARGE-SCALE DRAINAGE OF THE NORTHERN FENS

During the mid-1300s, Hatfield Chase returned to its status as property of the Crown, now a Royal Hunting Forest under the jurisdiction of the Forest Law. The latter applied to an area reserved for the Royal Hunt and associated pleasures. However, by the time of the 1608 survey of the Royal Forests and Chases, it was considered to be 'utterly wasted'. This is strange when the excellent hunting provided for the visit of Prince Henry in 1609 is considered. It seems again that the perspective of the beholder might have influenced the judgment made. In 1600 Parliament had passed 'An act for the recovery and inning of drowned and surrounded grounds and the draining dry of watery marshes, fens, bogs, moors and other grounds of like nature'. This was really intended primarily for the East Anglian fenlands, but was applied firstly to the Yorkshire Fens and specifically to the area around Hatfield Chase. The passing of this Act ultimately spelt the end for many of the wetlands in both the Yorkshire and the East Anglian fenlands.

Fresh from his exploits in the Low Countries, Cornelius Vermuyden was eventually contracted to undertake the work on behalf of King Charles I. This phase of the drainage affected around 59,997 acres (24,280 hectares) of wetland in Hatfield Chase, Wroot and Finningley, the Isle of Axholme, and along the River Idle. The intention was to reclaim large areas of land and so render them suitable for agriculture. From the project, in the core zone of the Humberhead Levels only the present-day areas of Thorne and Hatfield Moors remained intact, and beyond this the more outlying wetlands in the constituent river valleys, along with the larger carrs such as Potteric,

King Charles I. (1600s print)

remained reasonably intact but in an increasingly dry landscape.

On inspecting the area and the task, Vermuyden declared the reclamation quite practicable. After centuries of local inability to drain any significant part of the total 70,000 acres (28,328 hectares) of water from the area, the people of the region were not convinced that it was feasible. After all, every previous attempt had literally floundered. King James I summoned a local jury to consider the issue and the task, but they broke up after stating that it was impossible. Vermuyden was prepared to take on the work and bound himself to achieve what the jury had stated was impossible. However, before he could decide what to do, King James I died (in somewhat suspicious circumstances) and was replaced on the throne by his son, King Charles I. He was familiar with the ongoing negotiations and, under serious financial pressures as typified his reign, confirmed the necessary agreements. On 24 May 1626, articles previously drawn up were signed by Vermuyden and for the Crown. Vermuyden was contracted to reclaim the drowned lands and make them fit for tillage and pasturage. For this, he and his fellow Adventurers would receive one third of the reclaimed area. He went back to Amsterdam to raise the necessary capital and no doubt to recruit the specialist skills needed for the undertaking. A company was formed almost entirely of Dutch investors and the work began. They brought with them a considerable number of Dutch and Flemish workers, which at once by-passed the difficulty of recruiting local labour from communities opposed to the undertaking. It also meant the Adventurers had a workforce experienced in living in and indeed draining great wetlands. Having previously been recruited to help drain Dagenham and Canvey Island on the Thames, some of the necessary labourers were already here. Others, including French Protestant Huguenots from Picardy, and Walloons from Flanders, had arrived in England because they were fleeing religious persecution.

The plan for the drainage operations was reasonably straightforward. The principal mechanism for the drainage scheme was the cutting of a new channel to take the River Don northwards to the Turnbridge Dyke and the Went, and then at a later date the cutting of the Dutch River to take the combined flow of the Don and the Went eastwards to the Ouse. This took away the southward flow of the Don that formerly ran into Thorne Mere and south then east to the Idle, and across the south of Thorne Moors. The River Don was diverted north, prevented from entering the Level by means of embankments, and taken north through the Turnbridge Dyke into the Aire. This was problematic because the channel was too small to carry the water and the result was flooding of the 'old lands' around Fishlake, Sykehouse, and Snaith. The remedy, undertaken after Vermuyden had left, was to cut a new deep channel called 'The Dutch River' to take the water directly to the River Ouse near Goole. The solution worked but at an enormous extra cost and to the detriment of many of the Adventurers.

In the south of the area, the River Idle was to be diverted by straight channels into the Trent, taking out the meandering watercourse across the Levels of Hatfield Chase. Deep cuts took the water from the main lakes and meres on the Level, and the Idle was blocked at Idle Stop and partially diverted into the existing Byker's Dike and down the newly cut New Idle, and the Double Rivers to the River Trent. The River Torne was also diverted north-eastwards through a new cut, the New River Torne, and passed under the New Idle at Tunnel Pits. The scheme also involved a general straightening and deepening of rivers and other channels.

However, there were problems with the local people in the northern part of the area. They resented the project and the workers who were brought in to do the job. They decried the newcomers as foreigners and marauders. Dissatisfied with the efforts of the Crown, they took the law into their own hands. They rioted and broke down the embankments and assaulted the Flemish workers; several people died in the conflicts and legal disputes ran for years. Often not recognised was the fact that Vermuyden did attempt to satisfy some of the grievances of the locals. Clearly, the main issue was the loss of their lands and traditional rights. There was nothing to be done about this whilst undertaking the work as commissioned. However, a further trouble was the employment of 'foreigners' to do the deed, adding insult to injury.

To try to encourage a more positive attitude, Vermuyden did employ large numbers of native workmen and paid them considerably above what they were used to. Apparently, he also tried to alleviate the obvious suffering of those adversely affected by the scheme, but it was of little avail. R. Ansbie wrote to the Duke of Buckingham from nearby Tickhill Castle in 1628:

> What has happened betwixt Mr. Vermuyden's friends and workmen and the people of Axholme these inclosed will give a taste. Great riots have been committed by the people, and a man killed by the Dutch party, the killing of whom is conceived to be murder in all who gave direction for them to go armed that day. These outrages will produce good effects. They will procure conformity in the people, and enforce Vermuyden to sue for favour at the Duke's hands, if not for himself, for divers of his friends, especially for Mr. Saines, a Dutchman, who has an adventure of 13,000 l. in this work. Upon examination of the rest of Vermuyden's people, thinks it will appear that he gave them orders to go armed.

According to Dugdale, the works did reduce unemployment locally, and where the country about had been 'full of wandering beggars' these had all disappeared. There was good employment at high wages for all willing to work. The reclaimed land, freed of waters, was to be made into valuable agricultural holdings, but this would require further long-term cultivation. On 6 January 1629, Vermuyden received a knighthood from Charles I, in 'recognition of the skill and energy that he had displayed in adding so large a tract to the cultivable lands of England'. He also took a grant from the Crown of all the 24,500 acres (9,915 hectares) of land reclaimed in the manor of Hatfield, at an annual rent to the Crown of £193 3s 5½d, one red rose ancient rent, an improved rent of £425 from Christmas 1630, and a cash sum of £16,080. Additionally, Vermuyden was permitted to erect one or more chapels for the Dutch and Flemish settlers to worship in their own languages. They also proceeded to build houses, farmsteads and windmills, with the clear intention of long-term settlements on the lands recently won from the waters.

Henry, Prince of Wales.

For the locals though, this was all serious provocation and caused major and continuing bitterness. They continued to take issues into their own hands and obstructed the work on the drainage scheme. On 10 April 1629, a complaint was laid before the Council Board at Whitehall by the Attorney General and by Vermuyden with regard to the riotous behaviour of Robert Portington esq. and others, in beating, wounding, and killing workmen employed in the undertaking, and 'for spoiling the walls made for the draining of the lands'. The relationship of Robert to Roger Portington, who entertained Prince Henry in

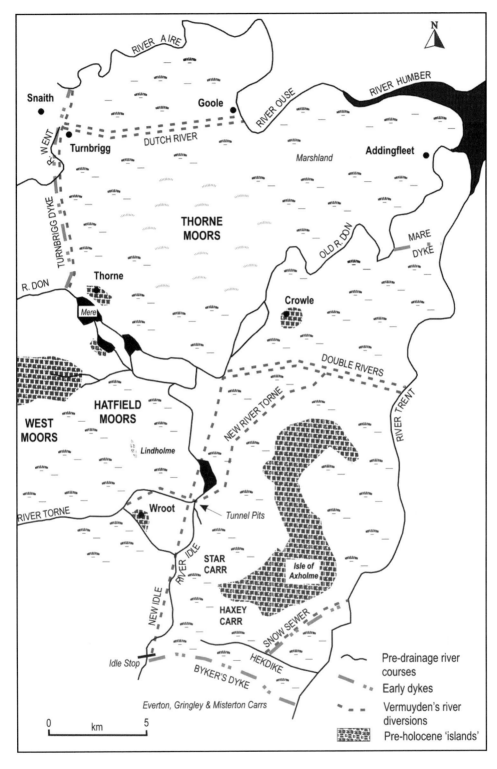

Vermuyden's drainage of Hatfield Moors.

the famed deer hunt in 1609, or perhaps to his son or brother, is not entirely clear. Roger Portington of Tudworth had removed to the manor hall at Hatfield, having received an inheritance from Sir Roger Portington of Leeds. *The History of Thorne* suggests that they were not actually related but that Sir Roger's widow left the estate to Roger Portington of Tudworth because he was her former husband's name double.

It is likely that the Portingtons were long established in the region, and had a keen interest in the Chase and the hunt. It is unlikely that they would have appreciated the imposition of Vermuyden on 'their patch' and worse still, having a clearly detrimental impact on their enjoyment and possibly livelihood. Yet there is a further twist in this tale. When Roger Portington entertained Prince Henry to such wonderful hunting, one of the other guests of the party was in fact Cornelius Vermuyden. Indeed, this was when he first conceived the idea of draining the Hatfield Chase and surrounding areas. If Henry had lived to be King, with his passion for the hunt, it is unlikely that the undertaking would have come about. However, Henry died, Charles succeeded, and Vermuyden drained. The problems of violence by locals to the imported drainers, and of new flooding to old lands by the malfunctioning drainage project, were to rumble on for many years.

The matter was taken to the Privy Council, with complaints of lost rights and damage done to the surrounding districts by the drainage works. This resulted in an inquest held by the Earls of Clare and Newcastle, and Sir Gervase Clifton. As might be expected, the hearing went in favour of Vermuyden. He had already subpoenaed many of the original inhabitants for damages done to him and his agents, and several were apprehended and taken to York Gaol. The bitterness of the locals to the Dutch intruders grew stronger and the situation continued to deteriorate. Eventually Lord Wentworth, the President of the North, intervened and determined that the legal suits should cease. He also directed Vermuyden to assign to the locals certain tracts of moor and marsh to be enjoyed by them in common. Finally, after unsuccessfully disputing the directive, Vermuyden withdrew altogether from the adventure. He first put his interests in the hands of trustees and then pulled out completely.

After Vermuyden left the area, the damage caused by the scheme to the 'old lands' was relieved at great expense by the cutting of the Dutch River. There were serious difficulties in raising the necessary capital for the works since all the problems had ensured the value of the Adventurers' shares had plummeted. However, money was raised and the new river was cut, thus alleviating the serious cause of complaints in the north of the area. There followed a period of relative calm during which the settlers, dispersed across the reclaimed areas in individual houses, set about cultivating the land. However, the tranquillity was not to last, because, promoted in part by the attempts to drain the Cambridgeshire Fens to the south, the English Civil War broke out. With the Yorkshire Royalists very active across the River Don, the Parliamentary Committee, based in Lincoln, watched over the region. It seemed that Sir Ralph Humby was about to march into the Isle of Axholme with a small force, and so to prevent this, the order was given to breach the dykes and to raise the sluice gates at Snow Sewer and Millerton Sluice. The result was catastrophic inundation across the region that undid the drainage and cultivation efforts of many years. This was estimated to have caused damage to the settlers of around £20,000 (a massive sum at that time) in just one night. The local activists went further, wreaking revenge on those who had dispossessed them. The settlers' houses were wrecked, corn in the fields was destroyed, and fences were torn down. When the settlers resisted they were forced at gunpoint to watch the area re-flooded, the rioters swearing that they would see the Levels drowned again and the foreigners swim away like ducks.

Following the floods, the commoners set about claims as participants in the lands that remained dry, and which were now, at last, free of the Dutch settlers. Colonel Lilburne, in charge of a force of Parliamentarian troops, took occupation of Sandtoft, apparently driving out the local Protestant vicar and stabling their horses in his chapel. The Colonel struck a bargain with the commoners that assigned 2,000 acres (81 hectares) of Epworth Common to him personally, in exchange for the remainder assigned to them. He agreed to uphold the claims of the commoners and prevent any redress by the now deposed settlers in terms of any claims to their own losses from the recent events. Despite Lilburne's influence and dogged-ness, the former settlers did get a ruling in their favour some eleven years after the event. The form of the settlement, however, prevented any major compensation, but some were able to return to their former dwellings and holdings. For years after the legal settlement, the com-moners continued at war with the settlers. Both sides took legal action and neither was averse to brute force. Mr Reading was engaged to defend the rights of the participants and settlers, but the commoners still resisted and at one point tried to burn him and his family in their home. It was said that Mr Reading lived to 100 years of age, but he spent fifty of those years fighting battles with the fenmen. He reckoned to have been involved in 'thirty-one set battles' with the commoners in defence of the drainers and the Adventurers.

As in the East Anglian Fens, a fundamental problem with draining these peatlands was that once dry they shrank and so ended up lower than the drains and, as previously stated, this subsequently necessitated the cutting of the Dutch River to alleviate problems of flooding the reclaimed land. As with many of the major drainage schemes of the time, the problems were not immediately solved, and breaches in the flood defences, accidental or deliberate, caused disaster and damage. Further manipulation of the original project was needed for the next 200 years as more cuts were dug and innovations to drainage and pumping were applied. The Mother Drain was constructed in the south between 1769 and 1803, to take water from Everton, Gringley, and Misterton Carrs. It was here at Misterton Sluice that the first steam-powered pumps were installed. So began the final phase of human dominance over an intransigent nature. Engineering works continued throughout the period and in 1862, as specified in the original agreement signed by Charles I, the Participations were incorpo-rated by Act of Parliament.

THE SOUTHERN FENS: SOUTH LINCOLNSHIRE AND CAMBRIDGESHIRE

Vermuyden, far from being disappointed in the outcome of his northern adventure, now knighted, turned his attentions to the south and the scene of the earlier disastrous inunda-tions. In July 1630, the Earl of Bedford wrote to Sir Harry Vane, recommending him to join Vermuyden and the earl in the enterprise. Busy as ever, before the end of 1630, Vermuyden entered a contract with the Crown to purchase Malvern Chase in Worcestershire, which he enclosed and improved. He paid £5,000 for this, and went on to spend £12,000 on land at

Sedgemoor in Somerset. However, despite his enthusiasm and energy, his past was catching up with him and, around this time, there seem to have been a series of legal suits, which resulted in a short stay in prison. Not only were the commoners of Hatfield still on his case, but the Dutch investors were also unhappy, the costs incurred having been far greater than expected and the benefits not so good.

Despite these setbacks, he was soon proceeding with his greater vision for the draining of the Great Level of the Fen in Cambridgeshire. Despite some earlier piecemeal attempts at drainage, the general neglect of the rivers was taking its toll and the districts formerly drained were now regularly under water again. Even the older farms and settlements across the region on the islands were under threat of ruin. The Commissioners of Sewers in Huntingdonshire were attempting to raise funds through local taxes but seemed to have no great success. With problems stacking up, and few apparent solutions, the Commissioners of Sewers meeting at King's Lynn called for Sir Cornelius Vermuyden. At their meeting, he offered to undertake the necessary works and even to raise the requisite capital. He required from them that he receive 95,000 acres (38,445 hectares) of reclaimed lands in recompense. The Commissioners then entered a contract with Vermuyden on these terms but the local outcry against such a contract 'with a foreigner' was such that the offer was immediately withdrawn.

However, one of the original group interested in the drainage was Francis, Earl of Bedford, the owner of numerous areas of old Church lands in the Fens. He was a more acceptable face and so was brought into the scheme as the chief undertaker. Other adjacent landowners also joined the adventure and contributed large sums of money, generally in exchange for proportional rights in the reclaimed lands. Vermuyden was still needed though, since it was his surveys and plans upon which the whole project relied. Importantly too, it was he who

Francis Russell, Earl of Bedford 1641.

had the experience of the practicality of such large drainage enterprises and he had a considerable workforce of experienced labourers, mainly Flemish, at his disposal. The Adventurers did consider the proposals of another Dutch engineer, Westerdyke, but eventually it was Vermuyden's proposals that were accepted.

As in previous 'adventures', the difficulty in raising the necessary capital was a major obstacle. The Earl of Bedford suffered serious financial difficulties and had to raise money against many of his other properties. Some of the lesser undertakers were financially ruined. Shrewd or perhaps devious, Vermuyden energetically ensured means of paying his Flemish workforce but against assurances in the form of reclaimed lands allotted to him from the Adventurers. This meant in effect that even before the works were undertaken, the landowners and other speculators were already significantly in his debt. For them, the original contract with the King's Lynn Commissioners would have been a more cost-effective route. However, the stage was set and the work began.

The new works included the Bedford River (the 'Old Bedford River') extended from Earith on the Ouse to Salter's Lode, with a cut 70ft (21km) wide and 21 miles (33.6km) long. The intention was to relieve and take off the high floods of the River Ouse. Another cut, Bevill's Leam, ran from Whittlesea Mere to Guyhirne, and was 40ft (12m) wide and 10 miles (16km) long. Sam's Cut, 20ft wide and 6 miles (9.6km) long, ran from Feltwell to the River Ouse. There were also Sandy's Cut near Ely which was 40ft (12m) wide for 2 miles (3.2km), Peakirk Drain at 17ft (5.1m) wide running for 10 miles (16km), and other drains like Mildenhall, New South Eau, and Shire Drain. The scheme also included new sluices at Tydd on Shire Drain, at Salter's Lode, and at the Horseshoe below Wisbech. Some of these opened and closed horizontally like a gate, and others rose perpendicularly like a portcullis. A sluice of the latter form, known as a 'clow', was installed at Clow's Cross to control tidal influxes, and a major freshwater sluice was built at the upper end of the Bedford River. Such was the grand scheme.

However, as had happened earlier in the north, the local fenmen, the 'fen slodgers', were set against these plans. They refused to work on the project and laboured to fill-in the cuts that the Flemish workers had dug. There were also riots and the locals mobbed the Flemish workers so that they frequently had to undertake their labours under armed guard. For the locals these were their commons, upon which their geese grazed. They were not going to lose them without a fight. For them, the annual floods brought wild-fowl and fish, peat, withies and reeds. The fenmen carried out a policy of harassment and haranguing, generally making a difficult undertaking very unpleasant indeed. Furthermore, there was simmering beneath the surface, both in the rural fens and the nearby towns. This was a deep resentment towards these 'foreigners', mainly Flemish and Dutch, who were taking the drowned lands from the local commoners. As one objector in the tract *The Drayner Confirmed* (1629) put it:

> What is the old activitie and abilities of the English nation grown now soe dull and insuf-
> ficient that wee must pray in ayde of our neighbours to improve our own demaynes? For
> matter of securitie, shall wee esteem it of small moment to put into the hands of strangers
> three or four such ports as Linne, Wisbeach, spalding, and Boston, and permit the coutrie
> within and between them to be people with overthwart neighbours; or, if they quaile
> themselves, must wee give place to our most auncient and daungerous enemies, who
> will be readie enough to take advantage of soe manie fair inlets into the bosom of our
> land, lying soe near together that an army landing in each of them may easily meet and
> strongly entrench themselves with walls of water, and drowne the countrie about them
> at their pleasure?

As indicated by the above, one of the main consequences of the undertaking was consider-able unrest and disquiet in the countryside and also in the towns around and about the Fens. The objectors trod a delicate line because civil unrest was fraught with danger and the penalties were severe. One of the ways to unsettle the project was through general disquiet and the composition of songs, ballads and poems against the drainers. One of the most popular was 'Powte's Complaint'; '*powte*' being the Old English name for the sea lamprey:

Come Brethren of the water, and let us all assemble,
To treat upon this Matter, which makes us quake and tremble;
For we shall rue, if it be true that Fens be undertaken,
And where we feed in Fen and Reed, they'll feed both Beef and Bacon.

They'll sow both Beans and oats, where never Man yet thought it;
Where Men did row in Boats, ere Undertakers bought it;
But, Ceres, thou behold us now, let wild Oats be their Venture,
Oh, let the frogs and miry Bogs destroy where they do enter.

Behold the great design, which they do now determine,
Will make our Bodies pine, a prey to Crows and Vermine,
For they do mean all Fens to drain, and Waters overmaster,
All will be dry, and we must die —'cause Essex Calves want pasture.

Away with Boats and rudder, farewell both Boots and Skactches,
No need of one nor t'other, Men now make better Matches,
Stilt-makers all, and Tanners, shall complain of this disaster,
For they will make each muddy lake for Essex Calves a Pasture.

The feather'd Fowls have Wings, to fly to other Nations,
But we have no such things, to help our Transportations,
We must give place, O grevious CASE! To horned Beast and cattle
Except that we can all agree to drive them out by Battel.

Wherefore let us intreat our ancient Water-Nurses
To shew their power so great as t'help to drain their Purses
And send us good old Captain Flood to led us out to Battel,
Then Two-penny Jack, with Scales on 's Back, will drive out all the Cattle.

This Noble Captain yet was never known to fail us,
But did the conquest get all of that did assail us;
His furious Rage none could assuage; but, to the world's great Wonder
He tears down Banks, and breaks their Cranks and Whirligigs asunder.

God Eolus, we do thee pray that thou wilt not be wanting;
Thou never said'st us nay – now listen to our canting;
Do thou deride their hope and Pride that purpose our confusion,
And send a Blast that they in haste may work no good Conclusion.

Great Neptune, God of Seas, this Work must needs provoke ye;
They mean thee to disease, and with Fen-Water choak thee;
But with thy Mace do thou deface, and quite confound this matter,
And send thy Sands to make dry lands when they shall want fresh Water.

And eke we pray thee, Moon, that thou wilt be propitious,
To see that nought be done to prosper the Malicious;
Tho' Summer's Heat hath wrought a Feat, whereby themselves they flatter,
Yet be so good as send a Flood, lest Essex Calves want Water.

Then apace, apace drink, drink deep, drink deep,
Whilst 'tis to be had let's the liquor ply;
The drainers are up, and a coile they keep,
And threaten to drain the kingdom dry.

Why should we stay here, and perish with thirst;
To th' new world in the moon away let us goe,
Fir if the Dutch colony get thither first,
'Tis a thousand to one but they'll drain that too!

Chorus: 'Then apace, apace drink, drink deep, drink deep etc.'

Such verses were read or sung to rapturous applause in towns and villages throughout the fenland. There were also popular drinking songs such as 'The Draining of the Fennes', with verses such as:

The Dutchman hath a thirsty soul,
Our cellars are subject to his call;
Let every man, then, lay hold on his bowl,
'Tis pity the German sea should have it all.

PROBLEMS WITH THE UNDERTAKING

Along with the deep resentment caused by the works, there were serious difficulties with the engineering itself. Despite the deep cuts and drains that Vermuyden's workers dug across the Fens, the works largely failed to remove surplus water from the drowned lands. They acted as receptacles for excess water but did not really carry the water off. The problem was in the lack of effective discharge to the sea, an issue that had been one of the causes of the earlier problems and severe inundations. In Holland, particularly Zeeland where Vermuyden gained his earlier experience, the rivers were somewhat easier to embank and the water carried out to sea. The lower-lying lands were kept dry by pumping with windmills. In keeping back the sea on the one hand, and the freshwater of the river on the other, this worked. However, in the Fenland, the situation was markedly different and a key problem was the removal of water off the Great Level and its discharge to the sea. The ramifications of this misunderstanding and omission were to test future generations of engineers who followed Vermuyden and the Dutch drainers. The later solutions included the provision of more effective outlets for discharge to the sea, and the deepening, straightening, and constricting of the drainage channels. The latter was with the intention of increasing the velocity of water-flow and thus ensuring more effective scouring of the silts and sediments that otherwise blocked the discharge.

In the short-term, the efforts of Vermuyden and the others were at best limited. Some areas were drier because of the drains and the receptacles for excess water, but most of the Fen was still wet or at least seasonally inundated. In 1634, a Commission of Sewers met at Huntingdon and declared that the scheme was defective, with 400,000 acres (161,874 hectares) of the Great Level still inundated, especially during the winter months. Charles I took a personal interest in the draining of the region and began to plan a programme of reclamation. His intention was to convert the region to what was termed 'winter grounds' and to build in the centre of the Level a town called Charleville, as a celebration and commemoration of the great under-taking. Once again, Vermuyden was employed to carry out the King's design. Despite the obvious failings of the works so far, he seems to have been the only one available with signifi-cant experience in major drainage works. Therefore, he proceeded to implement the ideas put forward by King Charles. He had built an embankment on the south side of Morton's Leam from Peterborough to Wisbech, a navigable sluice at Standground, and a new cut between the stone sluice at the Horseshoe, and the sea below Wisbech. The latter was 60ft (18m) across and 2 miles (3.2km) long, and embanked on both sides. There was also another sluice in the marshes below Tydd at the outfall of Shire Drain. However, with the works is full progress, other matters across the kingdom were coming to a head that would take Charles' attention from his drainage schemes. The standoff with Parliament and the serious financial problems of the Crown were pushing the situation to the limit, and civil war was increasingly inevitable.

A key issue and problem for the Crown had long been the raising of monies and the control of income-generating business and innovations. This became especially problematic during the reign of Charles I and was one of the major drivers behind the King's interest in draining drowned lands such as Hatfield Chase and the Fenland's Great Level. The suggestion by the Parliamentarians was that the royal interest in the reclamation schemes was purely to fill the coffers without the need to resort to Parliamentary sanction. This, suggested Oliver Cromwell, member for Huntingdon, and others, meant that the King's personal gain was the objective and not the betterment of the kingdom or the needs of the commoners. In this way, the Parliamentarians were able to fan the flames of discontent across the Fens and the other low-lying wetlands.

Whilst there was truth in the fact that these were intended as major money-making schemes, the broader intent against the interests of the commoners was perhaps unfair. Charles and the Crown had often supported the interests of the commoners in maintaining their rights against incursions by both the greater aristocracy, and especially the lesser gentry. Indeed, it was probably this support that caused much of the underlying discontent amongst these increasingly politically influential groups. Cromwell himself used this opportunity to rise from relative obscurity and to campaign vigorously across the region against the under-taking. The predictable result was that Cromwell suddenly found himself increasingly popular across the fenland counties and a champion of the cause of the commoners. In fact, he was soon described as the most popular man in the region and hailed by fenmen as 'The Lord of the Fens', as he went from meeting to meeting, stirring up resentment and protest. Forster, in the *Lives of Eminent British Statesmen*, says:

> From that instant the scheme became thoroughly hopeless. With such desperate determination he followed up his purpose – so actively traversed the district, and inflamed the people everywhere – so passionately described the greedy claims of royalty, the gross extractions of the commission, nay, the questionable character of the improvement itself, even could it have gone on unaccompanied by incidents of tyranny, – to the small proprietors insisting that their poor claims would be merely scorned in the new distribution of the property reclaimed – to the labouring peasants that all profit and amusement they had derived from commoning in those extensive wastes were about to be snatched for ever from them – that, before his almost individual energy, King, commissioners, noblemen-projectors, all were forced to retire, and the great project, even in the state it was, fell to the ground.

The success of the Cambridgeshire fenmen reverberated around the kingdom and encouraged others to resist. Those in the northerly regions once again saw the possibility of getting rid of their own 'improvers' and 'drainers'. The Earl of Lindsey had succeeded in the enclosure and drainage of around 35,000 acres (14164 hectares) of the Lindsey Level, completed in 1636 at considerable expense. Part of the project involved inducing farmers to take up residence and to cultivate the reclaimed lands. Problems arose when the fenmen burst upon them and destroyed houses and property, killed their cattle, and let the floodwaters back onto the reclaimed land. Similarly, in West and Wildmore Fens between Tattershall and Boston, there had been some progress by Adventurers in reclaiming areas. They had been relatively successful in draining and then cultivating an extensive area of now richly productive land. However, with the atmosphere of almost open revolt now pervading the area, the fenmen gathered to deliver a body blow to the reclaimers. Apparently under the pretext of gathering for a football match, the games of which rampaged across the countryside and were violent in the extreme, they burst over the enclosures, burnt the corn and the houses, and killed both people and cattle. They then turned to the drainage works themselves, breaking the embankments and blocking the drains. When they left, the reclaimed lands were once again under water. Therefore, following a few years of prolonged insurrection, the Levels were once again a vast water-body and the drains to the sea were again silting up and failing to discharge. However, despite these problems, a grant was subsequently made to the same Adventurers to drain 72,000 acres (29,137 hectares) of fenland from the River Glen to Lincoln and the River Trent, and, in recompense for the outlay, they received 14,000 acres (5,666 hectares) of new lands.

In 1641, the Earl of Bedford applied to the Long Parliament for permission to continue and resurrect the engineering works. However, the general civil unrest across the region prevented any real action. The earl died soon afterwards, his considerable wealth vastly reduced by his involvement in this projected and so far unsuccessful undertaking. Surprisingly, with all the unrest and resentment, Vermuyden remained on the scene, still pursuing the idea of reclaiming this vast wetland. His political situation, as a close associate of Charles, must have been difficult as his eldest son, also called Cornelius, was a colonel in the Parliamentary army under Fairfax in the build-up to the Battle of Naseby. Cromwell wrote to Fairfax on 4 June 1645: 'The party under Vermuyden waits the King's army, and is about Deeping; has a command to join with Sir John Gell, if he commands him.' However, the younger Cornelius Vermuyden resigned his commission a few days prior to the Battle of Naseby, having suddenly found his presence required beyond the seas! It appears that he did not return to England until after the Restoration, but in 1665 he was a member of the Corporation of the Bedford Level.

Vermuyden senior was probably too focused on his drainage projects to be diverted into the political turmoil, at least more than could be avoided. He must surely have held allegiance to the Crown, as both Charles I, and his father James I, had been his staunch advocates. With civil war still raging, Vermuyden wrote his *Discourse on the Drainage of the Fens*. In this tract, he pointed out the works still necessary to bring about the drainage and reclamation of the 400,000 acres (161,874 hectares) of the Great Level. With much lobbying and pamphleteering over many years, there were petitions to Parliament to resolve the means of perfecting the drainage of the Great Level. Finally, in 1649, authority was granted to William, Earl of Bedford, to complete the works begun by his late father. Once again, the Dutch drainage engineer Westerdyke was summoned to criticise the works and plans of Vermuyden, but once again, Vermuyden won the day and was appointed to oversee the drainage.

The Dutch workers were gathered to begin this new phase of the endeavour. However, after a promising start, the project slowly ground to a halt because of a lack of money and presumably of confidence. Bearing in mind the costs and failings of the earlier attempts, this was perhaps not surprising. Some of the Adventurers sold their shares to reduce any risk of further liabilities, and others continued but under severe financial duress. The work carried on but now with a supply of cheap labour in the form of Scottish prisoners of war taken at the Battle of Dunbar, 3 September 1650. This was a battle of the Third English Civil War at which the English Parliamentarian forces (under Oliver Cromwell) defeated a Scottish army commanded by David Leslie and loyal to the future King Charles II, who had been proclaimed King of the Scots on 5 February 1649. On 23 June 1650, Charles II landed in Scotland at Garmouth in Moray and on his arrival signed the 1638 Covenant and the 1643 Solemn League and Covenant. He was then proclaimed King of Scots. However, in the midst of resignations from the army and political anger over the Scots' actions, Cromwell took leadership of the forces and marched north. Despite initially meeting stubborn Scottish resistance, and on the outskirts of Dunbar facing almost certain disaster, Cromwell turned the tables following a Scottish tactical blunder and won the day. The Scottish army fled the field, and the slaughter of the Scots soldiers, described by Cromwell as 'executions', extended for a distance of around 8 miles (12.8km). Finally, at the Battle of Worcester on 3 September 1651, Cromwell defeated Charles, who fled to mainland Europe. Cromwell became virtual dictator of England, Scotland and Ireland, and Charles spent the next nine years in exile in France, the United Provinces and the Spanish Netherlands. Following the death of Cromwell in 1658, political crisis led to the restoration of the monarchy, and Charles returned as King. On 29 May 1660, his thirtieth birthday, he arrived in London to general public acclaim; all legal documents were modified and dated as if Charles II had succeeded his father as King in 1649.

Left: King Charles II.
(1600s print)

Below: Oliver Cromwell.
(1600s print)

In the melee of these troubled times, a thousand of the prisoners, from several thousand taken after the battle of Dunbar, were set to work north of the Bedford River. Here they continued to labour, many dying, before England and Scotland reached a political settlement, and they could return home. On their departure, with again little support from the Fen districts, there were problems in getting the necessary labour. However, war again intervened, this time with the Dutch, and Blake's victory over Van Tromp in 1652, provided an influx, this time of Dutch prisoners of war. Five hundred of these new prisoners were immediately put to work on the Level.

THE NEW UNDERTAKING

This next stage of the reclamation of the Great Level of the Fens included a number of features that were important and would be clearly recognised today. The New Bedford River was cut from Earith on the River Ouse to Salter's Lode. This in effect halved its length from 40 miles (64km) to 20 miles (32km): a new river 100ft (30m) across and parallel with the Old Bedford River. On the south side of the new cut there was a high bank, and similarly along the north side of the old river. This created between these two great banks a large area, about 5,000 acres (2,023 hectares), called the Washes. Vermuyden described the function of this land as to allow the floods to 'bed in'. In other words, during times of winter floods there was land to receive the excess water. Other works were also carried out. The River Welland, for example, had a large bank 70ft (21m) thick and 8ft (2.4m) high constructed from Peakirk to the Holland Bank. The River Nene had a new bank from Peterborough to Guyhirne, and a further bank was constructed from Standground to Guyhirne. The latter protected the Middle Level from overflowing excess waters from Northamptonshire. The River Ouse was protected by high banks from Over to Earith, with a navigable sluice provided at the latter. Various other cuts and drains were dug, including Smith's Leam; Vermuyden's Eau (or the Forty Feet Drain) from Welch's Dam to the River Nene near Ramsey Mere; Hammond's Eau near Somersham in Huntingdonshire; Stonea Drain and Moore's Drain near March; Thurlow's Drain from the Forty Feet Drain to Popham's Eau; and the Conquest Lode that ran to Whittlesea Mere. Another major engineering construction was the Denver Sluice, intended to turn the tidal waters into the Hundred Feet River and to stop upland floodwaters from passing up the Ten Mile River towards Littleport. In the South Level, a major work was the cutting of St John's or Downham Eau (known locally as 'The Poker' owing to its very straight construction), a 120ft (36m) wide and 10ft (3m) deep, running from Denver Sluice to Stow Bridge on the River Ouse. With sluices at both ends, its function was to carry off floodwaters that descended from the rivers of the South Level. Most of the rivers were provided with new sluices to present the influx of high tides, and at the same time, old cuts and channels were scoured to speed the drainage when required.

Finally, in March 1652, the undertaking was finished and ready for inspection by the Lords Commissioners of Adjudication as appointed by Parliament. The inspectors sailed on the New River to Stow Bridge and back to Ely. They examined the new cuts and sluices and other works, and then listened to Sir Cornelius Vermuyden read his notes on the design of the undertaking and how the works had been achieved. He referred to the successes in the Middle and North Levels, where there were already 40,000 acres (16,187 hectares) of land:

> … sown with cole-seed, wheat, and other winter grain, besides innumerable quantities of sheep, cattle, and other stock, where never had been any before. These works have proved themselves sufficient, as well by the great tide about a month since, which overflowed Marshland banks, and drowned much ground in Lincolnshire and other places, and a flood by reason of a great snow, and rain upon it following soon after, and yet never hurt any part of the whole Level; and the view of them, and the consideration of what hath previously been said, proves a clear draining according to the Act. I presume to say no

more of the work, lest I should be accounted vain-glorious; although I might truly affirm
that the present or former age have done nothing like it for the general good of the nation.
I humbly desire that God may have the glory, for his blessing and brining to perfection my
poor endeavours, and the vast charge of the Earl of Bedford and his participants.

There was then a public thanksgiving to celebrate the completion of the works. On 27 March
1653, the Lords Commissioners of Adjudication of the Reclaimed Lands, accompanied by
their officers and the Company of Adventurers led by the Earl of Bedford, with leading men
of the districts such as magistrates and others of note, were present at a vast public service at
Ely Cathedral. The sermon was preached by Revd Hugh Peters, the chaplain to the Lord-
General Oliver Cromwell. It appeared that at last the Adventurers and drainers had prevailed
over nature, but at a cost.

The protracted works, much undertaken during the period of the most bitter conflict ever
fought on English soil, had left Vermuyden broke and indeed in debt. In order to pay the
wages of his Dutch and Flemish workers, he had sold all the land allotted to him or which
he had purchased in areas like Hatfield in Yorkshire, at Dagenham on the Thames, and at
Sedgemoor in Somerset. By 1654, he had sold the Hatfield estate and was selling even the
lands allotted to him in the Great Level. Then, in spite of clearly having lost all, in 1656,
his debtors pursued him for further redress and he appeared as a humble petitioner before
Parliament, seeking assistance and support. After this, he disappears from the public record and
it was assumed until recently that he went abroad and died a poor, broken old man. All the
extensive lands reclaimed from the wastes, the drowned lands recovered for the nation, were
dispersed to others who had lacked the tenacity of Vermuyden but would now reap the benefits. For someone who was so prominently in the public eye, it is surprising that the death
of Sir Cornelius is shrouded in mystery. There was even a rumour that began in the 1800s,
that he was the same person as Sir Cornelius Pharmedo or Fairmeadow, noted in An Act
of Naturalisation of certain Noblemen and Gentlemen of England, passed by the Scottish
Parliament in 1633. Following this lead, and with an absence of other information on his
death or the whereabouts of the burial, it was then suggested that he was buried at St Martin-
in-the-Fields, London, in 1683. However, the story was totally unfounded and according to
the children of Cornelius Vermuyden the younger, Sarah and Bartholomew, their father died
of a seizure and the documentation of 1694 relates to Chancery Suits concerning disputes
over his estate. They further stated that his father, Sir Cornelius Vermuyden, 'was seised of
the same and died about 16 years ago' (Bartholomew), and 'died so seised … about 16 or 17
years ago' (Sarah). This would place his death at about 1677-78. However, after some persistent
research the burial place was located in the register of the church of St Margaret, Westminster,
with the statement: 'Sr Cornels Vermooden, on 15 October, 1677'. Therefore, it seems he died
at the age of eighty-seven in the 'Great House in Channel Row, Westminster'.

6

THE PROGRESS OF 'IMPROVEMENT'

No doubt whilst Vermuyden wasted away in penury, and the commoners mourned their losses, others must have gained considerably from his activities in both north Lincolnshire and South Yorkshire, and in south Lincolnshire and Cambridgeshire. The regions could no longer be described as boggy wastelands, and certainly in good seasons were covered by fields of waving corn where once the tops of reeds had swayed in the breeze. As the drainage took effect, settlers moved onto the land, and farms and cottages sprang up on the new lands; hard work could be re-paid and rewarded by good crops. To all intents and purposes, the objectives of the original charter, as granted by Charles I, had come to pass as written in 1861:

> In those places which lately presented nothing to the eyes of the beholders but great waters and a few reeds thinly scattered here and there, under the divine mercy might be seen pleasant pastures of cattle and kine, and many houses belonging to the inhabitants.

Yet the drainage of the Fens was by no means complete. Generally, the improvements became more permanent and the risks of regression and loss less serious, or at least less frequent. Perhaps the arduous nature of wresting the land from the waters and protecting it as such had also honed the enterprise and skills of the farming communities that colonised and cultivated the new lands. Over the decades the 'improvements' gradually went on across both northern and southern regions, with rivers flowing through artificial banks and often into new channels. In the Southern Fens, the River Nene remained comparatively 'natural' until relatively late. New dykes and drains, cuts and channels and eaus were formed and new embankments and sluices were built. Other channels were dredged and deepened. Mills were needed to actively pump the water from side drains into main drains and from wetlands into ditches and drains. First, there were windmills like those in the Netherlands pumping water from the Polders. Then came steam pumps and then oil and electricity. Sluices were constructed to keep freshwaters from backing up, and to stop seawater flooding the low-lying lands. Great embankments lined the rivers, both 'natural' and man-made, and protected coastal areas from high tides. Where once nature held sway, now all was to be contained and controlled. It is estimated that in the Southern Fens alone, around 680,000 acres (275,186 hectares) were converted from 'dreary waste' into the most fertile and productive agricultural land in Britain. As Samuel Smiles wrote in 1904:

> The soil of England is sufficiently fertile; but it has been made so principally by the industry of its people. A large portion of it, and that the most fertile, has been reclaimed and embanked from the sea. The two thousand square miles of land in Lincolnshire and Cambridgeshire, forming the Great Level of the Fens, would, but for human skill and industry, be lying under water, the haunt of wild birds. The prophecies of the decay that would fall upon the country, if 'the valuable race of Fenmen' were deprived of their pools for pike, and fish, and wild-fowl, have long since been exploded. The population has grown in numbers, in health, and in comfort, with the progress of drainage and reclamation. The Fens are no longer the lurking places of disease, but as salubrious as any other parts of England. Dreary swamps are supplanted by pleasant pastures, and the haunts of pike and wild-fowl have become the habitations of industrious farmers and husbandmen. Even Whittlesea Mere and Ramsey Mere – the only two lakes, as we were told in the geography books of our younger days, to be found in the south of England – have been blotted out of the map, for they have been drained by the engineer, and are now covered with smiling farms and pleasant homesteads.

Nevertheless, it is worth considering too the period from the demise of Vermuyden and his Adventurers in the late 1600s, to the situation that seemed so pleasant to the eyes of the industrialising and agriculturally improving Victorians. Vermuyden is the name that almost everyone associates with these great drainage schemes, but there were other equally eminent engineers who followed. There were also other factors and issues, which finally swept almost the last vestiges of these once great wildernesses from the map. Perhaps the most significant of the engineers was John Smeaton, born in Whitkirk, 4 miles (6.4km) east of Leeds, on 8 June 1724.

Whittlesea Mere after drainage. (Victorian print)

Probably most famous for the iconic Eddystone Lighthouse, Smeaton worked in many areas of civil and mechanical engineering, and these included fenland drainage. One of his major works was the drainage of Potteric Carr in South Yorkshire.

THE DRAINAGE OF POTTERIC CARR

Potteric was the greatest of the South Yorkshire carrs, lying west of the greater Humberhead Levels and at the edge of the Great South Yorkshire Fen. It covered around 4,250 acres (1,720 hectares) of low-lying ground south-east of Doncaster. By the mid-1700s, the area had two drains running through the north-western area and into a small lake, the Old Eaa. From here, the water flowed down a stream into the River Torne. The Torne was now embanked for much of its length, and the stream entered the river via a sluice. A small area north of St Catherine's Well Stream, which was also embanked, was drained by the Huxterwell Drain and entered the Torne at the same sluice. Since, despite the bigger schemes, much of the land was still subject to severe flooding, consideration was given to the need and potential of effective drainage and protection from inundation for the whole area. To this end, the Corporation of Doncaster and one of the major landowners, William Dixon of Loversall, commissioned a feasibility report from Smeaton. He had previously submitted plans to drain Lochar Moss near Dumfries, though his plans had not been taken up. Smeaton visited Potteric in July 1762 and took a series of levels across the area. In September of that year, he reported on two possible schemes. The first proposal was to take the water from a new main drain in the carr, via a short tunnel under the ridge that carries the Doncaster to Balby Road. The water would then flow in an open cut to meet with the River Don a little upstream of Friars Bridge. The second possibility was to lead the main drain or 'Mother Drain' to an outfall on the River Torne around three quarters of a mile below Rossington Bridge, entering via a sluice. The latter was to have doors directed towards the river but also a draw door on the landward side to hold water back in the event of drought. This second scheme was the simpler of the two, but might incur objections from landowners downstream on the Torne if they felt that increased flooding might occur.

The levels survey indicated that the lowest ground of the carr was about 5ft (1.5m) above the level of the River Torne. The general guidance for land drainage was that the water in the ditches and dykes should be at a minimum of 2ft (0.6m) below the land surface. There would then be a fall for the drain of about 3ft (0.9m) over 3.5 miles (5.6km). However, there seems to have been some sort of error in the surveys. Whereas the levels in the carr and the Torne were accurate, there was a problem with those across to the River Don. In fact, the land at Friars Bridge, rather than being below Potteric Carr, was actually at about the same level. In other words, there would be no fall. By November 1763, Smeaton's fees of £26 5s were paid and in January 1764, he was asked to prepare estimates for the works to be undertaken. He spent a further six days on site in March of that year at a charge of £1 8s 6d (one guinea plus 7s 6d expenses), to undertake the necessary additional work to produce the costs for the first scheme. Evidently, the drain to the River Don was the preferred option. Works of this nature required Parliamentary approval and so a petition went to Parliament in January 1765. The Town Clerk for Doncaster, Richard Sheppard, drew up the Bill, Smeaton presented evidence, and the Act was obtained in April 1765.

THE LARGE COPPER BUTTERFLY

In 1864, the large copper butterfly (*Lycaena dispar*) was made extinct in the Southern Fens and in England. This extinction was due to loss of habitat across its core range of the Fens and East Anglia. The endemic English sub-species *Lycaena dispar dispar* was lost in 1848 due to the drainage of the only remaining sites, mostly around Whittlesea Mere. Its food plant is the great water dock (*Rumex hydrolapathum*) which occurs along ditches at Wicken Fen; in 1927, there was a reintroduction, albeit with the Dutch sub-species, *Lycaena dispar batavus*, to both Wicken Fen and Woodwalton Fen. The former was at first the most successful, but the wartime drainage of Adventurers' Fen put paid to that. In part, the population at Woodwalton has been maintained through artificial support ever since. The marsh fritillary butterfly (*Eurodryas aurinia*) was also finally lost in the early 1940s. This habitat loss and fragmentation are a problem for mobile species as suitable habitat becomes smaller in extent, and is separated by greater areas of inhospitable countryside; climate change makes this worse for many species.

However, it seems that there was some suspicion that all was not well, for in May 1765, James Brindley, engineer, was asked by Doncaster Corporation to 'take a Levell of Potterick Carr to find which will be the most effectual way and method to drain the same'. He received a fee of 8 guineas plus 1 guinea for travelling expenses from Barnsley. It is likely that one of the Commissioners named in the Act, perhaps Thomas Tofield who lived nearby, had realised the errors in the levels. However, it appears that Smeaton had already been on site and was working up a detailed proposal for the second scheme. It was this more detailed proposal that was eventually undertaken. The River Torne was diverted in a long cut through a new bridge to be built adjacent to the existing Rossington Bridge. The latter would accommodate the new Mother Drain. The outfall was built on Doncaster Corporation land to avoid any legal issues with adjacent landowners. This was around half a mile upstream from the point originally chosen. There were problems with this in that the gradient of the fall, so important in major drainage projects, was reduced to around 5ins per mile (127mm per 1.6km). To compensate for this, Smeaton decided that the Mother Drain would have a considerable bottom width of about 18ft (5.4m) and be carried on a horizontal plane with a depth of 6ft (1.8m). This was 2ft (0.6m) below the river level at the outfall. The new channel for the River Torne was to be at least 20ft (6m) wide and with bank slopes of not more than one-in-one. He also planned to take the water that ran into the carr from the 'uplands' (not a large catchment), via catch-water drains around the edge of the main body of the carr.

The work to completion was then reasonably straightforward and undertaken in three stages. The first phase was completed by 1768, with the new Rossington Bridge built, the new Torne channel cut, and the upstream channel enlarged with raised and extended embankments. The Division Drain and the Lady Bank Drain were enlarged and the Mother Drain was cut to the old course of the River Torne.

Following the successful completion of the first stage, there was a delay as land forming the northern part of Potteric Carr was allotted and enclosed as per an award dated 1771. This was land also owned by Doncaster Corporation, but presumably with common rights attached. The second phase of work commenced in 1772 and was completed in 1774. This included the extension of the Mother Drain under old Rossington Bridge, the building of the sluice, the cutting of Rossington Drain, and the enlargement and extension northwards of Huxterwell Drain. In total, there were around 4.5 miles (7.2km) of new cuts on the River Torne, the same for the new Mother Drain, and about 8 miles (12.8km) of other cuts.

Smeaton's approach to Potteric Carr and its drainage accords with some of the main principles of fenland and carr drainage. The scheme separates what are termed the 'living waters' of the rivers and tributary streams from the 'land waters'; the latter being those generated by rainfall actually within the site to be drained. A process of embanking watercourses, and straightening or deepening channels to improve their flow characteristics, achieved what was required. The intention was to stop them overflowing onto the land in times of flood, and to remove water from the area as quickly as possible. This reduces the necessary function and capacity of the drains within the target area, which deal with the rainfall onto the site itself, and any smaller amounts of water flowing in from higher ground not taken directly to the main river. These drains must then have enough capacity to carry the water off the site and should discharge downstream as far as is possible. In order to prevent a backflow reversing up the drains when the river is in spate, a sluice may be necessary. However, there is often a need to ensure some water supply for agricultural needs, and so some capacity to hold back the flow may be necessary. The prime agricultural demand, however, is to lower the water-table, and so the water levels in the drains are to be kept several feet below the level of the surrounding ground. The resultant storage capacity in the drainage system means that there is a buffering effect during high flows, and peak discharges are smoothed out. It seems that many of the engineers made their detailed plans and designs based on personal experience. There are no simple or easy answers to some of the complicated issues of channel flow and water movement. Smeaton noted:

> Flow occurs within the full cross-section of a channel even when the bottom of the channel lies below the level of the outlet; i.e. there is no 'dead water'.

> As an equal quantity of water must, in the same channel, pass in a given time through every section, the velocity will vary inversely as the area of the section.

> For a given flow the grater the velocity (under equal circumstances) the greater will be the gradient, and *vice-versa*.

> For a given cross-sectional area and gradient, the flow increases with the ratio (R) of area to wetted perimeter; that is, the hydraulic mean depth.

This last fact justifies the extra expense of making drains with a horizontal bottom, rather than a sloping one, where gradients are small, and for digging the bottom below the level of water at the outfall, as at Potteric Carr.

These points were set down in a letter to Tofield and Grundy concerning an enquiry about drainage at Deeping Fen in 1770. The approach, combined with the basic principles, will generally achieve the effective drainage of a fen or carr. It is important to realise that all this work was undertaken at a time before detailed calculations of relationships determining flow in channels had been developed.

SMEATON AND THE YORKSHIRE AND NORTH LINCOLNSHIRE FENS

Whilst working on the successful drainage of the greatest of the South Yorkshire carrs, Potteric Carr, Smeaton also turned his attention to Holderness (in 1763), Hatfield Chase (in 1764), and then Adlingfleet Level near Trent Falls (in 1772). In Holderness, he worked with engineer John Grundy on a scheme to improve the drainage of around 11,000 acres (4,452 hectares) of low ground in the Hull Valley. Grundy was the engineer working on a new sluice at Deeping Fen in Lincolnshire. At Adlingfleet, the construction of a comprehensive drainage scheme in 1772 removed flooding from around 5,000 acres (2,023 hectares) of low ground, some of which was permanently under water. He had first visited the site in 1755, at the request of the landowner at Haldenby Manor. His suggestion at the time was that in order to avoid the expense of the necessary Parliamentary Act for the construction of new drains, the existing drains should be enlarged and the Ousefleet Sluice re-built. John Grundy also visited the nearby estate at Eastoft in 1759 to report to the owner, Mr Marmaduke Constable. His view was that the land had sufficient fall to facilitate drainage but that the existing drains were too narrow and had too many bends. However, there were problems in implementing any improvements since numerous landowners were involved and the scheme would come under the Court of Sewers. Without an individual Act of Parliament, the difficulties might be too complex to overcome. His suggestion was to leave any attempt on this bigger improvement for now, and to build a wind-driven scoop, engine, or windmill to lift water off the land directly.

The ultimate solution was a collaboration of the major landowners in presenting a Bill to Parliament for the necessary act in order to progress the works. Smeaton, working with a detailed survey and map from Charles Tate, reported on the scheme in December 1764. Whilst the existing drainage network might be satisfactory if improved by enlarging and straightening the drains and rebuilding the sluice, it was advocated that a new drain be cut from the Green Bank in the south to an outfall on the River Trent. With a lower low tide here, this meant a better fall and the sluice could remain open for longer than at Ousefleet. The lowest points in the land to be drained were at Haldenby Common (4 miles from the outfall) and at Eastcroft Moor (5.5 miles from the outfall). The calculation suggested a fall of about 1ft per mile (0.3m per 1.6km) and a drain water-level at around 2ft (0.6m) below the land; all-in-all very satisfactory for effective drainage.

At this time, Adlingfleet had no major river across its boundaries, the whole site being very flat and the old River Don diverted by Vermuyden. The latter had made little attempt to effect any drainage of this area and so Smeaton's scheme required barrier banks to be raised along the southern and south-western boundaries to prevent flooding from outside the area. These effectively enclosed the area, with the natural levees of the old River Don raised to the east and the Whitgift drainage system to the west. This meant that the only incoming water was from rainfall on the area itself and drainage could be effected by simply taking this water off. The advice was heeded and the Act of Parliament for the major works to the River Trent was obtained in March 1767. Smeaton was paid £28 16s 4d for his fees and expenses, and the work undertaken by John Grundy. It was completed in 1769, and the Enclosure Commissioners made their Award in 1772. This set out the details of the allotment of the now drained land, field by field, together with the Mother Drain and the embankments. The total cost of draining this area of around 5,000 acres (2,023 hectares) was about £7,000. The main drain, nearly 6 miles (9.6km) long, involved around 170,000 cubic yards (155,448m) of material excavated at around 3d per cubic yard (0.9m). There were just over 12 miles (19.2km) of lesser drains, generally about 6ft (1.8m) deep and about 5ft (1.5m) wide at the bottom.

Smeaton was also working on improvements to the drainage of Hatfield Chase, Vermuyden's first major fenland scheme. It was over 100 years since the original undertaking, and the tax revenue from the 14,000 acres (5,666 hectares) allotted to Vermuyden and his fellow Adventurers (the 'scotted' land), and from the 3,000 acres (1,214 hectares) allotted to local landowners (the 'decreed' land), was largely spent on the ongoing maintenance of the rivers, channels, drains and embankments. There was also the need to pay off the initial capital expenditure, and as seen in the Southern Fens, the costs were rarely met. One issue was the restriction of water flow at Misterton Soss. Vermuyden had built a tidal sluice at Misterton with embankments between the sluice and the outfall, and a further barrier bank between the north side of the River Idle and higher ground near to Misson. The River Trent was already embanked to prevent high tides flooding over into the adjacent land. With the river in flood, the rise in high tide could be 14 to 16ft (4.2 to 4.8m) above normal at this point. These works ensured that tidal waters and freshwater floods were kept off the lower grounds north of the barrier bank. The carrs of Gringley and Misterton had been converted into 'summer grounds', i.e. pasture land flooded only in winter and so available to stock gazing at other times. To relieve the constriction of the flow, Smeaton recommended additional sluice doors to be constructed and the cut widened to allow this. The water would rise to a lower height, the waters would also run off more quickly, and the carr pasturelands would be improved. However, the benefits of the proposal were largely for lands outside the scheme, e.g. the carrs, and so the landowners proceeded only with the raising of the banks. Later, in the 1790s, the Everton, Gringley, and Misterton carrs were completely drained by engineer Jessop. The additional sluices, as originally designed by Smeaton, were included, but were eventually replaced by a new sluice and floodwater pumps in the 1900s.

The Snow Sewer was an old watercourse enlarged and extended as a main drain to take water from the carrs south of the Isle of Axholme. It runs for 6 miles (9.6km) and has an outfall to the River Trent at Owston. There were problems with the water overflowing at high tide and Smeaton re-constructed the banks and sluices to resolve this. Another problem was with the flooding that still occurred with the River Torne during periods of high rainfall. Vermuyden had constructed a cut that ran north-east and with four right-angled bends close to Hirst Priory. At this point, it picked up the water from the short main drain and carried this east via the 'South River', to an outfall with a sluice on the River Trent at Althorpe.

The Adventurers' scheme had also had a main drain, called the New Idle, which flowed from Idle Stop, under the Torne at Tunnel Pit, and so to Dirtness Bridge. From there, as the 'North River', it went north-eastwards to Hirst Priory and to a large sluice at Althorpe. Following the Vermuyden project, another link had been cut between the North and South Rivers at Hirst Priory. The idea of this was that under severe flood, the two channels would each flow at their maximum capacity and ensure the most effective discharge. Smeaton identified problems such as the lack of height in some of the embankments and the lack of sufficient depth in parts of the new cut River Torne. Various suggestions to improve the situation had already been made, but the costs were considered prohibitive. In addition, the works would have necessitated a specific Act of Parliament. However, by the 1770s, there was a renewed enthusiasm to undertake the necessary works and surveys were carried out. In 1776, Smeaton reported in detail on the problems and issues of the River Torne drainage. In this report, he points out that:

> … as I understand that the whole Course of the proposed outfall Drain, lays thro' Parishes and Lordships wholly unconnected with the Participants concern in Hatfield Chase; in case Difficulties should arise in reconciling these different interests, it seems to me of consequence to that Body of Gentlemen, and the Country at present depending upon their Undertaking, to shew how these Levels of Hatfield Chase may be drained, in a very competent Manner, without going out of their own Boundary.

He goes on to explain how he proposed to achieve this. He was to cut a new and improved drain from Tunnel Pit to the Trent to carry off excess floodwater and to provide this with an effective outfall sluice. The project involved deepening the bed at key points, new cuts, and the straightening and shortening of the channels at critical points. The embankments between the Torne Bridge and the Ross Bridge were also to be raised. The total costs were estimated as £13,500 for the actual works, excluding legal fees etc. The works were to a large degree, but not totally, successful.

Further improvement had to be undertaken at a later date by Matthias Scott, the Surveyor of Works, who had already been involved in the enlarging of the North River from Crowle Bridge to Althorpe in 1773. Smeaton probably omitted these additional works on grounds of cost. Having obtained the necessary Act of Parliament in 1783, Scott designed a new cut in the north to Keadby, and a new sluice and 30ft (9m) wide cut. The work was carried out by Scott's successor, Samuel Foster, largely following Smeaton's original plans for the new Torne and the South Idle drain. There were significant improvements through the provision of separate outfalls at Althorpe to the River Trent. Along with widening the existing drains, the new works included 10 miles (16km) of new cuts, considerable new embanking, three new sluices, and a number of new bridges. The total costs incurred over the period from around 1776 to 1789 were about £23,000. Now in Smeaton's words, Hatfield Chase had been drained 'in a very competent manner'. Although more works would be undertaken in the centuries that followed, the combined efforts of Smeaton, Brindley, Scott, Foster, and Grundy sealed the final fates of many of the wetlands that survived Vermuyden and his Adventurers.

DRAINAGE IN THE WIDER LANDSCAPE OF
THE YORKSHIRE AND NORTH LINCOLNSHIRE FENS

The greatest challenge was in draining the huge floodlands and raised mires at the core of the great Yorkshire Fen, and its achievement ranks as one of the great engineering feats of the time. However, there was also a deal of activity happening across the wider fenlands and in the wetlands that were strewn along each of the constituent river valleys. In the Ancholme Valley in 1637, a new cut was dug between Bishopsbridge to the Humber, and at South Ferriby a new tidal sluice was constructed. These were intended to improve navigation and to control flooding, but were only partially successful. The carrs of Routh and Swine were successfully drained but the lands further north were still vulnerable to flooding. By the nineteenth century, the Beverley-Barmston Drain and the Holderness Drain were cut and the River Hull was dredged from Driffield to Hull, and many of the problems were solved. Across Holderness, there were still numerous post-glacial meres present in medieval times, and they were considered valuable for fowling and for fishing. However, many of these were drained during the 1200s and 1300s for agricultural improvement. The major period of drainage of the meres was the 1500s and 1600s, after which only the largest, Hornsea Mere, remained by 1858.

In the Vale of York, Walling Fen survived until the cutting of the Market Weighton Canal in the late 1700s, and the River Derwent has retained intact washlands to this day. The Lincolnshire Marsh was less problematic to reclaim. With alleviation and coastal sediment accretion, extensive storm beaches, and the building of the sea-bank, there was little need for the cutting of more than local drainage channels.

From the 1700s onwards, a further impetus to drainage and reclamation came from the drive to enclose and thus 'improve' open common land and 'wastes' through Parliamentary Enclosures. Each area targeted had an individual Act of Parliament and the process continued until well into the 1800s. This not only facilitated reclamation of the former wetlands but also created a completely new landscape and social structure. The open fields, with the nationally notable exception of around the Isle of Axholme, had largely gone, replaced by dispersed farms scattered around the older nucleated villages and other settlements. As part of the process of improvement around the tidal zones of the Humber Estuary, there was applied what is believed to be a unique system of reclamation: 'warping'. This was the embankment of fields to retain mineral-rich sediments carried by tidal floodwaters, undertaken for a number of years and used extensively in the region during the 1800s and early 1900s. The process effects two major changes. The first is that it buries the unproductive peat soils under a layer of rich mineral soil. The second is that over time, it raises the areas of land above the level of regular floods. This system was called 'flood-warping' and there was an alternative where flood management was difficult to apply, called 'cart-warping'. As the name suggests, this was where the silt was carried onto the land by cart, and was similar to the use of mineral-rich sand transported to land-improvement sites in the south-west of England, such as along the Camel Estuary in Cornwall. Warping was applied to large areas along the lower Trent Valley, to the northern parts of Thorne Moors, and to the lower reaches of the Vale of York. Thomas Bunker, in 1876 (in Limbert, 1983), described the process of warping:

It appears that considerable tracts of poor land and moor are very low, in fact lower than high water mark at spring tide. Advantage is taken of this by raising a bank perhaps 10 feet high round a field of perhaps 20 to 40 acres and allowing the tidal waves to flow from the river by means of a large drain into the field; at high water, when the current ceases, a large portion of the mud held in suspension settles on the land, and the comparatively clear water runs off as the tide ebbs. This mode of proceeding is continued for some years and the result is the deposit of as good a soil as need be wished for.

As the major flood management and the big drainage schemes kicked in, farming in the wider landscape played its part too. Across the entire region, the lowland fields cut out of open fields and waste by improvers had drainage ditches or 'wet hedges' around them. Then within the fields themselves, there were increasingly effective drains and drainage systems imposed. By the 1800s, lime and marl were being applied to improve soil condition and fertility, and by the twentieth century, the period of intensive agri-industrial farming added synthetic fertilisers and other chemicals to drive production upwards.

One of the most important people involved in drainage of the area in the nineteenth century was the engineer Makin Durham of Thorne. Locally he was known as 'the second Vermuyden' and was also 'by far the largest proprietor on Thorne Moors'. Durham was born in 1805 and died seventy-seven years later, in March 1882. He began work as an apprentice to Richard Pilkington, the Thorne surveyor, who was particularly involved in enclosures across northern England, and later took over Pilkington's practice. However, Durham retained a strong local interest and concentrated on practical and financial matters of drainage and land reclamation in the Thorne and Hatfield area. He oversaw the effective and scientifically based drainage of lands across the region. Locally focused Acts were passed and local finance was raised to undertake the work. With the first Dun Drainage Act in the 1830s, Durham was made the Commissioner for an extensive area of riverside land between Bentley, Doncaster, Stainforth, and Fishlake. These lands were to be drained and the Commissioners made their award in April 1839, with Durham appointed as the engineer to both make and then maintain the necessary works 'of great importance to the district'. Durham was also appointed as engineer to the Corporation of the Level of Hatfield Chase – a post that he had held for their predecessors, the Trustees of Decreed Lands. He undertook the design and the engineering of the drainage of the Levels into North and South Districts, each drained by steam-driven pumping engines. His projects included drainage schemes along the Went and in other areas too. Overall, his contribution was effectively to 'mop up' much of the wetland that remained after the earlier great schemes and the piecemeal land improvement under the enclosures.

THE SOUTHERN FENLAND

In the wider landscape, in both the Northern and Southern Fens, along with drainage and protection of the major areas, there was an increasing move from the 1700s onwards towards enclosure and 'improvement' under individual Acts of Parliament. At the core of this process was the mechanism to take lands sometimes owned by or with common rights attached, for many people, and to re-distribute the same to a few. In many ways, this provided the incentive and the economic means to undertake the subsequent 'improvements'. Then, in the farm-land that was taken from fen and from heath or waste, there was a progressive and insidious intensification of the farming practice over the next 200 years. A significant part of this was a process of drainage of both wetlands and of relatively drier areas of agricultural land through under-draining and other mechanisms.

Large areas of the fenland remained even after the efforts of Vermuyden and the Adventurers. Then, in 1762, an Act was passed for the improvement of the low grounds on the River Witham. The river was straightened and deepened, the Grand Sluice at Boston was constructed, and the surrounding fens were effectively drained and reclaimed. The Witham Act was followed by similar ones for the better drainage and the reclamation of Holland Fen, and of the Black Sluice District in 1765. In 1801, an Act was passed for the enclosure of the East and West Fens.

Despite these works, the region was still subject to regular threats of inundation, especially from high tides and severe storms. Particularly damaging high tides occurred in January 1779, in October 1801, and in November 1807. In the latter case, the storm waters were so high as to enter Boston church, flowing right up to the pulpit. Further high tides caused damage in 1815, and in March 1820, when it was the highest ever recorded. All along the East Coast was the ever-present threat of major inundation, a situation that in some cases remains to this day. Over the centuries, there have been constant efforts to protect and re-build the embankments and the other defences to keep the sea at bay. There are signs now that in some areas at least, either the battle has been lost, or the will to continue the fight has dwindled. However, in the seventeenth and eighteenth centuries the agricultural improvers and reformers were quick to see the opportunities coming from wider landscape drainage.

WHITTLESEA MERE

The drainage of Whittlesea Mere in the Southern Fenland was one of the most celebrated achievements of the Victorian improvers. Whittlesea Mere began to form sometime around 2,000-3,000 years ago, as climatic change caused progressive, though fluctuating, sea level rises after the last Ice Age ended. This prevented the rivers draining to the sea and the conse-quent flooding created the great fenland landscape. The area was a mosaic of wetland habitats including reed beds, pasture, wet woodland and open water. Much of Cambridgeshire was covered in a deep layer of organic peat soil of the 'Black Fen'. This factor would test farmers and drainage engineers alike for many generations when the age of improvement began. The mere was central to the local economy, providing large numbers of wildfowl and fish, as well as raw materials such as reed, sedge, fen litter (dried peat used for animal bedding) and peat fuel. It was also a source of recreation famed for its skating and regattas in early Victorian times. People travelled miles to watch, or to participate in, the activities.

However, the mere was under threat as the wider fenland was subjected to drainage and improvement from the 1600s onwards. In fact, the land immediately around Whittlesea Mere, and the mere itself, were now isolated as one of the last remaining areas of extensive undrained fen. During the sixteenth and seventeenth centuries, the pre-industrial drainage of the Fens had transformed the landscape from wetland wilderness to tamed farmland. The industrially

SKATING RACES IN THE FENS.

Skating on the fens. (Victorian print)

driven drainage of the eighteenth century hammered the last nails into the coffin. This remarkable and ongoing 'adventure' and 'undertaking' created a significant proportion of Britain's best quality farmland, but at a huge environmental and sometimes social cost.

Whittlesea regatta, early 1800s. (Victorian print)

Perhaps if the mere had survived a few more decades into the agricultural depression of the later 1800s, then maybe it would still be there today. However, the certainty of higher profits for local farmers, and the application of newly developed steam pumps and other technologies, meant its drainage was inevitable. In the end, the mere was completely drained in the early 1850s. The Victorian historian W.H. Bernard Saunders (1888) stated that 'the soil was found to be rich, and largely impregnated with animal matter, so that the wind, which in the summer of 1851 was curling the blue waters of the lake, was, in the autumn of 1853, blowing in the same place over fields of yellow corn'. This was celebrated as yet another victory of Victorian endeavour over brute nature and wilderness, turning to good profit that which had been unproductive. Yet the ecological interest and hence the nature conservation value of the mere was massive, and around half the plants now extinct in the former County of Huntingdonshire were lost with its drainage. The adjacent sites that remained, such as Holme Fen and Woodwalton Fen, suffered the effects of low water levels for the next 150 years. Today, over 99.9 per cent of the Fens has been drained.

William Wells, the local squire who was one of the architects of the drainage, realised the likely scale of ground shrinkage from observations elsewhere in the Fens. In order to gauge this impact he erected the Holme Fen Post to record the change. It was buried so that the top of the post was at ground level, and today it has dropped about 4m, which amongst other things has released huge quantities of carbon dioxide into the atmosphere. The release of carbon dioxide, and perhaps other aspects of these landscape changes, has contributed to

Floods of the Ouse over the embankments near Littleport, March 1947. (Astbury, 1958)

The River Ouse in flood into the South Level, March 1947. (Astbury, 1958)

current human-induced climate change. The land that was formerly Whittlesea Mere is now the lowest-lying ground in the Fens and perhaps in England. Most of the wider fenland is now below sea level and needs active pumping to allow productive agriculture. As noted, there have been several major flooding events in the Fens, including the devastating floods in the winter and spring of 1947, and in 1953. During the latter event, around 2,000 people died. The general view is that the absence of further catastrophic flooding in the Southern Fens has been in part due to luck and in part to the necessary vigilance and good management by the network of Internal Drainage Boards and the Middle Level Commissioners (MLC). The latter control the main drains that characterise today's Fens.

We leave this phase, which might be called 'The Great Draining' and move on to the twentieth century. With the main drainage accomplished, this was not the end of the process. Some intractable sites still hung on, and many clung tenaciously to life until the 1940s, when American technology, with tracked vehicles and tractors, bled the last vestiges of life out of the old fens. There then followed the excesses of government-funded intensive agriculture in the post-war years, which firmly nailed the lid down on the coffin of the old fenland scene. Only in a very few places could nature hang on at all, and finally, at the end of the twentieth century, we see the pendulum of change begin to swing back towards a more sustainable future. At Whittlesea, the act of draining this iconic site, the largest natural lake in southern England, was herald to the final stages of the great drainage.

7

STRIPPING THE FLESH
FROM THE BONES:
THE FENLAND PEAT CUTTERS

Peat and peat cutting are at the very core of the fenland landscapes: the former a manifestation of wet nature, and the latter of human utilisation. The mark and the legacy of the peat cutter are written deep in the landscape of all fenland regions. However, in both the Northern and Southern Fens, the intensive agriculture that followed peat winning has often erased most of the obvious evidence. Go to the Somerset Levels for example, and you can still see the evidence of recent peat-winning activities. Across most of eastern England, the bulk of the evidence has long-since been ploughed away. There are some remaining sites and landscape features still marking where old peat cuts or turbaries were, but beyond that, the main thing is the absence of peat. In some cases, these turf pits became flooded and have remained as ponds or pools in the landscape but now in a sea of arable land.

The cutting of peat as fuel was always important to the peoples of the wetlands. The Roman writer Pliny, in his *Natural History* in the first century AD, described peat cutting by German tribes along the Rivers Elbe and Ems. 'They weave nets of rushes and sedges to catch fish; and form mud with their hands, which, when dried in the wind rather than in the sun, is burned to cook their food, and warm their bodies chilled by the cold north wind.' There is very early archaeological evidence for peat cutting in Denmark and both the Fens and Somerset Levels in the pre-Roman period, and peat cutting tools and even cut turves over 2,000 years old have been found. A Classical description of the Celtic Batavi tribe suggested that they were so wretched that 'their drink is the drink of swine, and they burn their very earth for warmth'. In other words, they drank beer and burned turf. Early writers referred to peat as 'combustible earth', so Cardinal Piccolomini, in 1458, described how the people of Friesland made 'fires of combustible earth, since they lacked firewood'.

Associated with traditional community peat cutting and use, were distinctive tools and implements, and long-standing cultural attachments and folklore. The ways in which peat was cut, processed, and used, varied through time and between regions to give a rich tapestry that is now in danger of loss from cultural memory. Local rural history museums preserve some implements and even buildings complete with traditional hearths, so you can get a real feel for the past. A deep sense of history and mystery concerns the traditions of common rights and their attachments to buildings or hearths. Never allowed to go out, famous cottage or farmhouse fires, or particularly those in old inns, burnt continuously over decades, or even centuries. Local people placed huge importance on these.

Peat was 'worked' on a small, domestic scale for millennia, and the impacts were generally quite limited. There were few people and huge fenland landscapes to exploit. What's more, the peat was still building more rapidly than people could cut it. However, as the population grew and society moved towards industrialisation and urbanisation, the demands changed. New technologies swung into action to drain and improve these vast wetlands and so-called 'wastelands'. Peat cutting played its role in the transformation of these landscapes. When the peat-based fens were drained, sometimes there was a deep peat resource to be harvested and sold. This was a bonus to the land improver. Furthermore, any remaining peat was cut and burnt on the surface of the land as a fertiliser and soil improver. Known as 'paring and burning', this improved future cultivation and cropping. Along with 'marling', 'claying', 'liming', 'warping', and of course draining itself, it was part of the armoury of the improver. Many of the peat areas were allocated to individuals on the enclosure of improved and drained areas of fen, and these were then worked as commercial peat turbaries. Around Wicken and Burwell for example, this continued to the 1940s at least. The trouble with peat cutting, as already described, is that it lowered the shrinking land surface further, and potentially exacerbated difficulties in drainage. In the Cambridgeshire Fens, some of the peat-cut lands lay derelict for some years before new technology allowed them to be effectively cultivated. In the Northern Fen, the great peat mass of Thorne and Hatfield Moors remained reasonably intact in parts until well into the twentieth century.

From the mid-1800s emerged commercial peat extraction and processing industries – in some cases the end of the peatlands and often part of the lingering death throes of the fenlands. With this mode of extraction, the contemporary culture mixed with older local traditions. During the late nineteenth and twentieth centuries, peat fell out of domestic use, with firewood and then coal, gas, oil, or electricity more convenient, but peat extraction still continued, the later phases including massively destructive extraction firstly for horse litter, and then for horticulture. Indeed, in this way, during the late twentieth century, most of the English fenlands ended up on the manicured gardens of middle-class England. Some small areas of industrial peat extraction for horticulture have lingered on, but mostly it has stopped. We now destroy other people's fens and peat bogs and import their peat to Britain, so the environmental destruction is out of sight and out of mind; we can carry on gardening with a clear conscience. In the later twentieth century, the final stages of this process in South Yorkshire became a bitter *cause célèbre* for conservation in this disputed landscape.

PEAT WORKING IN THE FENLANDS

To extract peat from a bog or fen the site has to be relatively dry, although there are some exceptions to this. The Dutch, for example, used dredges to take wet peat out of the polders. However, in Britain this approach was localised and instead, attempts were made to lower the water-table either permanently or at least temporarily. In simple terms, this is generally easier on high ground where essentially the key is to cut a drain and take water off downhill. Individual bogs are in part drained and the dry edges of the bog worked or cut for peat. However, in low-lying areas, and particularly in extensive fenlands, this operation becomes more difficult. Unless you can drain an entire landscape, the water from your neighbours will flow back onto your land, the sort of problems experienced by Vermuyden and the others.

To undertake effective drainage in the lowlands you need control over large areas of land, by either ownership or co-operation of the community. You then need the necessary technology and skills to cut dykes or drains, and to move water from the flat land into these. In addition, as we see repeatedly across the fenlands, you need money and available skilled labour. Even then, the projects frequently failed. Very often drains are higher than some areas of the surrounding landscape, and so it is necessary to pump water off the land into the drain. This is a difficulty which gets worse in peaty landscapes as the drainage takes effect. The small drains must then flow seaward and into larger drains or canals. The intention is that the network of drains and dykes across the land will carry the excess water away. Once the land is relatively dry, then it is possible to cut, extract and dry peat or turf from the fen or bog. This is carefully dried and eventually carried away for storage, use, or sale.

However, there are some serious difficulties in this whole scheme, which is why many areas remained unreclaimed and un-worked for many centuries. One obvious problem, that apparently did not strike the early drainers until rather late, was that if you drain a peat bog or fen, it dries and shrinks. This means that very quickly, your site is lower than the surrounding land and of course, water will flow back in. The only solution is active pumping to a drain that is now markedly higher than your original ground. (Drive through the Cambridgeshire or Lincolnshire Fens today and you will see how the drains and often the roads are higher than the surrounding landscapes.) To do this requires pumps, originally wind or animal-powered pumps, then steam, petrol or diesel, and then electric. The water is carried to great channels with high embankments and then off to the sea; the typical landscape of the modern East Anglian Fens. The final problem is that in a landscape such as the Fens or the Somerset Levels, the 'fall' or drop in height from inland to the coast is negligible. This presents difficulties in getting the water to flow, but it also leaves the areas vulnerable to inundation from land or sea in the event of a storm, or worse still if there is a rise in sea level. Repeatedly this has been the fate of such 'reclaimed' lands. The Norfolk Broads, which was a massive medieval peat cutting, was finally abandoned to water as the land shrank and sank, and the sea level rose.

In regions such as the Northern and Southern Fens, the modern landscape was imposed on the extensive wild lands of fen, bog and water in a period from the 1700s to the 1900s. Much of the land was 'enclosed' by Parliamentary enclosure, with each administrative area (generally a parish) requiring its own Act of Parliament. Within this mechanism, there was the possibility to establish areas such as fuel allotments and poor lands; those with common rights often received small pockets of enclosed land as part compensation for the loss of their privileges. In some areas, this led to a complex system of drains or ditches, that divided the land into small rectangular units, and then occasional odd-shaped corners left over. The landscape gradually developed the characteristic patterns we see today, with roads and farms all following the patchwork pattern of individual ownership of large landowners and smaller plots.

In South Yorkshire, the settled Dutch drainers cut linear strips into the vast peat bog of Thorne Moor, cutting and then cultivating as they went. This produced the typical 'cable' landscape still present today.

Within these areas, some of the plots were essentially peat bog or fen, still very wet and often with several metres of peat. By the late 1800s, many such sites were worked by owners for domestic use as fuel but also as a commercial business. Much of this was for peat fuel, but there was an increasing demand for animal litter. With a growing market for horticultural peat during the mid to late twentieth century, there was also a move from traditional hand cutting to commercial machine milling and destructive opencasting. Many of the traditions were lost almost overnight, and sites such as Thorne and Hatfield in the Northern Fens were partly obliterated. Left unfettered, the industrial exploitation would have undoubtedly resulted in the total removal of these uniquely important ecosystems and cultural landscapes. Even with the conservation measures brought in because of public and expert outcry, catastrophic and very avoidable damage was already done.

Once the first stage of exploitation (a degree of drainage in order to make the site workable and reasonably safe) has been achieved, the next step is to develop the necessary access to get people, equipment and often animals (such as donkeys or ponies to carry the peat) onto the peat grounds or turbary. There need to be working areas set aside plus places to rest and to eat. The working area needs spaces for specific tasks of treating the cut turfs or peats, and then stacking them to dry, and turning them whilst drying. There is often at least a further process of drying in larger stacks. Finally, the peats are carried off site by sledge, cart or pannier to be stored in a covered stack or a barn close by the cottage for use as required.

The techniques used and the implements employed in the fenlands evolved over centuries, probably from before the Romans. However, it is to them that we owe the invention of the primary tool of this trade – the spade. There were wooden and perhaps bone peat spades used in earlier times in both the Cambridgeshire Fens and the Somerset Levels, but a spade made of iron or steel was the invention of Roman military technology. Given the basic tool over the intervening period of perhaps 1,500 to 2,000 years, a diversity of regional approaches and implements has evolved to address the same problems but with distinctive local character. The basic techniques and tools were similar from the fenland lowlands to the Cumbrian valleys, the vast Irish bogs, or the Scottish Isles.

In the East Anglian Fens, the main tool used in the cutting was a 'beckett': a rather slim straight spade, in appearance a bit like a cricket bat but with a flange at right angles to the main blade. This made two cuts in one movement and pushed easily through the peat without use of a foot. They came in many slightly differing shapes and sizes; locally and individually made with a shaft of willow. The blade was made from cast-off iron tools and other scrap. The metal blade might leave some wood exposed as this helped the turf slip off more easily, and the flange was around an inch less than the blade width. The result was a sharp-bladed tool that cut a neat, brick-shaped turf that was easy to handle, to carry and to dry. Dried turves were sold by measure, and in the Fens, this was based on a small beckett measuring 14ins by 3ins (356 by 76mm) used at Isleham Fen in the 1850s. The small size created turves that dried quickly but took longer to cut. However, at Wicken a blade was developed that was around 16 by 4½ins, to produce a larger turf, after shrinkage 11 by 3½ins.

Isleham small turves were sold in a thousand and Wicken large turves were sold as 600 'to a thousand'. Eventually, the Wicken beckett size and measure were adopted by turf cutters across the East Anglian Fens.

The earlier tool for digging turf in the Fens was the 'moor spade' or 'sharp shovel', designed for use with a strong push from a foot. Some were constructed from iron, making digging hard and slow. The digger would make out the line of his cut and then use the spade to clear vegetation from the top 15ins (381mm) or so. The next step was to 'crumb up' or shave the exposed peat to produce a level platform for cutting. Vegetation around the side might also be cut away to facilitate stacking of the cut turves. A 'peat knife' or 'turf knife', a crude metal cleaver, was used to cut down through the sides of the pit or trench. Either this or the cutter would begin with the beckett immediately. The digger made two cuts for each turf and worked backwards, cutting one spit down (i.e. the depth of the beckett) and four spits across. Each turf was broken off and lifted easily to the side of the pit. The trench was cut the length of the field to be worked, with the surface cleared and thrown back into the previous pit. He then worked back to widen the pit to four spits and, with the turves opened and set back, would dig along the other side. Depending on the field and the number of men working, he might open another pit too, but leaving plenty of room between the trenches to allow for barrowing and stacking. Once dug, the individual field was abandoned for perhaps thirty years before being dug again. By that time, the site would have levelled off and some new peat formed. However, the new peat was not the objective of the turf cutter, but the now available deeper old peat. This might be a further spit depth below the original cut. Some sites might produce two or even three spits, but others, such as the South Adventurers' Fen, might offer up four or even five spits of depth. In such cases, pumping water out by windmills, and holding floodwater back by dams, became a real task, and critical to any long-term exploitation. This is one reason why so many peat turbaries were simply abandoned when workable peat was exhausted.

Barrowing peat at Burwell, Cambridgeshire, 1920s.

Individual turves weighed about 6–7lb, and the pit left would be around a yard wide (0.9m). The digger lifted to his side to leave a row of three turves in height with a broken row on top. These were commercial piecemeal diggers so speed, quality and consistency were of the essence. The operation was more difficult once the digger moved onto a second spit depth and a narrower trench (only three spits wide). Around the early 1900s, the piece-rate rate was about 5s per 1,000 turves to include opening, digging, turning, barrowing, stacking, and boating; with digging and laying paid at 2s 6d per 1,000 (i.e. a Wicken 600!). The fenmen worked from 6 a.m. until 3 p.m., to dig about 3,000 Wicken turves per day. The highest recorded digging rate was an amazing 6,000 per day, but poor weather often restricted the work. Once dug and stacked, turves were left to dry, generally for around three weeks, but varying depending on the weather. They were then opened or dressed, which meant re-stacking but with gaps to allow air circulation to speed the drying process. Each turf was handled individually and a skilled digger could dress around 3,600 an hour. After perhaps six weeks, the turves would be sufficiently dry to be barrowed and stacked by the drain. Since the better drying weather would be later in the summer, the early priority for work was the digging itself. The final shaping of the turves was also done with the beckett or perhaps sometimes with a special trimmer. Those that were not up to standard were cast to one side as 'bits' to be sold cheaply to local people.

Peat cutting was physically demanding and thirsty work, with men stood in an airless peat pit in the summer heat, with high humidity and thousands of biting flies. The water of the bog and the surface drains was not suitable to drink but the diggers could slake their thirst from the clear water of the drainage 'lodes'. With bad weather and in the deeper pits or trenches, the digger, in greased leather thigh-boots, was standing in water. To avoid slipping they wore either broad boots over the thigh-boots, or even a short wooden board strapped beneath the sole. In other cases, they used flat-bottomed stilts strapped to their calves. With all this, the heat, the humidity and the flies, working at the turbary must have been an unbelievably hard experience.

The weather forever caused difficulties and once stacked, the turves could be soaked again by heavy rain. They then required further turning and drying, tasks often done by young lads. These youths also did much of the barrowing and learnt to cross the drains and the bog using wooden planks and trestles. The open wheelbarrows measured 6ft (1.8m) from the front of the wheel to the end of the handles, and carried sixty Wicken turves a load. At the storage site, the turves or peats would be stacked on a bed of litter to keep out worms and other problems. They were marked with a reed or a missing turf every thousand. Sometimes turves were taken directly to the boats, or they were stacked and stored for later shipping. The planks along which the barrows were trundled were around 14ins (356mm) wide and made of narrower spars bolted together. They were slippery, flexible and bouncy, and the lads charged with the task had boots with spiked clips to help them grip. The men were expected to barrow around 200 turves at a time, the youths rather less. The next task would be to ferry the load of peat away along the lodes, with due regard to water depth and the handling of the flat-bottomed boats pulled by trained donkeys. Each small boat might carry around 2,200 Wicken turves. In some years, great stacks of peat were left close to the turbaries to be ferried away the next year. The boats carried their burden of peats to storage sheds owned by the major operators with an annual mooring fee paid to the parish council. The peat was then stored in sheds when space allowed, or otherwise in more open exposed conditions. In the sheds, the turves were placed on wooden slats to allow air to circulate.

Turf was needed all year round, since it was used not just for heat but for cooking too and so the supply to households was an important business. Taking Wicken as an example, turf hawkers came from Soham, Fordham and Burwell to fill their carts. They would take up to 1,500 turves at a time in small carts pulled by ponies or donkeys. Around the immediate neighbourhood of a turf-digging village like Wicken, the diggers themselves would sell and deliver peat. Some locals got their peat straight from the storage sheds, buying quarters in a sack or more if they brought a barrow. In many cases, the diggers' wives helped unload turves from the boats for storage, and helped with the loading up of hawkers' carts. In later years, in some areas, peat was bought off the back of a petrol-driven lorry, and the turf often sold in towns and villages some distance from the Fens themselves. Even as late as the 1980s you could buy peat turf off a lorry in Barnsley of all places.

THE CAMBRIDGESHIRE AND SOUTH LINCOLNSHIRE FENS

Here in the Southern Fens, peat, peatlands and water were central to the development of the landscape and its communities. Traditional peat cutting remained until the mid-twentieth century but then dwindled to become a vague memory. The main reason for cutting stopping was simply the dramatic removal of the peat landscape by agricultural improvements, with some of the last major sites obliterated as part of the 'war effort' of the 1940s. Other fuels also came in, and the railways (and then improved road transport), made change almost inevitable. Wentworth-Day describes the typical fenland peat fire and the local peat diggers:

> Men of both villages lived on, and by, the fen. In summer they dug peat, which we burnt on the great, whitewashed kitchen hearth within the half-circle of an iron cartwheel rim. It glowed and smouldered, in a creamy ash, night after night. It bloomed with a soft, red core, day after day. A fire which never went out from year's end to year's end.

The everlasting nature of the peat fire was one of its important attributes, especially in a society where in the early days matches were scarce or unavailable. He goes on:

> One felt, somehow, that that kitchen turf fire was as old as the house, a glowing house-heart, soft and warming, whose scent, delicate and penetrating, had bewitched the nostrils of Victorian grandfathers and of far, far distant Georgian and Carolean grandmothers. It was part of the very bone and spirit of that old family house.

The famous bird artist and pioneer of the Field Studies Council, Eric Ennion, moved to Burwell in Cambridgeshire in 1926 to join his father's GP practice. From then until the early 1940s he was able to observe the wildlife and people of the dying fenlands, captured in his evocative book *Adventurers Fen*. He wrote of the turf cutters and the old turf pits in the early twentieth century, with barges carrying loads of cut peat and the land surface already dropped below the surroundings. Describing how the area around Adventurers' Fen still had two skeleton wind-mills to pump out the water, he noted how the others had fallen into disrepair once the land had been stripped of turf. Ennion explained how the system of drains and sluices lowered the water as needed in order to work the turf; and furthermore, how the marsh vegetation thrived in the resulting conditions. Ennion also repeats the observations about peat regeneration:

> The welter of rushes and flowering marsh plants was called litter. Some was cut as a coarse hay for cattle but most of it dies down to add its debris to a future layer of peat: small wonder that peat replaces itself by a foot every twenty years. The turf was cut during spring after the March winds had sped the mills and drained off surface water. It was stacked and left to dry all summer … In autumn the turf boats, often towed by a donkey, came down the lode bringing planks, trestles and barrows.

The fenland peat lies deep in some areas but shallower in others, occurring at the surface if recently formed or under layers of silt and clay if ancient. This is due to the processes of flux-ing levels of sea over the centuries, with periods of freshwater and salt-water inundation at different times, and the meandering nature of the great sluggish rivers that snaked their way across the unfettered primeval fen. The best peat for fuel is at the deeper levels, well decom-posed and heavily compacted. Younger, more fragmented peat could be cut and used but was less favoured as a fuel.

The re-flooding of worked turbaries was good in that it produced the conditions necessary for re-growth of peat. It was suggested that 4 to 6ins (102 to 152mm) of peat could grow back in under ten years, though much of this was re-settling of the uneven cut peat surfaces, maybe washing down of peat fragments, and some younger undecayed plant material. Where the peats are deep and lie at the surface (as they do, or at least did, around Ely) the areas are often, for obvious reasons, called the 'Black Fens'. The idea of the cutover peat surfaces regenerating is highly contentious, with conservation bodies generally refusing to believe that it takes place.

It is likely that peat cutting here began with or even before the Roman settlements. With trees scarce over much of the area, and often needed for building, peat fuel was the obvious choice of the early fenman. The only alternatives were dried cattle dung, or dried vegetation such as sedge or flag. Dung is still widely used in India and Africa, and in terms of good hus-bandry, it is preferably applied to the land as fertiliser. Peat or turf were dug where conditions, especially water levels, allowed. This would need to be close to settlements because transport across the fen was difficult. Then, as land-ownership was more formally established, and use of resources became engrained in legislation or common rights, the exploitation was more controlled. Gradually, from the early medieval period, there were attempts to drain larger areas of the Fen, and so more peatland became available to the turf cutter. Here, perhaps more than anywhere else in lowland England, the communities were sat atop a huge reservoir of peat fuel, and by the 1800s, its exploitation was becoming industrial. The village of Wicken near Wicken Fen was a centre for the extraction of what was called 'turf' rather than peat. This extraction and use finally ended soon after the outbreak of war in 1939. The last peat cutter was apparently a man called Bert Bailey, who lived to ninety-five, and died in 1982 having joined his father to dig peat at the age of twelve in 1899.

During this period, local homes relied on peat fuel, as did Wicken Village School until the 1920s. By then, as in many places throughout Britain, coal was being imported to replace the traditional turf. Furthermore, mineral coal was needed for modern ranges and for the smaller modern fireplaces. Peat needs a big hearth with a flat base and was favoured by the early Fen people in their squat cottages with few or no windows. The turf would smoulder slowly and aromatically to give a cosy heat, leave just a pale ash, and the fire would burn all year round. These ancient cottages full of acrid smoke that burnt your eyes would have generated some discomfort, but this was perhaps of benefit too. The Fens was an area famous for the mild form of malaria, the 'ague', and it is likely that the peat smoke kept the malarial mosquitoes at bay. When Linnaeus first visited the Laps of northern Europe, he found that they burnt turf in their primitive houses to much the same effect in order to keep mosquitoes and midges to acceptable levels. If you did not like peat smoke then the alternative was being bitten to death by midges and mosquitoes.

Although peat was important to local people, there were few references to turbaries or peat bogs in the Southern Fens in the Domesday accounts of 1086. This may be because they were just local resources for common use and not regulated or taxed. By the 1300s, they were subject to disputes in legal and other documents. For example, in 1321, when Lady Mary Bassingbourne founded a poor hospital in Wicken, she provided for a supply of free turves for its heating. This apparently continued until around 1870. In the Fens, common land was hugely important to the local communities, with pasture vital for grazing stock and common turbaries essential for survival. Records show that the lord of the manor and the Church also exacted their dues in the form of reeds, turf, litter, fish and fowl. These were productive landscapes and everyone expected their cut.

At Wicken, the common turbaries were in Wicken Poor's Fen and Wicken Poor's Piece, both set aside for the maintenance of the poor. In 1684, producing peat fuel and sedge for litter, these were called 'Wicken Sedg Fenn' and 'Turf Fenn'. The peat diggings here are described as rough and random, and a sharp contrast to the industrial exploitation in organised serried ranks of the 1800s and 1900s, as found in nearby St Edmund's Fen and North Adventurers' Fen. Common use of the resources was not necessarily free to all, nor was it disorganised. It was generally available to those with very specific rights and it was organised and administered very carefully by the community.

To be sustainable, turf extraction had to be controlled, and so there were restrictions on peat digging in the turbaries. At Wicken, this meant that those with rights could not dig before the third Monday in July and they were not allowed to hire assistants. The aim was to prevent commercial exploitation of the common resource – a commoner being able to dig, dry and cart all that they needed for the rest of the year. Should they need more, then certainly by the later part of the period it was possible to buy it. By this time, the competition was from mineral coal. Although weight-for-weight peat has only about half the calorific value of coal, it was generally available for much less than half the price. In the Southern Fens, turf could be bought as turves by the hundred, the half hundred or the quarter. However, you could also buy (for much cheaper) the broken turf called 'bits' in a bag. Judging quality was important, and 'pipey turves' with 'reed torts' were considered poor and had plant roots in amongst the part-decomposed peat, with a tendency to flare up rather than burn smoothly and slowly.

Following the widespread enclosure and drainage of much of the Fens, and the advent of improved transport allowing in supplies of coal, the imperative to have either communal or individually owned turbaries was less important. Peat turf was still significant but more so as a commercial product for fuel, for animal litter, and then increasingly for horticulture. The tendency was then for owners to either sell or lease the turf digging rights, or to employ men to dig for them. In Wicken, the price paid varied and it depended on the period allowed for digging and the depth of peat to be dug. The value also depended on quality and it is said that the diggers could gauge this from the vegetation above ground. Sometimes between £50 and £80 per acre (0.4 hectares) was paid for a long deep dig, but in other situations a price of £22 an acre for a dig of one spit deep was reasonable. Some of the smaller owner-diggers carried on until the early to mid-1900s, including those around Burwell. Josiah Owers, the builder and carpenter at Wicken, Bill Norman the local postmaster-cum-shopkeeper, and Mark Bailey a farmer, all had fields here and hired local men to dig for them. Others, such as a Mr Harrison and a Mr Badcock, actually lived in tiny hovels in the middle of their fields and peat turbary holdings. Here they survived until the mid-twentieth century, their crude shacks being given ironically splendid names such as 'Lapwing Hall' and 'Ragamore Castle'. Some of the small owners even constructed their own windmills to pump out water from their turbaries. These were relatively small and the design reduced to a basic skeleton of tarred timber supporting a four-blade mill. The mills were called 'outliers' and were visible all over the Fens with their scoop wheels lifting water into the main drains and away from the peat bogs. They ran from the first week in March until the last week in August; the fenland turf digging season beginning (if they were lucky) from early April. On windless days they would stop, and rainy days might flood the peat pits. A regular problem was the tide being high in the Wash, and the rivers unable to take more pump water. Making a living in the fenland was always a matter of balancing water, land and the elements. In wintertime, the Fen landscape was once again mostly covered by water. The peat harvested was taken to dry and would be usable within about six months. As we discuss later, this situation greeted Alan Bloom when he arrived to begin farming in the late 1930s.

Then, with the outbreak of war, much of the traditional fenland peat extraction finished. It seems from descriptions of the time, however, that many former peat turbaries were already worked out and abandoned. During the 1940s, when the War Agricultural Committee oversaw the reclamation at great expense and with little success, of the former Wicken turf bogs, all but Wicken Sedge Fen, Poor's Fen, and St Edmund's Fen were turned to agriculture. Just these three were left remaining high (and dry) above the surrounding land, which shrank and turned to dust. The water-pumping windmills were abandoned; they rotted and later collapsed, with just the odd one ultimately restored and preserved for posterity.

PEAT CUTTING IN THE FENLANDS OF YORKSHIRE AND NORTH LINCOLNSHIRE

As in the Southern Fens, the cutting and burning of peat fuel must have gone on in the Northern Fen for millennia. Certainly, the Romans were cutting peat in sites like Askham Bog and Skipwith Common near to the major Roman settlement of York. John Goodchild, writing in the early 1970s, or at least editing an otherwise anonymous contribution to the *South Yorkshire Journal*, described the history of peat cutting in and around the Thorne and Hatfield Moors area.

Much of this was based on the remarkable find of an archive of documents and other materials at the ruined peat works on Thorne. Without this find, our knowledge would be very limited; indeed, as the original journal is hardly known today, it is worth repeating the notes. There is more written elsewhere, especially by Martin Limbert (i.e. Limbert, 1986), but space here does not allow a more detailed account. Goodchild notes the absence of detailed accounts of the earlier periods but states that in the absence of any other easily available fuel in the area, peat turf must have been widely used from an early date. He set about remedying some of the information vacuum based on this archive of notes found in the abandoned peat works on Thorne Moors. He suggests too that the peat when cut was transported out by boat, and notes the difficulty in using any other form of transport in the area.

The evidence that does exist suggests that peat fuel was clearly important across the area, and there is evidence for Roman usage to the north around York. Areas perhaps used in the South Yorkshire and north Lincolnshire part of the Northern Fen, must have long since been lost to agricultural improvement. Absence of evidence, however, is not proof of absence, and it would make sense for the Romano-British to have exploited this abundant fuel supply. Goodchild suggests that Thorne and Hatfield certainly became 'turf' moors in post-Roman times, but notes that relatively little is known until the eighteenth century. However, he does provide interesting records of use of peat turf in York. In 1388, peat or 'turbarum' was being brought into York by water to supplement the city's own turbary on the Tillmire near Heslington. He suggests that peat was not available from other sites on the main rivers near York and so additional supplies were needed and the Yorkshire Fen was the obvious choice. It is believed that coal from the Leeds area was burnt in Roman York, but there is little evidence of peat use at such an early date. However, by the seventeenth century, the amount of peat turf consumed increased with improved transportation along the new Dutch River. Created for drainage, the new river also provided a deep, navigable watercourse from Goole as far as Thorne. Transport by smaller boats was possible upstream as far as Doncaster as long as the tide was favourable. References to a Thorne 'Keel man' (1687) and a Doncaster 'Waterman' (1717) confirm such use of the waterway. Transport was still possible up the old Dun to Turnbridge until the late 1600s, when it had become too 'warped up', i.e. silted. By this time, with peat extraction from the moors increasing, drainage allowed access and turbary, and then agriculture followed.

In York in 1643, there was reference to the illicit selling of turf, when nine men were accused of 'selling turfs contrary to my Lord Mayor's price'. Admitting guilt, they were fined ¾d each 'according to an Order made in the like case the 9 November 1593'. This latter reference was to four men reprimanded and fined for a similar offence. In the 1643 entry for fines paid to the Corporation of York, it is stated that money was received as 'of watermen for selling turves before the price was sett by my Lord Mayor 8/-'. The notes refer to the month of November, so perhaps a time when the cold was making turf especially important.

References indicate that during the seventeenth century, peat was cut and marketed across a wide area of the old Yorkshire West Riding. There are references to 'Turf Mosses', to 'wayne leades of dryed peates', to the use of carts for carrying dried peat, and to 'the turfpitt' from places such as Giggleswick, Thruscross, Barwick-in-Elmet, Bentham, and Fishlake. In the latter case, the notes refer to the theft in 1652 of 'one Catch loade of Turves & wood' with a total value of £7. This was by four men, one of whom was referred to as an 'Airmyn Waterman', and the 'Catch' was a ketch, one of the traditional open sailing trading barges that plied up an down these watercourses.

There is little detail on the actual organisation of the turf cutting industry until the eighteenth century. As drainage allowed, further encroachment took place into the great peat mass of the raised mire of Thorne. The turf moors were worked from a series of cuts next to the canals that extended short distances into the bog, mostly running westwards and out of the moor. There is reference on a plan of 1752 to 'The Cutt by Thorn into Trent used by the Tenants instead of the Old River Dun'. By 1790, this canal and drain was used by around thirty to forty boats carrying turf, which was then transferred into Dun barges or ketches. Still called 'The Boating Dyke' in the 1970s, in 1817 it was known as 'the Ancient Drain and Canal called Boating Dyke'. Prior to the opening of the Stainforth and Keadby Canal in 1797, the cut turves were carried down navigable drains that ran across the moors. After cutting, the turf was dried on the areas of moor set aside for this purpose. Turves were laid on the ground and built into heaps of twelve turves, on Crowle Moors, called 'walls'. The dry turves were then stacked in peat stacks called 'pyramids' until they were boated away.

However, it seems that the use of peat turf from the Northern Fens as fuel declined in the late 1700s and early 1800s. This was undoubtedly due to competition from collieries that were opening and supplying mineral coal across the region; but perhaps also because of the requirement to pay dues on the new canal system. This changed situation decreased the economic competitiveness of the peat. However, the other factor that was coming into play was directly relevant to our story. The impact of drainage and then enclosure of the area was leading to the conversion of large amounts of former peat moor into arable land. In fact, the issue of peat cutting was raised during the enclosure process. The 1811 Act for the Inclosure of Hatfield, Thorne and Fishlake, stated that 'no person was to pare, dig, cut, or take away any wood, turf, sods or soil of any part of the commons which were to be inclosed, until the allotments were made', although the 'Peat Moors, known by the Name of Thorne Waste, and which have Time immemorially been considered, used, and enjoyed as the Estate, Right and Property of the Person or Persons whose Estate abuts or adjoins the same, shall not be divided'.

Indeed, in many ways it is this proviso of the Act which meant the fragments of the original Northern Fen, today remaining as Thorne and Hatfield Moors, survived at all. The rights of turbary in the part of Hatfield Chase within the Manor of Hatfield were to be reserved, and the cutting and leading away of 'Turves from the peat or Turf Mosses' was to continue. However, this was to be for the use of local inhabitants only, for domestic use and not for commercial sale. Even so, they were allowed to take the turf away in 'Carts, Waggons, and Carriages'.

With inclosure there was a new drain cut along the edge of Thorne Moors or Thorne Waste from Broadbentgate to the North Soak Drain. Like the other moorland drains, this was used to carry small boats and loads of peat. However, in 1829, this stopped because it was decided that 'boating was injurious to the drainage'. The extent of the navigable system of drains and dykes was quite significant; the main drains on the 1840s maps included at least 6 miles (9.6km) that could be navigated as Boating Dyke. Nevertheless, from around 1815, the turf trade dwindled and the remaining commercial activity supplied mostly Hull and York. There were only about eight or nine boats still operating and these were 'chiefly confined to the moors'. By 1837, White's directory reported that there were formerly about thirty boats operating but now only seven or eight. These were carrying to York, Hull 'and other markets'. There are reports of peat turf used in metalworking at sites close to Sheffield at about this time.

Areas of the moors were being improved for farming by 'warping' (described earlier) and in 1848, the Thorne Moor Drainage and Improvement Act established the Thorne Moor Improvement Company to reclaim the 'swampy bog'. At its establishment, the company had capital of around £37,000 in £20 shares with a remit to improve small parts of the 'Waste'. The process involved either a charge levied on private landowners for the service provided, or the purchase of the lands for the company itself. The work involved warping and it targeted areas in Fishlake, Hatfield, Thorne and Swinefleet. However, although these operations had an impact on local land use and water levels, they probably did not affect the overall integrity of the core peat mass and its high water-table. The Level of Hatfield Chase Act of 1862 may have resulted in some lowering of the water-table, but the central peat area still remained very wet.

As time progressed, the gradual efforts from a number of players (the Participants, the Improvement Company, and individual private landowners) began to have an impact, and agriculture began to squeeze out the now much smaller turf cutting industry. However, the potential business interests were changing and, in 1854, E.H. Durden had presented a paper to the *Yorkshire Geological Society* on 'the application of peat and its products to manufacturing, agricultural and sanitary purposes'. Now the peatland, 'formerly a swampy bog', was becoming 'efficiently drained and prepared for improvement'. There was a further twist, however: by the 1880s, the market for peat moss as animal bedding to service needs in the army and especially in the rapidly spreading urban centres of Victorian England, was to become the new big industry. The process of moorland reclamation was speeding up dramatically and a new industry was emerging. It was suggested that:

> … .the moors have been developed in an extraordinary manner by the manipulation of the surface for peat moss litter which has now become a most important trade, the Thorne Moors finding employment for 350 hands in stripping the surface of the waste for litter. When the surface has been cleared, sluices made for the purpose are opened to admit the tidal water from the rivers Ouse and Don, which brings up rich earthy matter called 'warp' and deposits it on the land; by this treatment, pursued for about 3 years, extensive tracts of the waste have, since the beginning of the 19th century, been converted into fertile land of the most valuable kind.

It is believed that this process began in earnest in around 1884, a result of growing demand for peat litter for animal bedding, for warped land for agriculture, and through the initiative of local business-minded people.

By 1901, the Hatfield Chase Peat Moss Litter Company was working an irregular area, with a series of parallel drainage channels and an access road over the moors. This network of canals was imposed on the earlier landscape and was not necessarily derived from the earlier system of drains, which had doubled-up to provide waterborne transport. To give some indication of the emerging demands for peat moss litter, there was an increase of around 98,353 working horses between 1901 and 1906. These were employed by railways, tramways, omnibus companies, and various local authority undertakings, and, of course, many other businesses. Peat moss litter made an ideal bedding material for them.

Peat wastage dust storm, Isle of Ely, 1949. (Astbury, 1958)

By the late 1890s, the British Moss Litter Company had been formed, and it took over a number of established peat works across the region between the Rivers Don and Trent. Alongside the system of canals and boats there also developed a network of narrow-gauge railways and connections beyond to the wide rail network. A new 'pressing mill', still known today as the 'Paraffin Mill' or the 'Paraffin Works', was being built in 1895. This was to produce, from raw peat, gas for fuel, ammonia water, paraffin, creosote, methyl alcohol, tar, and even alcohol for motor cars. Peat dust was used to pack fruit and peat was even fed to cattle. However, these diversifications did not last long and the mill closed in 1922. With declining use of horses for industry and transport, the moss litter business also collapsed. Nevertheless, during the 1930s and '40s, there emerged the interest in horticultural peat. Described later, this very nearly erased the entirety of the remainder of the great Northern Fens.

In both Southern and Northern Fens, the craft of the peat cutter was vital to community and life for many centuries. However, as common rights developed into commercial enterprises, the intensity of the industry grew and the need to drain became more pressing. The peat turf industry helped improved farming to move in and so terminated its own existence. As was so often the case, these wet landscapes were disputed territories. Agriculture grew in power and influence, and the enabling role of the turbaries was the cause of their own demise. Industrial peat cutting during the late twentieth century was to prove a most destructive force in the final reduction of the peatlands to their present minuscule extent.

8

DESTRUCTION AND REBIRTH: FENLANDS FROM THE LATE NINETEENTH CENTURY THROUGH THE TWENTIETH CENTURY

THE SOUTHERN FENS: SOME ACCOUNTS OF THE MODERN ERA AND THE FINAL STAGES OF RECLAMATION

From the late 1800s and through the 1900s, we witness the final death throes of the Fens in both the northern and southern regions. Increasingly isolated in the landscape, desiccated and also exploited for peat, the remaining sites clung on; a few hundred acres here and there, usually by dint of their intractable physical nature or simply by chance. Gradually, however, lowered water-tables and intensive farming led to the destruction of soils in the surrounding areas, often simply blowing away as dust. The inevitable shrinkage and lowering of ground surface followed. Traditional uses of the remaining fens ceased and, combined with low water, led to ecological successions with fen turning to wet woodland and meadow to scrub. The few sites that remained in the Southern Fens were valued by naturalists and by wildfowlers; those in the Northern Fens were exploited for peat fuel and then peat moss litter. Some areas were abandoned during the First World War and the Depression years, but, with the outbreak of war again in 1939, and the advent of newly imported technologies for farming, we enter the penultimate time of the great fenlands of eastern England.

A STORY OF WARTIME RECLAMATION

Of the numerous accounts of the Southern Fens, there are three which give a real insight into the core of the issues and the final death throes of the greater fenland. The first is a short book written in 1943 by Alan Bloom called *A Farm in the Fen*, which is the story of wartime reclamation and 'improvement' for agriculture at Priory Farm between Wicken and Burwell. In the author's note at the beginning of the book, he states, 'I venture the hope that those who read this book may become conscious of a conviction that land, good land, now that it has been so hardly won back from dereliction, should never again be neglected or diverted from its true purpose.' This is a fascinating account of the day-to-day, blow-by-blow process of draining one of the last great fens and turning it to agriculture. Down in the Fens to buy a farm, he arrives in the area to find rivers perched high above the land so that barges go past above head level, and tiny rises in topography referred to as 'hills'. He is also shown 'Rothschild's Thirty Acres', given to the National Trust by Lord Rothschild, where according to the locals:

> … on summer nights you see people with nets and sheets and lamps come down after butterflies. College gents, I reckon they are, yes, and young women too. Some of that land used to be farmed when I were a boy. Good land, too, some of it, though a lot's been dug for turf.

The price was around £2,000 for 200 acres (81 hectares), including the farm buildings. His guide also spoke of how the land had been in the past, with turf digging lowering the surface, and how fen litter had been as valuable as good hay. Turf digging and litter cutting had both ended by the close of the First World War. On his second visit from the top of Cock-up Bridge, about 15ft (4.5m) above the surrounding land, he could see a huge area with 'no sign of cultivation at all: it was a scene of utter desolation'. He had heard there was derelict land at Burwell Fen, and inspection of the Ordnance Survey maps indicated 'swamp' here and there, with the words 'Adventurers' Fen' between the lines marking Reach, Burwell, and Wicken Lodes:

> Here were many hundreds of acres, over which wild nature had completely gained the mastery, and I could concede no sentiment … a sea of reeds, dead reeds, with their plumes tossing and waving in the wind … For almost a mile it was nothing but reeds except for clumps of bushes here and there. Among them, close by, was the glint of water. A few rotted haystacks stood near the bank – the fen litter …

Observing the overgrown Rothschild's Thirty Acres close by Priory Farm that he was about to buy, and derelict windmills, and wild reed beds, Bloom 'felt the urge to take up the fight becoming more and more insistent. Damn it all, there was that elementary drainage law that, if a farmer pays drainage rates, he has the right to be drained'.

Once the work to reclaim the farm began, he met with the Burwell Drainage Commissioners' rate collector and fen reeve, a Mr Fred Peachey. The Commissioners had been established when the drainage of Burwell Fen was promoted through an Act of Parliament in 1846. With steam pumps available it was deemed feasible to drain the fen, but at considerable cost. In order to raise the necessary funds to rid the 3,000 acres (1,214 hectares) of water, a mortgage had been taken. In the time that had elapsed, only half the fen had been drained, and £16,000 of the loan remained outstanding. Over 1,000 acres (405 hectares) of the lowest land remained 'derelict', i.e. wet. It was suggested that the lower lands had been worked by turf diggers but they had never paid back any of the mortgage loan; thus the land depreciated but drainage work was not undertaken. Some farmers gave up cultivating the lands affected to try to avoid paying drainage rates; others tried to give their fields away but there were no takers. So around 1,000 acres (405 hectares) were considered derelict and wasted, and a millstone around the necks of the would-be farmers.

The National Trust had acquired the 300 acres (121 hectares) of Adventurers' Fen to add to their holding of 500 acres (202 hectares) at Wicken Sedge Fen. The Commissioners felt that by 1930 things were pretty hopeless, and conditions steadily deteriorated. In 1930, there came the Drainage Act, which assessed land within the drainage area on its annual value rather than on a flat rate. This upset the Commissioners because the annual value from land considered 'derelict' was almost zero. Furthermore, there was a clause in the act to the effect that land classed as 'non-agricultural', such as the nature reserves, should pay only a small fraction of the agricultural charge. Naturally the National Trust took advantage but this was much to the chagrin of the Commissioners and their constituent farmers. Following complaints by Bloom to the Ministry of Agriculture, the Burwell Drainage Commissioners were wound up in late 1939, and their duties passed to the River Great Ouse Catchment Board based in Cambridge.

With the outbreak of war there was an upturn in central government interest in farming improvement and drainage. By the spring of 1940, Alan Bloom was considering more ambitious plans. 'There were other more or less waterlogged and inaccessible parts of the Fens, and why should I not try to get a few people together with money to invest, and make a big thing of this reclamation job?' His scheme didn't get much support but it was a hint of things to come, and by June 1940, he was investing in a caterpillar tractor to allow access onto wet and difficult land. Bloom goes on to describe how, in his view, Priory Farm had become a battlefield on which the forces of dereliction had paused in their encroachment on the farmed land. In fact, for years the advantage had been with 'wilderness' and nobody could farm against water, but now the tables were turned.

This very personal account begins to give us an insight into the processes and drivers at work in this bitterly contested landscape. Bloom felt that he had got to 'fight the National Trust, or rather, I supposed, the local governing Committee ... men with mainly academic interests. They could not see things in the same light as those whose interests were agricultural'. The final stage seemed to be set over the potential to bring into cultivation around 15 acres (6 hectares) of the flooded lands at the request of the War Agricultural Committee. However, this scenario quickly changed when it was decided at a higher level that Adventurers' Fen would actually be used as a bombing target; both Bloom for Priory Farm, and the National Trust for the nature reserve, received the appropriate requisition notices. Then the situation changed abruptly again when the requisitions were cancelled.

In August 1941, the Biology War Committee presented a Memorandum on 'R. frangula as a source of charcoal for munitions' to the Joint Committee of government research organisations. This plant was *Rhamnus frangula* or *R. catharticus*, the alder buckthorn, long-known to provide fine-grade charcoal needed for explosives. Unfortunately, it is uncommon in Britain and, with maritime blockades overseas, supplies had been halted; so this was an urgent matter of national security. As a result of the report, a survey of the distribution of the species was commissioned (November 1941), and it had been found on Adventurers' Fen. This brought a temporary stop to the reclamation work as Bloom and other farmers were commissioned to clear scrub and selectively harvest the alder buckthorn, and for this the National Trust got paid. Essentially the work involved cutting or coppicing the buckthorn and it was anticipated that it would take at least three years for any significant re-growth. However, within a few months the buckthorn was pretty much all cut out and the War Agricultural Committee was fretting over the state of the fen, anxious to bring it into cultivation. The proposal was now for the entire 286 acres (116 hectares) of Adventurers' Fen; the rules of engagement had changed: 'the Catchment Board engineers and officials, the overseers and their men – were of the opinion that Adventurers' Fen could be and would be drained.' Apparently, some of the local farmers were still against the scheme, saying that it would be a colossal waste of money and would not work. But the battlefield was soon to receive a visit from the chairman of the War Agricultural Executive Committee, and then, not many months after, by the King and Queen and their entourage.

The War Agricultural Committee had already begun work on reclaiming the southern part of the Adventurers' Fen prior to March 1941, and the hope was that they would be cropping the whole site by summer that year. Apparently the Catchment Board men had already deepened the drain to the immediate north of Rothschild's Thirty Acres, and the impact in lowering the water-table was considerable for some distance inside the reserve; for Bloom this was a good sign. Apparently, across the fen the National Trust had done a thorough job of making a swamp, with not a drop of water allowed to run into the drainage system. The water could only drain away very slowly and the consequent impact was to render the site exceedingly wet. This was good for the purposes of conservation but was regarded as a major hindrance to those wishing to shed superfluous water from the Burwell Fen and surrounding lands. The first job was therefore to dig out and clear all the dyke out-falls into the 'interline' and the old main drain, and then to drain off the surface waters to allow ploughing on land adjacent. Major new drains, 'new dykes – in long straight gashes', were cut across the ancient landscape to release the pent up waters. As Bloom wrote, 'It was sheer delight to watch that water running full pelt from seven or eight points along the boundary of the Fen out of those grips we had been digging.' After a drying breeze for a few days they could begin the process of burning off the surface vegetation, and the end of an era was finally closing in on the Adventurers' Fen. Lighting just a small pile of sedge litter, the flames burst up as if the area had been doused in paraffin:

> The flames crackled and licked the lower growth, and ran up the bare, hard reed stems to consume first what plumes remained over winter, leaving them twisted and burnt like spent match sticks. All beyond became hidden in smoke, mounting, swirling higher and higher, black at first but turning a rusty-white against the background of blue sky. Out of the smoke bushes came into view, blistered and gaunt as the flames swept on … the smoke … seemed to be hundreds of feet up in a billowing cloud.

The result was clear within less than thirty minutes; the fen had changed completely in appearance, with the dull buff-grey turned to black and, except for occasional reeds persisting in damp turf pits, the charred bushes and smouldering sedge hassocks were all that remained. Bloom and his companions grinned through their blackened, sweaty faces as they surveyed their victory over ancient nature. The cultivation costs were grant aided at £2 an acre plus the cost of ploughing. Half of the grant was to cover costs and half went to the landowner or farmer. The tenancy on this land was to run for three years after the end of the war, the same as the power of the War Agricultural Committee. However, as Bloom admitted, it was clear by later in 1942 that the costs of the work had been significantly underestimated, but, as he said, 'there was nothing I could do about it. We had our work cut out to get the two hundred and eighty-six acres cropped by 1943, let alone 1942', and this despite a colossal investment of public money and a huge effort by Bloom and his colleagues. It was shortly after this time that King George VI, Queen Elizabeth, the Minister of Agriculture, the Duke of Norfolk, and Mr Tom Williams MP, plus a huge number of pressmen, visited the area to inspect the efforts to feed the landlocked country. They were no doubt impressed. This was just the sort of stirring stuff that the country needed.

By February, the area was losing a massive amount of the topsoil, and the losses got progressively worse through March. But the land was soon sown with oats and barley, plus beet and potatoes. With dry weather there was the ironic spectre of a drought. The solution was to get permission from the Catchment Board to abstract from Wicken Lode; action that would certainly have drawn down the water-table on the remaining nature reserve fen even further. In May, there was an even worse gale which swirled up great black clouds of dust from Swaffham, Waterbeach, Soham, and Islcham, giving the sky 'a queer, dark tinge for hours'. This was apparently the worst 'blow' for years, a certain result of the War Agricultural Committee's efforts. Dust settled across a wide area and was reported from homes in Bury St Edmunds over 20 miles (32km) away. The ancient fenland, robbed of its water, was now just blowing away. A further complication of the wind-blow was the infilling of dykes that needed to be re-dug, and the replanting by some farmers of the same crops two to three times. But that summer they were harvesting wheat and barley and plenty of sugar beet. The best crops of all seemed to be off Rothschild's Thirty Acres nature reserve. By the end of 1943, Alan Bloom's initial work was done and the land was moving towards intensive, industrial agriculture. As he says:

> Adventurers' Fen and Priory Farm had proved that crops equal to any other black fens – and better than some –could be grown. Those ideas and hopes, that for so long I'd been pushing back into the pigeon-holes of my mind, could now begin to emerge. More complete fertility, extended mechanization, more and better buildings, a thorough livestock policy, alternative leys to give some of the much-cropped land a rest in turn.

He goes on to consider how the improvement of these 300 acres (121 hectares) had cost the nation so dear, but this was, he felt, the fault of the previous generation and the intensive two years was simply making up for time lost twenty or thirty years before. But he was looking towards what he felt was the permanent recovery of agriculture in Britain and an end to the neglect. He saw signs that 'the welfare of the land must in future run parallel with that of the nation', and the main thought of millions of people 'was that cheap food, abundant in quantity and variety, is the only thing that matters'. So this was the vision that oversaw the final demise of the ancient fenland in the southern area. Little did he realise how rapid mechanisation and agri-industrial development, spurred on by the post-war zeal to be self-sufficient in food, subsidised by the public purse and petrochemicals, would totally transform the landscape and the communities. These factors would make all of Alan Bloom's vision come true, only a hundred times bigger. But perhaps too, he did not foresee or approve of the loss from the land and the villages, of the families and communities that for generations had been there. His vision was of vibrant communities living and working around the farms and learning to love the land and the landscape. If only he had known …

Alan Bloom, MBE, plantsman, was born on 19 November 1906, and died on 31 March 2005, aged ninety-eight. He was one of the great pioneers of British horticulture in the middle to late twentieth century. His vision and passion drove the move to reclaim what he saw as the derelict and wasted fens for the good of the nation. I would have loved the chance to ask him what he felt about them, looking back from the following millennium.

THE LAST OF THE OLD FEN

Not long after Bloom's wartime account, that most prolific of countryside writers, James Wentworth-Day, wrote his *History of the Fens*. As with much of his work, Wentworth-Day writes from the gut, full of incisive observation and passion. He was raised in a thatched farm-house close by the fens which Bloom came to 'improve', and his ancestors had lived there for generations before. Here he experienced:

> …. in the witch-hours before dawn, the smell of the fen. A strange indefinable smell, scent of reeds and peaty waters, of sallows, and meadowsweet, of rotten lily pads – and of fish. That smell of freshwater fish which is penetrating, ineluctable, indefinable. An old, strange, blended smell, a smell as old as Time, compounded of scents that belonged to an untamed, undrained England, the England of the Saxons.

He goes on to describe the whimper of wild ducks' wings at night, with the thin whistle of the teal, and the pig-like squeal of water rails. There was the 'kerk-keek' and 'ker-erkk' of moorhens moving from lode to lode at night, and then the 'br-ooomp-oomp', hollow and ghostly, of the bittern in May and June. This was the quiet chorus of secret voices of the

Stalking sledge. (Victorian print)

fens during the manless hours, that carried on the soft fenland breeze. This was the fen of Wentworth-Day's childhood, and by the end of his life it had been reduced to just the rump of Wicken Sedge Fen; all else was gone. But whilst Wicken remained undrained, it was, as Wentworth-Day observed, not unchanged.

> Still a place of dense reed-beds, of sedge jungles, of forests of sallow bushes and creamy oceans of meadowsweet. But the old village proprietors, the fen owners, who each had their few acres of the wild fen, where they cut their reeds, mowed their sedge, and speared their eels, have sold out.

He notes that the National Trust now owned the fen, almost to the last acre; cutting neat grass rides and placing signs on white posts to tell you where to go. But the villages had changed too; the mud and thatch cottages tumbled down back into the earth from which they came. They were replaced by 'hideous villas of staring white Cambridge brick, with their grim, unsmiling roofs of alien slate, under which no swallows nest, on whose rooftrees no starlings whistle'. It was the same in all the villages around in Wicken and in Burwell, they were 'divorced from their brown and smiling mistress, the fen. And the villages are the poorer'.

In 1935, Wentworth-Day bought a part of the old fen: 'a half-drowned, stinking swamp of disused peat diggings, red-beds, and interlacing dykes'. He stopped up the drains to hold back the winter flood-waters on the land and the meres were instantaneously re-created. This miniature oasis close to the remnant Wicken Fen, in a very short time, drew in huge numbers of wildfowl and an amazing diversity of water-birds both common and rare. Wentworth-Day recorded pintails and goldeneye, common and arctic terns, six cattle egrets and a great white egret, mallard, teal, garganey, gadwall, shoveler, curlew, curlew-sandpiper, green sandpiper, common sandpiper, greenshank, a yellowlegs, bar-tailed godwits, ruffs and reeves, little grebes, common snipe and great snipe, and much more. He had starlings coming to roost in flocks half a mile long (0.8km) and 100 yards (91m) deep. There were even nesting black-necked grebes. Hen harriers and marsh harriers swept over the reed beds and Montagu's harriers bred there. 'A wild and lovely place, which dwells in the memory as a very perfect picture of the older England, the England of Hereward the Wake and St Guthlac, the Saxon hermit.' On Wentworth-Day's little fen, 'Coots clanked, ducks splattered, snipe drummed, pewits wailed, and the redshanks sprang on flickering wings, ringing their carillon of a thousand bells', and up to 50,000 sand martins swirled in massive migration roosting flocks. It was, in just this few hundred acres of Adventurers' Fen, 'the old spirit of the Great Fen that once covered half Lincolnshire and Cambridgeshire'; but it was destined not to last long. The war came along and then:

> They drained the fen with a great clamour of bureaucratic self-praise. The waters went away and the fish died by the cartload. The reeds stood rustling and dry above the black mud. Then they set fire to the reeds, and for a day or more my secret fen roared and crackled in a tawny yellow, red-hot sea of flame. Great billowing clouds of black smoke rose up and polluted the blue skies and swept away on the wind until dust, ashes, and smoke fell like a grey pall on the roofs and the green heath of Newmarket, away on its windy upland.

The duck rose up and were away, and the moorhens, rails, bitterns, warblers and others too. When the wind blew the dust, smoke and ashes away, all that was left of the secret fen was:

> … burnt and black and scorched. An insult to the high fen skies. An altar of burned beauty. A sacrifice to man's neglect of pre-war farming, a burnt offering to humanity's failure to live together in harmony. And thus, in a funeral pyre vanished the last and loveliest remnant of what had been a recreation in all its wild glory of the ancient Fens of Eastern England.

He had bought the fen 'to preserve it, to save for all time the essential Englishness of it, to love and enjoy the sight of birds and clouds, the wind in the reeds, herons fishing in summer shallows, gulls wheeling against May skies, the sting of winter sleet'. But now it was no more. Wentworth-Day questioned the wisdom of it all:

> Is the world any better for this change in my fen, or in the ten thousand acres of other Fens which they have drained, burned, grubbed up, and cultivated during the War? Materially, yes. Spiritually, no. Economically, again no. Those are the answers in a nutshell. On my fen they spent thousands of pounds in expensive drainage, in constructing concrete roads which will probably crack, sink, and become derelict in a few years. The bill for our County Agricultural Executive Committees is estimated to be in the neighbourhood of £25,000,000 a year. Do the Committees grow £25,000,000 worth of food each year? The answer, I think, is no.

His argument was that the extravagant, ruthless, soulless form of efficiency was destroying not only the beauty of the English countryside with its wildlife and heritage, which was bad enough. No, he also felt that this was killing the spirit, the soul and the independence of the countryman, and driving individuality out of the villages. He cited the ugly brick buildings, the concrete tractor houses, the glaring asbestos roofs, and most of all the growth of a hard materialism; all part and parcel of a sour material outlook. Wentworth-Day's lament for his lost fen concludes with some thoughts on Wicken, by this time the last fragment of fenland remaining. His concern here was that the landscape remained intact but divorced from the community and the traditions; it was essentially what I would describe as the severance of its cultural integrity. This meant that it was perched high above the surrounding land and was bound to get drier. Combined with the cessation of traditional uses, and crafts such as reed and sedge cutting, small-scale peat digging, fen hay or litter extraction, etc., the site would go through a gradual successional change. Already, he noted, that whilst it still held sanctuary for some of the great fenland rarities, others had gone, and many species were less numerous here than they had been in his Adventurers' Fen. 'The fen is safe. But it is not, and never will be, the same village fen again. Its life is divorced from the village life. It has become a scientific playground, a donnish pleasance … it is a place divorced and apart, alone with its past, mournful with its memories.'

It is almost impossible to add anything to what Wentworth-Day says, except perhaps to wonder if he and Alan Bloom met, which I'm sure as neighbours they must have done; the old fenman born and bred and the incomer. I'd love to know what was said. It is a shame in many ways that Wentworth-Day's generally right-wing High Tory views on society and his open racism and xenophobia diminished the impact of his otherwise richly informed rural writing.

Perhaps his views stemmed from the bitterness of seeing what he cared so much about destroyed wantonly during his lifetime. Born in 1899, he died in 1983 and would have witnessed the worst excesses of post-war agri-industrial destruction of the landscape. His social views can in no way be condoned, but perhaps his bitterness can be understood.

ADVENTURERS' FEN

The third writer to help inform our view of the final stages of the demise of the great Southern Fens is Eric Ennion, pioneering bird painter, educator, and founder of the Field Studies Council. Born in 1900 and dying in 1981, Ennion was described by Robert Gillmor as 'a man of great humanity, intelligence, energy and fun'. He was born in Northamptonshire, went to Cambridge University and then, in 1926, joined his father in medical practice in Burwell. From an early age he had been fascinated by wildlife and was a natural and talented bird painter. His account, *Adventurers Fen*, was published in 1942 as the dust of the burnt peat and vegetation settled over the hinterland of the Fens. He noted the changing social scene as old customs were lost, the brick buildings and slates arrived, and thatched tumble-down cottages did just that and tumbled down. The reed beds and sedge stood unwanted and unused, and the focus of activity now was not to control the waters but to banish them completely. The aim was to dry the fen, plough in the sedge, plough deep and marry clay with peat; to lighten one and prevent the other from blowing away. They wanted to grow wheat, barley, mustard, and beet. He witnessed some fields being pipe-drained, with lines of earthenware pipes in trenches all leading to a ditch; others were turf-drained. Topsoil was removed to expose the underlying clay and then gutters were dug, back-filled with peat turf, and the topsoil put back.

Ennion noted how, in 1630, the Adventurers had said, 'Is not a fat sheep better than a goose, a stalled ox better than a dish of eels?' But the 'Bailiff of Bedford' (i.e. the floods from the Bedfordshire watershed) had destroyed their plans, and in the 1930s, he would strike again. Ennion described the processes of the improvers and reclaimers gradually making their incursions into the old fens, and the toll that wind and water took on the attempts to grow wheat. Next the farmers grew crops of sugar beet and then potatoes, and these were followed by bulbs; and once again, as Ennion noted, the English fenland was beholden to the Dutch.

The changes of course wiped out the old fen plants and animals, and corn buntings, skylarks, and partridges moved in. In his quiet and unassuming way, Ennion observed the wildlife in these dying days of the Great Fen, and the people and their activities too. He noted that there was only a little arable land in the area, and whilst the wetlands were by no means virgin fen, they were still excellent wildlife habitat. Flooding was at a peak in April and by July the same land might be subject to drought; it was these extremes that kept the farmer at bay and made it testing ground for fauna and flora. When lands that had been cultivated were abandoned, they quickly sprang back to life from a dormant seed-bank in the soil with mints, loosestrife, comfrey, thistle, parsley, willowherb, orchids, bedstraw, vetch and many others.

During the 1930s, the combination of a period of depression for farming, extreme floods (1936-7), and a gale in 1937 which blew down the mill, put paid to the efforts to farm the wet fen. Ennion then set about surveying and later writing about the wildlife of the Adventurers' Fen during these last days of flooding:

Men of the Fens are used to floods. One way or another they've had to deal with them all their lives … The flood of 1936-37 was a bad one; you stood and saw nothing but water around for miles and miles, but it was worse, far worse, in the daily papers than in the fen.

By the early 1940s, Adventurers' Fen was drained, and nature was subdued; at least until 1947, and then 1953 …

Ennion closes with: 'Adventurers' fen in all its loveliness has gone but nature goes on elsewhere.' Of course, he was writing in the late 1930s and early '40s; the next fifty years would squeeze the pulp to the pips out of most of the nature that was left. It is now time to look at the few sites that have survived to some extent.

WICKEN AND WOODWALTON

Until the early seventeenth century, the bulk of the extensive peatlands and wetlands of the great fenland basin of East Anglia was still unreclaimed. Two centuries later there was only a small area left unchanged, mostly in the western corner of the basin, its centres being the last great mere, at Whittlesea and across the north-east of Cambridge at Wicken. Whittlesea Mere, whilst around 1,500 acres (607 hectares) in extent, and this rather variable, was a very shallow water-body. When the drainage engineers and their pumps finally sucked it dry, they extinguished the largest natural lake in southern England and a unique wealth of wild flowers, birds and insects.

With the mere gone, it was also possible to dry out the surrounding fen, and to open up the area to the activities of the peat cutters. By the 1870s, there were parallel drains cut east /

Cutting reed. (Victorian print)

west to allow the cutters to take their turf out by boat. This was taken to the Great Raveley Drain which ran down the eastern edge of the fen. Peat cutting continued as the main activity through the rest of the 1800s, and some of the southern area was taken into a farm holding to provide grazing, hay, and in the south-east section some arable. The extraction of turf appears to have ceased shortly after 1900, probably as the saleable peat had been exhausted. The area was then largely abandoned, except as land for rough shooting.

You can imagine the landscape described by Eric Duffey in the later twentieth century, as being a wide open fenland but scarred with the water-filled trenches of abandoned peat cuttings which ran north-south between the cross drains. The older cuttings would have reed beds spreading rapidly across them, and the more recently exposed peat would have short sedge-dominated vegetation establishing. The site was described in 1905 as consisting of open areas of 'litter' fen, with growth of scrub very localised. Exploitation of the site, apart from some cutting of reed, ceased. The commercial reed cutting continued until 1939, by which time the site was turned over to mostly scrub and developing woodland. By 1952, the basic early successional process was largely complete. Over the same period of time, as the changes happened within the site, the land use was changing beyond and around it. With peat cutting abandoned and drainage more effective, the surrounding land was reclaimed to intensive agriculture. This meant that the now much modified fen was isolated; a raised island of peat fen surrounded by increasingly desiccated black fen soils.

As discussed earlier, the demise of birdlife and of other wildlife was described by the eminent naturalists and sportsmen of the period. With Cambridge on the doorstep of the Fens, they were noted both for their natural history interest and their opportunities for wildfowling. The loss of both of these was viewed with some dismay. However, at this time, both conservation and ecology were only fledgling disciplines, and the over-riding perceptions of the changes was that they were an inherently 'good thing'. By the late 1800s, the National Trust had been established to try to halt the rapid loss of heritage lands, buildings and sites across England, and in 1912, the Society for the Promotion of Nature Reserves was inaugurated, though the process may have begun as early as 1904. The latter was driven by the eminent and wealthy entomologist Nathaniel Charles Rothschild, to acquire and take into management for conservation at least some of the sites that were under imminent threat. Being so close to Cambridge, and famed for their insect life, both Woodwalton Fen and Wicken Sedge Fen were obvious candidates. At this time the intention was not for the SPNR to actually take on ownership and management but to seek others to do so. Rothschild privately, personally and sometimes anonymously helped to encourage those with money and in authority to take on the task. He funded much of the work and personally contributed hugely to the costs of the acquisition of both Woodwalton and Wicken. Surveys of potential sites were undertaken and in 1915 a provisional list of candidate areas was submitted to the government's Board of Agriculture, and many of these are now sites that are protected as of the highest conservation value. At the time, however, Rothschild's ideas were ahead of the day and the list had little impact on the policies of a government driven by the problems of war-time food supply and then subsequent agricultural recessions.

By 1918, Rothschild was terminally ill and he died in 1923; his ideas and aspirations were in effect shelved for another twenty to thirty years. However, the fact that even a handful of the fenland sites survived in the Southern Fen is a testimony to his vision and commitment.

In terms of early conservation, Charles was described as 'The dependable one, and Charles did his duty, even did it with distinction [including being head of the Rothschild family and their banking interests] but at heavy personal cost … when to this burden was added mortal illness, the load became too much to bear'. The first place where he had become fascinated by the study of butterflies was Ashton Wold in Northamptonshire, and here, in 1923, at the age of forty-six, he took his own life; a tragically early death of a pioneering conservationist and champion of the wild fens.

In 1910, Rothschild had bought 300 acres (121 hectares) of Woodwalton Fen in what was then Huntingdonshire, to safeguard its unique wildlife from naturalist collectors and from the agricultural improvers. It was the largest tract of fen remaining in that county, and had a number of species that were either absent or very rare elsewhere. The plants included abundant fen violet (*Viola stagnina*), heath dog violet (*Viola canina* ssp *montana*), and fen woodrush (*Luzula pallescens*, now *Luzula pallidula*), all recently found. Their survival here was attributed to the remoteness of the site from the nearest railway station and also to the fact that the area was so wet as to require a boat for its thorough examination. This, it was felt, had deterred all but the most fervent collectors. The purchase of sites was deemed expensive and furthermore there was the added problem that it might advertise the presence of rarities to would-be collectors. A century on, across the country the same arguments are still debated by conservationists!

The fauna of Woodwalton Fen has been well studied and, by the 1970s, there was detailed information on twenty-one invertebrate and five vertebrate Orders (major taxonomic groups) including birds, butterflies and moths, beetles, sawflies, dragonflies and damselflies, and spiders. For the butterflies and moths alone there were 665 species recorded and for the beetles 750. There are many rarities, though a few are also known from other East Anglian fen remnants. In the 1970s, Eric Duffey suggested that unlike the flora, the fauna lacked the obvious links to the pre-drainage conditions; perhaps they have been more sensitive to the abandonment of micro-habitat disturbance of traditional management, and maybe some of the fauna are better able to move to new sites than the plants. The exceptions to this are the ultra-rare species such as the large copper butterfly and the large wolf spider (*Lycosa paludicola*). Associated with acid peat areas and unknown from other sites in East Anglia, the latter could be a link to primeval conditions.

The first of the fen sites to be acquired was not Woodwalton but Wicken Sedge Fen. This site had never been drained but when the main drainage scheme was implemented, it was embanked to hold back high land water in times of flood to help the rivers downstream cope with the additional flows. Fen litter or marsh hay and sedge were cut in summertime, and when these no longer paid then an alternative use was sought. When setting up the first council of the newly established National Trust, a member named Herbert Goss was included, nominated by the Entomological Society. At the meeting in April 1895, he reported on the need to acquire parts of Wicken Fen and the potential to purchase at least some of this important site. It was known that this was indeed the only remaining large area of East Anglian fenland that remained undrained. Famous amongst entomologists and especially to butterfly collectors, the site is about 17 miles (27.2km) north-east of Cambridge. So popular was it amongst collectors of both butterflies and moths since the 1850s that, in 1879, there were complaints that the number of lamps in use on the fen at night gave the impression of street lights. As noted by the National Trust, Wicken was an example of the incredibly fragile habitat that it sought to preserve, but which was threatened not only by habitat loss but from over-use by those enthusiasts (and also commercial collecting interests) who valued it so highly. Goss told the National Trust Council that 'Wicken Fen was the haunt of much wild life and of the rare swallow-tailed butterfly' and urged the desirability of acquiring some portion of it. There had also been rumours since the early 1890s, that the Wicken Sedge Fen was about to be drained. This had certainly encouraged naturalists and especially entomologists to actively seek ways to safeguard their precious site.

In 1899, the first 2 acres (0.8 hectares) of Wicken Fen were bought for the Trust from J.C. Moberly, an entomologist. In making this purchase, the National Trust had acquired its first ever nature reserve. More important perhaps was that in this process of acquisition and its move towards nature conservation, it drew in pioneers such as Charles Rothschild. The latter contributed to the costs of acquisition and the Council of the Trust noted that Wicken Fen was 'the first instance in which a property has been acquired partly on the grounds of its scientific interest' and how 'the value of the work of the National Trust to all lovers of natural science' should be recognised.

By the 1970s, Wicken Fen had grown by piecemeal acquisition to around 730 acres (295 hectares) of reed and sedge fen, open mere, and areas of dense alder and buckthorn scrub or carr. This was the last substantial remnant of the once 2,500 square miles (4,000km²) of the Southern Fen. With almost all the rest drained, Wicken remains in many ways as it did in earlier times, though isolated and now above the surrounding land which has shrunk. For a wetland this is a serious problem, and combined with processes of ecological succession because of drying out and also the loss of many traditional uses, presents a huge challenge to managers. Fenland sites managed for nature conservation require a careful balance of sometimes quite intensive work. In the absence of active management, the build-up of organic matter (decayed plant remains) from this productive environment leads to dramatic changes, with invasion by scrub and woodland leading eventually to a relatively dry oak-ash forest. Long-term management has sought to balance different needs and habitat requirements to include reed fen, sedge fen, carr and open water.

The site has been subject to detailed ecological studies since the 1800s and boasts over 5,000 insect species, including the reintroduced British sub-species of the swallowtail butterfly. The lists include 700 butterflies and moths, and 200 spiders of which six are unique to this site. Wicken has 300 species of flowering plants, and the birds include bittern, grey heron, marsh harrier and Montagu's harrier, shoveler, mallard, great crested grebe, wigeon, teal, bearded tit, and others such as owls, waders and smaller marshland species. During the twentieth century, the site's fame was maintained and specialists from all over the world came to study and to use the purpose-built laboratory and observation facilities. Needless to say, the collection of specimens is no longer allowed except by permit. Taken together, Woodwalton and Wicken total around 1,200 acres (486 hectares) and this is about one eight-hundredth of the original fen that ran as a nearly continuous blanket of bog and fen, of sphagnum moss, and alder carr, and open meres. Even this remnant suffers the effects of drainage of the sites themselves and especially of the surrounding lands. However, they still form today what is a wonderfully rich complex of damp woodland, fen, open water and wet heath.

Woodwalton Fen, managed by the Wildlife Trust and Natural England, is dissected by water-filled dykes and by damp droves between areas of reed bed, damp meadows, wet heath, and carr woodlands. The heath areas, with their purple heather and heaths, provide a sharp contrast with the fen and marsh where common reed, yellow loosestrife, common meadow-rue, milk parsley, purple and wood small-reed, fen violet, and fen woodrush grow and mix. The open water areas are fringed with marsh sow-thistle, bladderwort, flowering rush, water dock, and water violet. The insects here include the hornet clearwing moth, the marsh carpet moth, and many other interesting and rare species. In particular, Woodwalton is home to one of Britain's earliest reintroduction programmes with the large copper (*Lycaena dispar batavus*), extinct in the late 1880s, re-established from European Holland in 1927. The colony has been carefully nurtured and young even reared by hand and protected from predators. The original fenland species was *Lycaena dispar dispar*, but this is now extinct and the Dutch stock was the closest to the native.

One of the key challenges in managing or maintaining a site like Woodwalton, is to keep the water levels high and the water nutrient levels low. Just as in the Northern Fens, this area is one of low rainfall and here the maintenance of the extensive bogs, marshes and fens relied on water running off higher ground to the west. At Woodwalton it was found that yearly rainfall was about 21.5ins (546mm) with around 10ins (254mm) in summer. Evaporation results in losses of around 4.6ins (115mm). The situation is worsened by the fall in water level in the Great Raveley Drain, from -6ins OD (-150mm) in 1900, to -32ins (-800mm) in 1962. Of course with the land outside the nature reserve still shrinking, the water levels in the drain must fall further to avoid widespread flooding.

By the 1970s, a plan was in place to work with the then Drainage Authority to use the fen as a washland to take excess flood water off the surrounding lands during heavy rain. At the same time, the authority agreed to clay core the banks around the reserve to diminish seepage, and to channel drainage water through the site during dry periods in order to maintain the water levels. The whole scenario was recognised as carrying considerable risks because the behaviour of the flooding patterns were radically different from pre-drainage times, and also the water quality was changed. However, the alternative would be to allow the continued and inexorable succession of vegetation on the site to relatively dry woodland.

HOLME FEN NATURE RESERVE

The other main remnant fen site but much altered is Holme Fen Nature Reserve, now under the custodianship of Natural England. This area is located about 2 to 3 miles (3.2 to 4.8km) north-west of Woodwalton, and was originally only a short distance from Whittlesea Mere. By the early 1980s, it consisted of 652 acres (264 hectares) of what was described as birch woodland. It is old fenland that was turned into farmland and then disused, to form what has been described as the finest lowland birch wood in England. Much of the site is pure birch but some areas have alder, elder, oak, and willow. Relatively recent peat extraction left flooded peat pits, which ironically have added to diversity by maintaining some wet areas in this otherwise desiccated habitat. In the 1980s, it was also suggested that the addition of further disused peat workings as they closed would enhance the reserve. The nature reserve holds species that are considered to be relics of the former fen, including heather, cross-leaved heath, bog myrtle, sphagnum mosses, and fen woodrush.

THE NORTHERN FENS

Remote from centres such as Cambridge and its university, the Northern Fens seem to lack the rich literature and awareness of their southern counterparts. Apart from occasional forays by the Yorkshire Naturalists' Union or the Doncaster naturalists, and a few passionate protectors such as William Bunting, there was little written or celebrated about this lost fenland. Even the accounts we have tend to focus on the still present, though severely battered, sites like Thorne and Hatfield Moors.

In recent decades there has emerged a new awareness of the importance of these core sites, and there has been an intensity of research to parallel that at Wicken Fen in the south. Just as with Wicken, there is far too much to even summarise here, but perhaps just a taste will whet the appetite. There is a vast literature on the archaeology of the Humber region, and especially its wetlands, co-ordinated by Robert Van de Noort and his team, formerly at the University of Hull, and now at Exeter. Palaeoecological studies at Thorne and Hatfield have been driven by Paul Buckland and others such as Nicki Whitehouse, both formerly at Sheffield University, the latter now at Queen's Belfast. These long-term and often intensive studies have placed the core sites and the landscape history of the region firmly 'on the map'. However, there have been other major contributions too, notably from the people at Doncaster Museum – Colin Howes, Peter Skidmore and Martin Limbert – who, with a team of co-workers from the local natural history society, have researched and recorded diligently the history and natural history of the sites.

There have also been individual researchers and writers such as Martin Taylor, who have considered the River Don and also Thorne Mere and their place in the landscape and its history, and of course the great regional and local antiquaries such as Abraham De La Pryme, and Joseph Hunter. In recent years there has also been new work and exciting projects developing around Sutton Common, a northern equivalent of Flag Fen in Cambridgeshire. At this site and at others, the Carstairs Trust and Ian Carstairs have taken a lead.

Yet despite all this, the Northern Fens have always had a problem of a wider identity and really of an identifiable unity, and in this they differ significantly from those of East Anglia. Furthermore, they differ too in their relationship with their catchment and their uplands. The Humber Levels and the great Northern Fens are separated from their wider central catchment by the Magnesian Limestone Ridge that runs north to south across England, and here is cut through by the river at the Don Gorge. Beyond Conisbrough, however, the landscape opens up again and the great wetlands extended north-west along the Dearne Valley into 'Old Moor' and 'Ferrymoor', both extensive medieval wet moors. These are now enjoying a re-birth at the hands of mining subsidence, post-mining recovery of water-tables, and the custodianship of the RSPB. Further to the south-west, the River Don cut through Rotherham and towards Sheffield, through what was 'Lake Meadowhall' at the Tinsley Viaduct, along what in medieval times was still impassable wetland in the flat valley-bottom of the Lower Don Valley. This network extended further along Sheffield's five rivers to join a vast upland wetland of peat bog, fen and mire across the Peak District and the South Pennines. At Rotherham, the River Don splits, with the Rother tracking southwards to beyond Chesterfield, and again this was a great wetland valley with the largest fen and marsh in Derbyshire situated at Killamarsh (Killa's Marsh). This intimate connectivity has never been fully appreciated and the region, unlike the Southern Fens, has lacked a unifying identity. Through history though, from the very earliest times, it did act as a significant barrier and boundary in terms of its physical presence and the difficulty in crossing it, and in the transfer of culture. This great network of impassable wetland functioned like Flanders Moss in Scotland, to separate upland from lowland. At the same time, the rivers themselves acted as arteries for movement and trade.

The complexity of the Humber wetlands and hence of the Northern Fens is manifest further to the east too. In Yorkshire, great wetlands extended up the Hull Valley to Holderness, and along the River Aire towards Leeds, and the River Ouse and the Derwent to York and beyond to Lake Pickering. In Lincolnshire, the River Trent cuts through and leads to Nottinghamshire and Sherwood Forest. The River Ancholme runs in the broad valley between the Lincolnshire Edge in the west and the Lincolnshire Wolds in the east. Along the coastline around the Humber Estuary, the Northern Fens had connectivity with the Southern Fens through the extensive coastal marshes of Lincolnshire. The region retains a degree of this, though much reduced, along the coastal flats, dunes, and salt marshes.

Lacking any overall recognition or account of the region, to understand what happened over the last century or so, we must turn to the various individual accounts. For example, in 1991, Catherine Caufield wrote a short book called *Thorne Moors*, based on interviews with key individuals and especially the famously rude and irascible William Bunting, Thorne's equivalent of Wicken's politically-incorrect James Wentworth-Day. Born in Barnsley in 1916, the son of a greengrocer, Bunting left school at sixteen to become an engineer's fitter. His job was to make and mend machines and tools. He later moved into a more exciting and less conventional job as a courier for the *Reynolds News*, a left-wing Sunday paper, and was involved in smuggling money and messages to the anarchists during the Spanish Civil War. This was followed in the Second World War by various undercover operations for the British government in places such as Yugoslavia. At the end of the war, William Bunting and his family settled in Thorne and he became fascinated by the moors, their history and their wildlife. He died after a long illness in 1995.

Bunting described himself as 'a bad-tempered old sod'. I suspect that like Wentworth-Day in the Southern Fens, Bunting was bitter and disappointed by the impact of the modern social and political greed on this irreplaceable environment. Furthermore, in the early days there was the unwillingness, or inability, of either academics or the conservation movement to do much about it. Additionally, he believed most sincerely, and often had evidence to prove at least some of it, that much of the damage and the exploitation for private and individual gain were in fact illegal. In the case of his beloved Thorne Moors, Bunting was convinced that transfers from common rights and ownership to private interests, especially in the 1800s, were illegal. He also believed that because of the vested interests in mineral rights, and in the mid-1900s the peat industry, the trail was deliberately and illegally covered up. This, he felt, was why all his efforts were blocked at every end and turn. To his reasoning, the local authorities and their officers, and the public utilities and agencies, were all in cahoots; it was all conspiracy and bribery. The problem with Bunting's attitude was that whilst he had a very strong point, and a significant amount, though by no means all, of what he claimed was clearly true, he often did not discriminate in his ire towards foe and potential friend. He was often deliberately rude and even threatened violence simply to test people's resolve, and, of course, as a result many ran a mile. But whilst huge and irreparable damage was done, despite Bunting's efforts, much of what has survived is because of his passionate campaigning. He frequently took major utilities to court over what he felt were illegal acts, and to annoy them even more, he often won and did so publicly. It was not only for Thorne that Bunting campaigned, but for the remnants of Potteric Carr too, appearing at the public enquiry for the proposed M18 motorway. At the end of a typically long presentation by Bunting in the quasi-judicial arena of the enquiry, the long-suffering inspector apparently asked Bunting if there was anything which he could tell the Minister in order to help him decide on this particularly difficult case. I've been told that Bunting's response was along the lines of: 'Yes, you can tell him to **** off back down south!' Diplomacy was not Bunting's forte, but then perhaps he had a point.

In order to understand the transformations in this landscape, once the third largest fenland in England, we need to consider the issues of perceptions of wetlands and values. This is especially so in the Humber Levels, where in the shadow of the coal industry, rather than the refined spires and colleges of Cambridge, there was always the latent view that 'Where there's muck there's brass'. In the absence of a good economic use of a site or of land, there was clearly something seriously amiss. Given this prevailing view from the 1800s until the late 1900s, it is perhaps surprising that anything at all survived. Wicken held on in the south because of the early interest and its accessibility to entomological collectors; Thorne and Hatfield survived, though seriously damaged, because they were simply so big and intractable. Without Bunting and then other campaigners, they would surely have gone completely by the end of the twentieth century.

THORNE AND HATFIELD MOORS

The two core sites are the remains of the vast Humber Levels at the heart of what I call the great Northern Fens. Thorne, Goole and Crowle Moors, together with Hatfield Moors, are the remnant of the primeval wetland across the Humber or Humberhead Levels, with a history extending back over several thousand years. Together they cover around 8,201 acres (3,318 hectares), forming the largest complex of lowland raised bog in Britain. Today a large area of former peat workings is being managed by Natural England as a National Nature Reserve and this includes parts of Crowle Moor, owned and managed by the Lincolnshire Wildlife Trust. When wetness allows, the abandoned peat workings revert to bog, and these areas provide habitat for a rich diversity of fauna and flora with huge numbers of rare and unusual species. The whole area is badged by Natural England as the Humberhead Peatlands, and the two main component areas are Thorne Moors (located north of the M180 motorway and east of the M18) and Hatfield Moors (lying south of the M180). Thorne Moors are still extensively wet, whereas Hatfield in recent times has been mostly very dry. In the 1990s, the then Chief Executive of Natural England, Derek Langslow, was able to state:

Thorne and Hatfield Moors, on the South Yorkshire – Humberside border, are the last remnants of a vast area of peat bog and fen that once covered much of the land around this part of the Humber estuary. It is the largest area of peat bog in lowland England. We stand at a historic moment. Peat has been taken from the moors for centuries – with little thought for the future. Now, following an agreement reached between English Nature and Levington Horticulture plc, we can start to rebuild.

The moors have over 600 species of plants recorded and more than 3,000 species of invertebrates. These include numerous rarities and some almost unique to this area. Species include a population of nightjars that is of European significance, large numbers of adders, breeding nightingales, and rare butterflies such as the large heath. Plants include bog rosemary, cranberry, round-leaved sundew and much more.

A LITTLE HISTORY

Thorne Moors has been described as an unfortunate but 'classic' example of nature conservation and archaeological legislation failing to protect the archaeological and palaeoenvironmental resource of the area.

Having been severely affected by the drainage schemes of Vermuyden and those who followed, the once huge, double-domed raised bog was gradually encroached upon along the 'cables' of the implanted immigrant Dutch settlers. These typically narrow, linear fields with ditches or hedges to either side run in parallel groups into the outer moor. The same pattern can be seen in the landscapes of reclaimed peat bogs in lowland areas of northern Europe, and especially in Germany and in Holland. People had extracted peat for domestic use as fuel since the earliest times, certainly from the medieval period, but most likely since the Romans or before. However, the scale of the cutting was small in relation to the resources and it was also a time of active peat growth. By the early 1800s, William Harrison, a local botanist, a miller by trade, described to a friend how when he had moved to Thorne '… he could stand on his threshold and see Crowle Church across the Moors, but such had been the rapid rise of the surface in a comparatively short period, that the sacred edifice had become obscured from view'.

By the 1880s, the peat was being cut commercially for animal bedding and the Thorne Moors Improvement Company leased the moors to a number of peat-extraction businesses. The first task as always was to drain the areas to be cut; not an easy task as the bog was still incredibly wet. The ditch diggers needed to wear 'fen boards' on their feet, to stop them sinking into the mire. Eventually the cut peat was being taken off along paths constructed by tipping clinker from nearby blast-furnaces to stabilise the site. Shortly afterwards, a Dutch company began cutting canals into the moor and taking peat off by barges towed by horses, and then later a railway was built across the site to facilitate even easier removal.

Peat cutting necessitates drainage, and the lowered water-table changes the ecological conditions. With many of the animals and plants that have adapted to live in a peat bog being those specialised to an extreme and harsh environment, any major alteration may lead to loss and extinction. The rare mire pill beetle, for example, lives under the surface of wet peat and feeds on the leaves of moss. Change its habitat and it cannot adapt. The rannoch rush, similarly, is one of Britain's rarest plants and was discovered on Thorne Moors in 1831. Within fifty years it was lost due to the drainage. In the wet peat you can find its remains in abundance, but to see the living plant in Britain you would now need to travel to Rannoch Moor in Perthshire. Thus the process of extinction and the inexorable change in the peat bog due to drying out happens and is to a considerable degree irreversible. Even if the site were re-wetted, how would a plant like the rannoch rush get back; by train perhaps?

However, although the peat cutting during the late nineteenth and early twentieth centuries had a big impact, this was at least limited by an inability to dig too deep. Part of the peat cutters' legacy was to leave behind a series of abandoned cuts and wet trenches that quickly re-colonised and re-vegetated, to create a mosaic of rich wildlife habitats. The clinker tracks even helped the establishment of a base-loving alkaline fen and areas of base-rich grassland. Peat was cut by hand in the traditional ways and hauled from the moors in horse-drawn barges or carts. Intensification, mechanisation and railway transport were to change all this, and by the time Bunting arrived in Thorne, the future of the moors truly hung in the balance. At this time, the conventional wisdom of the conservation agencies and of leading academics on peat bog ecology was that Thorne was indeed already wasted. The view was that this rather unappealing northern wasteland had been so badly affected by peat cutting and by farming that it was now of little value and not worth saving. Also at the time, the conservation legislation was so weak as to be anaemic, and bodies such as the Nature Conservancy Council, whilst well-meaning, were toothless tigers and, as now, always grossly under-resourced. Often unable to act even if they did recognise a problem, Bunting of course viewed this as at best weakness and feebleness, and at worst the result of conspiracy and bribery.

So despite Bunting's claims about the interest and value of the moors, when the local authorities, across what was to become South Yorkshire, decided in the 1960s to tip ashes from coal-fired power stations, and perhaps municipal waste too, it was considered an inherently good thing. At one sweep it would resolve a problem of waste disposal and also turn a wasteland into a potential asset in the form of a regional airport. Originally put forward in 1962, and then again in 1969, the idea received considerable support. The airport proposal was again revived in 1971, and with the new South Yorkshire County Council established in 1974, the ash-tipping proposal was raised yet again, alongside a third proposal for an airport in 1976. By 1978, the reopening and upgrading of Thorne Colliery carried with it the threat of the disposal of coal-mining waste over the area. Despite all the big guns of the establishment set against him, Bunting battled on against each of the proposals in turn, and eventually every one of them was defeated. Gradually too Bunting's arguments were being heard and supported more widely and a nucleus of expert entomologists, botanists and palaeoecologists was growing with an interest in the area.

Despite this, the then Yorkshire Naturalists' Trust (based in York, and the main voluntary wildlife conservation body for the county) had in 1969 voted against objecting to the proposals to tip on the moors. However, lobbied vigorously by Bunting and dragged out onto the site to see it for themselves, the Trust changed tack and came out in support of the objectors. The Nature Conservancy Council was still to be won over and didn't designate the site as a Site of Special Scientific Interest (SSSI) until 1970. Despite recognition which perhaps influenced future decisions on minerals but at the time had zero impact on the now industrial peat extraction by Fisons plc, the deterioration continued. In 1963, Fisons had taken over the British Moss Litter Company, the latter being the eventual successor to the Victorian Thorne Moors Improvement Company.

By 1971, the final phases of conflict over this most strongly contested landscape were drawing to a head. Fisons now excavated several deep drains, cutting right through the heart of the site, and were in effect poised to destroy the Old Dutch Canal area, one of the richest remaining parts of the moor. Expert opinion was that the unique fauna and flora could not withstand such a direct assault and the consequent lowering of summer water-tables. The result was one of the most amazing acts in conservation history, a little like the tearing down of enclosures around London commons in the mid-1800s, or the fenland levellers before them. With a group formed from local naturalists, local residents, and students from various northern universities (Sheffield, Manchester, York and Nottingham), Bunting led them to direct action. This was the pioneer of Earth First, of Swampy and the rest. 'Buntings Beavers' trekked onto Thorne Moors almost every weekend during the spring and summer of 1972 and dammed the drains that Fisons had cut. With clay, stone, peat, logs and railway sleepers they held the flow of drainage water at bay to keep the precious water-tables as high as possible. The workers at Fisons tried to break the dams down and keep the drains flowing, but they were losing the battle. It was estimated that by the autumn some dozens of dams had been constructed, with individual ones up to 40ft (12m) thick. The activities made it to BBC television, after which Fisons dynamited eighteen of the dams. But undeterred the Beavers re-built them, and, following major bad publicity, Fisons caved in and let the dams remain. They then entered negotiations (from which Bunting, their *bête noire*, was of course excluded), with the Nature Conservancy Council and academics from the northern universities. In 1974, they agreed to protect a part of the site around the Dutch Canal and to repair and strengthen some of the dams built by Bunting's Beavers. The SSSI status placed upon the remaining 1,845 hectares of Thorne Moors in 1981 provided little more than notional protection to the site and especially to the archaeological and palaeoenvironmental resource. Peat extraction continued more-or-less unhindered and neither archaeological remains within the peat or below the peat were given any protection. Existing planning permissions and decisions were unaffected by the SSSI designation. Here, as is the case for many other wetland sites in England, the licenses and planning permissions for peat extraction mostly date from the 1950s and the post-war revival in the peat industry.

In 1985, they sold 180 acres (73 hectares) of the site to the Nature Conservancy Council for around £250,000 and it was declared a National Nature Reserve. Still too small and isolated an area to be viable and sustainable in the long-term, the site remained under threat. Fisons and then Levingtons continued to drain the wider peatland and then opencast the peat. The consequences for the ecology and the archaeology here were terrible, but the outcry continued, and following a landmark conference held in the late 1980s at Doncaster Museum into the conservation of, and the threats to, peat sites, the National Peat Campaign was established. This battled to change public opinion and to better inform the millions of gardeners whose hobby was destroying some of the most unique wildlife and archeological heritage that we possessed.

Over the next two decades the peat extraction interests were ultimately bought out with some millions of pounds of public money. But even this followed what seemed to be very questionable deals behind the scenes between the conservation agency and the peat industry. Locals felt that a deal was being done to save the Somerset levels and to sacrifice Thorne and Hatfield, and a meeting was held in Thorne at a local school hall. Packed with hundreds of objectors and protestors from Thorne and from groups across the UK, the senior staff of the NCC ended up providing assurances that the site in its entirety would be purchased, though the peat miners still exacted concessions on being able to work out areas they considered already badly damaged beyond repair. There had for many years been contentious and controversial debates about how much peat they should be allowed to extract and whether areas that had been surface stripped might as well be worked down to the base. Some conservationists such as David Bellamy had done surveys for Fisons and advocated that at least one metre of peat should be left if there was to be any hope of regenerating a bog afterwards. On the other hand, the archaeologists and palaeoecologists largely dismissed the idea of being able to re-create a bog which they contend is valuable for its unique profile and the 'fossilised' remains of plants and animals which it contains. For agencies and legislation, this idea of conservation has always been problematic, coming as it does somewhere in a no man's land between protection of living organisms, solid geological features, and heritage archaeology. For decades nobody seemed prepared to do anything meaningful to actually apply the law to protect this aspect of the natural landscape.

The key agreement was announced in 1992, but not actually signed until 1994. This meant the transfer of ownership or freehold of Thorne Moors from the peat producers (originally Fisons plc and then Levington Horticulture, then later Scotts Company (UK) Ltd) to English Nature, now Natural England. This transfer was on the basis of a leaseback agreement, so the peat producers continued peat extraction but leaving an average of 0.5m depth of basal peat to allow future restoration and conservation. Following the 1992 announcement, around 1,000 hectares of peatland was transferred to, and has since been managed by, the agency. Central to this agreement is the concept that the raised mire of Thorne Moors can be restored after peat extraction has been completed. The main focus of the management was the idea, based on published recommendations on mire restoration, that worked areas could be regenerated if water loss could be minimised. This concept is as yet 'unproved' but the prevention of water loss from the area has become a priority.

Much to the annoyance of archaeologists and palaeoecologists, the management plans do not acknowledge the protection of the archaeological and palaeoenvironmental resource. The rocky and often controversial road of the destruction and conservation of the Thorne Moors complex continued though. In the mid-1990s, the then English Nature announced its plans to de-notify from SSSI status the wider buffer zone around the core peatlands of the National Nature Reserve. This was because they felt this buffer of cut and worked peat no longer contributed to the hydrological integrity of the site; a point hotly contested by the Yorkshire Wildlife Trust and the Thorne and Hatfield Moors Forum. Furthermore, much to the chagrin of the archaeologists, this overlooked the palaeo-archaeological interest that might remain. So the disputes over the site have gone on almost to the bitter end. Now, embedded in a wider Humberhead Peatlands designation, the process of gradual rebuilding goes slowly on. Much has been lost that can never be reconstructed, but there is hope that a core site will develop as a wonderful wildlife and even tourism resource. Who knows, maybe over a few hundreds of years a raised peat bog will once again rise above the surrounding landscape. It's a shame that you and I won't be here to see it.

There is a vast literature on the issues described above, and on the extensive surveys of ecology, palaeoecology and archaeology of the sites. Space here does not allow more detail, but perhaps the reader will be tempted to follow up and delve more deeply. You will not be disappointed.

A good starting point are the *Thorne and Hatfield Moors Papers*, an occasional series edited by Martin Limbert formerly at Doncaster Museum, or the huge volumes on the wetlands of the region written and edited by Robert Van de Noort.

THE RE-BIRTH

There are now ambitious plans to reinstate sites in the Southern Fens around Woodwalton (The Great Fen Project) and around Wicken, and in the Northern Fens centred on the Humberhead Peatlands and Potteric Carr. These are exciting projects, though even at their best will nowhere near replace what we have lost. The process really began soon after the end of the war in the 1940s, when the reclaimed lands were under a new consideration for their future. Alan Bloom's frustration on hearing that the land he had so recently won back from nature would be allowed to revert must have been extreme. Laurie Friday and her co-authors recount a meeting between Bloom and a botanist walking on Adventurers' Fen. The botanist observed that it was 'such a pity that such a place … should have to be destroyed', and how it would 'take years to grow up again into its natural state'. This was a shock to Bloom, who ventured that 'the thought the Adventurers' Fen might ever be allowed to revert had scarcely entered my head … land, good land, now that it had been so hardly won back from dereliction, should never again be neglected or diverted from its true purpose'. So here we have the two diametrically opposed views, and each held with passion and a sense of righteousness. Indeed, it was these two views that essentially drove the bitter tensions between post-war agri-industry and the emerging conservation and environmental movements of the next fifty years.

At Wicken, a process of site and land acquisition has gone on and, by the 1990s, the National Trust was also in a position to develop and deliver a management plan and vision to encompass the wider site. Previous works and proposals had been rather piecemeal. Former arable land was brought back into either meadow or even wetland condition and there have been experiments to reintroduce the lost plant species from seeds at the core relict Wicken Fen sites. In the late 1990s, the Trust was reclaiming to nature around 128 acres (52 hectares) of arable land – with the purchase of seven fields from Priory Farm, the focus of Alan Bloom's Herculean efforts. This completed the cycle of acquisition that began in the late 1890s. This land had remained in agricultural production until 1994. There are still problems with water in both amount and in quality compared with what would have been there in the more natural landscape. Most of the site is hydrologically sealed behind banks and bunds of clay, but that doesn't necessarily ensure the necessary conditions. Furthermore, the loss of traditional uses (what I call 'cultural severance') is also hugely problematic. The Trust does go to great efforts to mimic former uses and to create the required environmental conditions that resulted. However, as Wentworth-Day pointed out in the 1940s, the Fens were formerly at the heart of village life and the subsistence utilisation made them what they were. This was a socially and economically driven process and not one subsidised by grant aid and volunteer efforts. The challenges remain very great. Indeed, these difficulties were alluded to by one of the great champions of Wicken Fen, the eminent entomologist Frank Balfour-Browne, in 1926. He stated that:

Various efforts have been, and are being, made to preserve the fauna and flora in the small area of Wicken Fen, efforts which, I venture to think, will prolong the existence of the remnant, at most, for a few years. In spite of the steps which are being taken, the natural conditions are changing rapidly and with these, the [water beetle] fauna is also changing.

This does get to the heart of the problem of changing conditions and the small size, relatively, of the remaining areas. The problems he notes were clearly about to get much worse for the next sixty years or so, and have only recently begun to generate a momentum of recovery.

The context of both the Southern and Northern Fen relicts also goes beyond just their current conservation value. These are also areas that have received the most detailed attentions and studies of scientists in the UK and perhaps in the world. Wicken in particular, being so close to Cambridge University, generated a series of meticulous studies into its fauna and flora. These were brought together in the books published as *The Natural History of Wicken Fen* (1925-1932) edited by J. Stanley Gardiner. In his final part of the introductory chapter, he noted, 'Scientifically, the more we study Wicken's three Fens, the more we are impressed by their importance … We want to put on record their conditions now, [to enable] our successors to compare them with what they are 50, 100 or hundreds of years hence.'

This is visionary stuff and light years ahead of thinking at the time. What they gave us is a baseline, just as the researchers at Thorne in the 1980s and 1990s did, against which future trends can be judged. Laurie Friday notes how Wicken Fen holds a place of huge importance in both conservation (as one of the first sites acquired by the National Trust), and in academic ecology as the focus of these detailed and meticulous studies. Over a period of around twenty years, the most eminent and successful ecologists and entomologists across the UK and perhaps in the world came here to research the site and its fauna and flora. Friday and Chatfield finish their 1997 book on Wicken Fen with the following:

We are sometimes asked what we are trying to achieve by all this activity at Wicken Fen. Perhaps the simplest answer is that we are trying to take the Fen backwards through time, to restore some of the biological diversity lost since the turn of the century. It is hard to read Alan Bloom's account of his struggle to drain and cultivate Adventurers' Fen or to watch the film he made of his efforts without admiration and heartfelt recognition of his excellent intentions. And yet we embark on undoing his work without regret: Britain is not at present in a state of food shortage and agricultural land all over the country is coming out of production. Now is an excellent time to attempt to restore lost wetland habitats and fenland species, and to recreate a landscape that has all but disappeared in 20th-century Britain.

Of course, for the environment and the landscape not all can be re-created and much is lost forever. There is also always the shadow of the vagaries and fluctuations in public opinion, the resolution or otherwise of agencies and politicians, and increasingly the pressures of world markets for grains and for fuel crops. There can be no room, even now, for complacency.

9

THE FUTURE FENS

At the end of this story of the almost total loss and annihilation of the Great Northern and Southern Fens, we bear witness to perhaps the greatest single ecological catastrophe that ever occurred in England. Consider too, that the process of 'improvement' also swept away vast, undocumented and untold expanses of rich wildlife habitat around and beyond the core of the Fens. The scale of destruction is almost beyond comprehension. What does the future hold? First, we recognise that we cannot recover what has been lost. Even today, there are new species discovered in the tiny and often tattered fragments of landscape which remain. Each of these is exciting, but they also act as a reminder that we have undoubtedly lost animals and plants that we did not even know we had. As one American politician tried to say a few years ago, though not in quite these words and not about fens: 'There are things we know we know about the fenlands, and there are things we know we don't know. We know some of the things we have lost, but the real issue is the things we didn't know we had but have lost; that's our real loss.'

It has also become clear that whilst we can never reinstate the old fen, much of what we have today is not sustainable in the long term. In a global environment of increasing food insecurity, there will be a need to produce food, and indeed more of it. Much of this will, of necessity, be grown intensively; this is the reality of our world. However, there is a need for compromise both for ethical environmental reasons but also for harsh pragmatic reasons. If we wish to grow food sustainably and intensively in both the Northern and Southern Fens, then we need summer water for irrigation. We also need to avoid the worst of the possible damage and disruption from both winter and summer floods. Clearly, the best way to achieve this involves 'working with the grain of nature and not against it'. So in the future, there will be wetlands that once again work for a living and work with local people. The new wetlands can be catalysts for local economic renewal too, as they generate new crops and products and trigger tourism income and other related benefits. The old fen was an intimate mixing of nature and people which created a wonderful and rich environment; perhaps the new fenlands can be the same.

To bring about the necessary changes there must be a vision, and that is something which has been gradually emerging across this great landscape. In the Southern Fen there are major projects centred on the Great Fen Project of Woodwalton Fen, the National Trust's visionary schemes for Wicken Fen, and the initiatives of the RSPB and others in Norfolk and Suffolk. For the Northern Fen, it seems that we still lack the bigger picture, although a more coherent approach is gradually developing. There are major projects at Potteric Carr and around Thorne and Hatfield Moors for example, but there is still no wider vision to restore the landscape on the scale necessary, or indeed to embed this within a maximisation of long-term economic gain. Surely, this must come soon and new initiatives for the Humberhead Peatlands, for example, begin to develop a more all-embracing whole. Yet even now, the new projects don't reach out to the outliers of the greater Yorkshire Fen – Holderness, the Vales of York and Pickering, or the Don and Rother Valleys. As the RSPB have demonstrated at nearby RSPB Dearne Valley Nature Reserve, and more recently with their partners in the Green Heart Project (centred on the Dearne Valley), these new wetlands can be the pulse of both economy and community.

Interestingly there is still a great north / south divide, and the Northern Fen projects today are mostly in post-industrial landscapes and in a context of deep-seated socio-economic deprivation. Despite this, great strides are being made. The core sites of the Humberhead Levels are Thorne Moors and the re-creation site of Hatfield Moor, and whilst belated progress is being made on conservation, the engagement of the local community remains at best minimal and the facilities for tourist visitors are bad. Peripheral sites such as run by the Lincolnshire Wildlife Trust are somewhat better, but as a tourist destination, there remains no coordinated vision. This engagement of local people and the development of the tourism potential are vital to attaching the future economic vibrancy of the region to these once vast wetlands. In the Southern Fen, the socio-economic situation is different and whilst there are pockets of deep-seated deprivation in the Fens, proximity to the emerging centre that is Cambridge, and even to London and the south-east, provide strong economic drivers. The projects in the south are much more developed in terms of visitors, tourism, and the local economy. This remains a huge challenge to the northern area, and RSPB Dearne Valley and its Green Heart Project show how this might be achieved.

RESTORATION AND RE-CREATION IN THE SOUTHERN FENLAND

THE GREAT FENS PROJECT AND ITS SITES:
WOODWALTON FEN, HOLME FEN AND THE SURROUNDING AREAS

Woodwalton Fen National Nature Reserve is one of only three sites in the Southern Fens where you can get a feel of a relatively undrained landscape. The other sites are Wicken Fen, and Chippenham Fen on the other side of the county. It is one of the oldest nature reserves in Britain, purchased by Charles Rothschild in 1910, and now owned by the Royal Society of Wildlife Trusts. In order to best manage the site, it was agreed between the Middle Level Commissioners and the Nature Conservancy (now Natural England, the site managers) to use the site as a flood storage reservoir. This performs the important function of keeping the reserve wet by maintaining a higher water-table than would otherwise be the case. A clay bank built around the fen keeps water levels high and, in times of inundation, floodwater can be stored on the reserve. Therefore, for example in 1998, the whole reserve of 514 acres (208 hectares) was under a metre of water. However, this important ecosystem service has an environmental cost because the quality and quantity of water from the flood events damages the reserve. Woodwalton Fen is a SSSI, Special Area of Conservation (SAC), a Ramsar Site, and a National Nature Reserve, designations that place a legal duty on the site managers to ensure that a favourable condition is maintained. A solution for this problem is required.

Holme Fen could have been the fourth fragment of surviving ancient fen in the county, but it is cut into four sections by major agricultural drains that keep water levels in the reserve well below what they should be. Fen and raised bog have given way to silver birch woodland, visible from the trains on the East Coast Main Line between Peterborough and Huntingdon. Unless there is action to reverse the trend towards desiccation then even the small areas of wetland that remain will disappear.

Climate change adds to the potential problems in maintaining these sites. It creates greater uncertainty in the natural environment, and may accelerate problems already experienced across the countryside. In this situation, there is an urgent need for imaginative and innovative solutions that make best use of the land. Current thinking is that rainfall patterns will change and so introduce a further driver for the Great Fen Project. In a situation of rapid climate change, Woodwalton Fen by itself is no longer enough to provide adequate flood storage to avoid risks elsewhere. This need for investment in flood capacity generates an opportunity to provide additional storage elsewhere, and to resolve the long-term water-quality issues for the nature reserve.

To address these issues and opportunities, there has been a significant amount of research undertaken to provide a firm scientific basis for the project. Eco-hydrological modelling shows how the project can create large areas of reed bed, wet grassland, fens and wet woodland. These combine with the right engineering to provide enhanced flood storage that will ensure future flood-risk minimisation for the local area. Unfortunately, because of the long-term changes in topography due to the wasting of soil and the sinking of the land, the actual re-creation of Whittlesea Mere is not possible. This is a shame, but open water will be created in areas where the mere once dominated the landscape. A further benefit of the restoration project will be the provision of new areas of countryside access where currently there is little existing provision. There are further ecosystem services provided too, since restoration and ongoing management will prevent further large amounts of carbon dioxide being released from the agricultural soils, and will begin the process of sequestrating or capturing carbon dioxide from the atmosphere. These are all positive actions to help minimise greenhouse gas emissions and lessen climate change.

The Great Fen Project helps demonstrate the beginnings of a new approach to fenland landscapes. It aims to address socio-economic and environmental problems by proposing that the land between the reserves returns to a mosaic of wetlands and other habitats. This approach will help conserve the remaining significant peat resource and at the same time create new areas of flood-water storage. There will be a huge area of wildlife habitat to be enjoyed by local people and visitors.

> ## A RECIPE FOR HERON:
>
> A heron if plain boiled for about eight hours becomes tender enough to afford a meal
> to a hungry person, and its flavour is only slightly fishy. It should be served with a thick
> white sauce flavoured with chopped parsley or fennel.
>
> Cameron, The Wild Foods of Great Britain (1917)

Since beginning in 2001, the project has purchased large areas of land. By late 2008, and due largely to a grant of £8.9 million from the Heritage Lottery Fund, more than 60 per cent of the target site was owned by the project partners. The grant was the biggest single heritage grant ever given in England. This funding provides for the purchase and restoration of land, and the provision of education and community-based activities to learn about and celebrate this undervalued but remarkable landscape. An important element of the Great Fen Project is that, for a long time, nature conservation has focused mostly on relatively small sites, and protecting the best remaining places for wildlife. However, a key task for the conservation movement in the future is to think bigger and to demonstrate the provision of important ecosystem services and potentially local economic benefit through tourism offered by wildlife-rich landscapes. The Great Fen Project is now showing how to achieve this in practice.

WICKEN FEN AND THE FUTURE

The National Trust and its partners have a strategy called The Wicken Fen Vision: 'Our strategy to create a large new Nature Reserve for Wildlife and People in Cambridgeshire'. It is this vision, consulted on in 2007 with the final version in 2008, which will guide the future and the recovery of the great wetlands. They are already a long way towards securing the necessary annual income and long-term finance to turn the vision into reality. This will not be quick and it will not be easy, but it is essential. The location of the fen is important, with Wicken Fen lying only 9.5 miles (15km) to the north-east of Cambridge, a rapidly expanding city. Now planned as a new town urban expansion area, there is major pressure for new housing and other built development. With the surrounding fenscape having some of the most intensively used and productive farmland in the UK, Wicken Fen has survived over the last 100 years as 'an island in a sea of intensive agriculture'. In the late twentieth century, nature reserve management focused on the protection of rare species through intensive management of their fen habitats. Despite this, as we have already seen, some species still died out. It was clear that it was simply impossible to protect all the species, no matter how intensive the management. This was because the wetland nature reserve was just too small and too isolated, and so emerged the idea of extending the site; and not only this, but enlarging it very considerably.

Consequently, in 1999, the National Trust launched its first 'Vision for Wicken Fen'. This vision aims, over 100 years, to work with others to extend the reserve sixteen-fold by taking in farmland to the south and east of Wicken. In doing this, the site will provide a landscape-scale outdoor living space for both wildlife and people, and a 'Green Lung' for Cambridge. This vision fits the aspirations of the National Trust founders of more than a century ago. Furthermore, in the twenty-first century, with climate change an increasingly important factor in our lives, adaptation to, and mitigation of, the effects of climate change must be at the core of National Trust actions. Here at Wicken this is very much the case.

It seems too, that the National Trust's core purpose of 'looking after special places, for ever, for everyone' makes them an ideal body to drive this partnership vision forwards. Since 1999, the National Trust has acquired sufficient land to double the size of the reserve. The 2008 version of the Vision brings the concept up-to-date and sets down an agenda for long-term change. The Trust will work in partnership with individuals and organisations at community, regional and national levels, to roll out programmes of land acquisition and management to benefit a great diversity of wildlife, to deliver huge ecosystem services, and to inform, engage and educate a new generation of local people, visitors and supporters. Lord Rothschild would have been both amazed and proud.

As in the north, there are problems here as well. First, despite the ambition of the under-takings, these sites are merely a tiny fraction of the size of the great Southern fenland. To compound the issues, the conservation sites for present are still isolated islands in now a sea of drought, a drained, desiccated arable environment. Water will always flow downhill to the lowest level and this remains a problem. Even a site like Wicken, with its substantial land acquisition and site re-creation, is limited by the surrounding land uses. Much of the restored area provides a landscape sense of the old fen, but it is dry and botanically very species-poor. Without a wider landscape-level approach to the water, the site will probably stay this way. The old fen is more secure in its bunds and embankments, and to a degree buffered by the new lands, but it is still an isolated and embattled fragment. The challenge for the future will be to re-wet the wider lands so that the expansive nature of Wicken becomes more than an illusion.

THE OUSE WASHES

The other main nature reserve in the present-day Southern Fen is the Ouse Washes, the land set aside in the later stages of the seventeenth century undertaking, in order to hold back winter floods. Ironically, since this was a key part of the success of the grand plan to drain the wider area, it has become a wonderfully rich wildlife habitat. The whole area covers around 6,178 acres (2,500 hectares) of winter-flooded wet meadows. The complex includes nature reserves run by the RSPB, the Wildlife Trust, and the Wildfowl and Wetlands Trust, the latter including a major visitor centre and viewing facility. The floodland lies between the two great cuts that helped straighten the flow of the River Great Ouse, and it takes excess water from the river in winter. The boundaries are the embanked Old and New Bedford Rivers, running roughly parallel for about 14 miles (22km). When flooded, there is usually a diversity of depths and levels from wet grassland to deeper pools, and this provides ideal conditions for a vast range of wildfowl and waders. In winter, there may be hundreds of thousands of birds – with, for example, up to 40,000 wigeon recorded, 1,000s of mallard, pintail, pochard, and teal, with gadwall, shoveler, shelduck, tufted duck, smew, and goldeneye. There are large gatherings of whooper and mute swans, and up to 3,000 Bewick's swans. Along with the wildfowl are wading birds, with lapwing, golden plover, snipe, redshank, ruff, avocet and others. The notable breeding birds include reed and sedge warblers, reed bunting, yellow wagtail, short-eared owl, marsh harrier, barn owl, garganey ducks, and waders such as black-tailed godwit and ruff, plus the more common species. Black terns and little gulls pass through in spring and breeding is always a possibility.

The flora of the wet meadows also gives some idea of what areas of the greater fenland might have looked like, with rushes, sedges, reed canary-grass, reed sweet-grass, thistles, docks, common meadow-rue, creeping Jenny, water dropwort, water–pepper, mousetail, sea aster, sea club-rush, wild celery, nodding bur-marigold, meadowsweet, purple loosestrife, and flowering rush. With abundant skylarks and meadow pipits, the meadows swarm with butterflies like common blue and small copper. Close to the osier beds, there is the chance of the rare large tortoiseshell butterfly, and feeding on marsh ragwort in the fields are the larvae of cinnabar moths. Uncommon moths include the cream-bordered green pea, the fen wainscot, and the obscure wainscot. In dykes and pools, there are numbers of dragonflies and damselflies, and attractive flowers such as fringed and yellow water lilies, frogbit, and sweet flag. This just gives some indication of the wildlife riches of this one area, and perhaps reflects the incredible wealth of the once great fenland itself.

THE COASTAL ZONE AND THE WASH

To find other areas of wild landscape, we need to go east to the fringes of the Wash, and both southwards into Norfolk along the coast, and northwards through Lincolnshire along the coast. Here, on the accreting salt marshes and flats, there is again a wealth of wildlife, and a feeling of space and of wild nature. Human activity still influences much of this land and people have reclaimed areas from the sea, which in turn created new marshes and flats. Squeezed out of the natural marshes and fens that ran inland along these coastlines, the wildlife still thrives in the nearly created wilderness. This helps connect the remaining sites in the Northern and Southern Fens, and other wetlands in Norfolk and Suffolk.

The Wash itself is also a hugely important area for nature conservation. The Wash National Nature Reserve is over 20,000 acres (8,800 hectares) lying on the southern shore of the Wash between the outlet of the River Nene and the estuary of the Great Ouse river. The reserve mixes open deep water, permanent shallow water, mudflat and salt marsh. With extensive intertidal mudflats and salt marshes, this is one of Britain's most important winter-feeding areas for waders and wildfowl. Large flocks of waders are present, and in autumn, large numbers of migrant birds such as grey plover, knot, dunlin, oystercatcher and bar-tailed godwit arrive to feed on the invertebrates found in the sands and mudflats, and to roost in safety. With a rising tide between September and early May, as the incoming water pushes the birds off the mud and salt marsh, they move onto the surrounding land. The entire sky can be full of wheeling flocks of birds. Winter also brings duck and geese to the area, with pink-footed and brent geese, wigeon, pintail and mallard. The salt marsh is also of great botanical importance and represents a valuable area for breeding birds, especially redshank, oystercatcher and increasingly, in recent decades, avocet. The Outer Trial Bank, an artificial island, is an important site for breeding seabirds, and common seal pups on the sandbanks during the summer.

ECOSYSTEM SERVICES –
UNDEVELOPED LAND & ECOSYSTEM FUNCTION VALUE

Much of the history which this book describes is based around loss and gain. The loss is of wildlife and a natural landscape; the reason given is often economic gain and benefit for society and increase of personal wealth for individuals. However, in recent years there has been a growing awareness of the huge services provided by ecosystems such as wetlands. Indeed, studies of such phenomena underpin the development of the Great Fen Project. With an increasing research literature, issues of land values and semi-natural ecosystems are addressed. Guidance from the former Office of the Deputy Prime Minister (ODPM) has proved useful in linking such assessments to real economic process and the competing demands of development. I undertook a study of the South Yorkshire site at what is now RSPB Dearne Valley, a thriving nature reserve with over 100,000 visitors a year. With derelict land such as at RSPB Dearne Valley, or perhaps agricultural land considered surplus to food production, as in the Southern Fens, the *Treasury Green Book* gives detailed and helpful guidance. In an attempt to give economic and functional values to undeveloped land, either as open countryside unaffected by industry or as land from reclamation projects, monetary figures allow comparisons and evaluations. The values differ with the habitat-type considered. The logic is as follows.

Changes in the provision of environmental goods and services may arise in a number of contexts resulting from a 3R intervention (Regeneration, Renewal and Regional Development). Projects that remediate contaminated land need to consider the environmental benefits (amenity, ecological, etc.) that might arise from soft end-use restoration (e.g. parkland), and which could be lost with a hard end-use option (such as commercial development). Similarly, such issues are relevant in considering, for example, the impact of liveability and quality of environments, and the role these factors play in encouraging or discouraging private investment.

A recent review of the literature on the value of Greenfield land suggests a range for different types of undeveloped land, present value £/ha:

- Urban core public space (city park) £10.8 million
- Urban fringe (greenbelt) £0.2 million
- Urban fringe (forested land) £0.5 million
- Rural (forested land, amenity) £1.3 million
- Agricultural land (extensive) £0.6m
- Agricultural land (intensive) £0.02m
- Natural and semi-natural land (wetlands) £1.3m per hectare

ODPM (2002) *Valuing the External Benefits of Undeveloped Land – A Review of the Literature.*

Using this approach we can place a value on the habitat creation at Old Moor (75 ha x £1.3 m = £97.5 m), and ultimately for RSPB Dearne Valley (200 ha x £1.3 m = £260 m). Heritage Lottery Fund support to RSPB and partners for this project has therefore generated an ecological service value of around £98 million. This will ultimately rise to around £350 million.

A further economic value can be placed on the absorption of carbon dioxide by wet grassland and wetland environments created and conserved here. This occurs from the moment the first wetland is created and organic matter begins to accumulate, and helps meet the UK government and regional greenhouse gas targets. The water management and flood alleviation benefits are also obvious, and then there's a fantastic landscape and wonderful wildlife that are literally priceless!

RESTORATION AND RE-CREATION IN THE NORTHERN FENLAND

The Humberhead Peatlands National Nature Reserve is at the heart of what was the great Northern Fenland. The reserve includes Thorne Moors, Hatfield Moor, Goole Moor, and Crowle Moor. Totalling 7,134 acres (2,887 hectares), it is the largest area of raised bog 'wilderness' in lowland Britain. The site is a SAC for its habitat and an internationally important breeding site for the nocturnal, insect-feeding nightjar. This bird led to the area being declared a Special Protection Area (SPA) under the European Birds Directive. Natural England's intention is to establish the moors as 'centres of peatland excellence' and to provide visitor facilities to match that aspiration. Go there today and you will realise the

challenge that waits ahead. However, once you manage to find it and to access the area, the site is stunning. Diverse habitats support 5,000 species of plants and animals recorded on the reserve, and these include over 4,000 insects. The adder population on the moors is nationally important too. Over 200 bird species have been recorded, and around seventy-five species have bred. Exciting species include winter visiting whooper swans, pink-footed geese, rough-legged buzzards, hen harriers, and short-eared owls. Summer visitors include woodlark, oystercatcher, lapwing, ringed plover, great crested grebe, and, at its most northerly English site, the nightingale. In recent years, evoking an image of the ancient fen, common cranes have appeared in the area.

Common crane. (Victorian print)

THE GREAT FEN PROJECT AND THE DRAINAGE OF WHITTLESEA MERE

The Great Fen Project is a landscape-scale restoration project located in the western area of the Southern Fens between Peterborough and Huntingdon. It is the latest of a series of dramatic changes (as described earlier) that have affected the area. This ground-breaking project aims to restore 7,413 acres (3,000 hectares) of farmland to become new wetland and other habitats. This is in order to protect the important National Nature Reserves of Woodwalton Fen and Holme Fen. It is a partnership between the Environment Agency, Huntingdonshire District Council, the Middle Level Commissioners, Natural England and the Wildlife Trust.

The term 'ecosystem services' describes the various benefits that semi-natural and even artificial ecosystems provide for society, such as flood and drought mitigation. The term is relevant to the Fens since the landscape provides many wider socio-economic and environmental benefits, including flood storage to protect local farmland and property. The Great Fen Project is located on the site of the once great Whittlesea Mere, southern England's largest natural lake. It seems appropriate that extensive open water will once again dominate parts of this big sky landscape.

THE HUMBERHEAD LEVELS NATURE IMPROVEMENT AREA AND NATIONAL NATURE RESERVE

In 2012, as one of twelve such projects in England, the Humberhead Levels Nature Improvement Area (NIA) was declared. It will receive a grant of £587,295 and additional resources amounting to £1,034,760. The area is part of the vast flatlands, the great Northern Fenland, straddling the borders of Yorkshire, Lincolnshire and Nottinghamshire. It is claimed that the area offers the best opportunity in England to develop a major multi-functional wetland landscape in a largely unrecognised biodiversity hotspot. The NIA covers 49,700 hectares within the Humberhead Levels National Character Area (the government's way of identifying and classifying distinctive landscapes). This is a different wetland model from others applied elsewhere, since the habitats are intimately interspersed within some of the most productive arable land in the UK. Most of the land is below sea level and vulnerable to climate change effects. It is accepted that novel approaches are needed to accommodate some of the rarest and most at risk wildlife that is found in this complex landscape. The Humberhead Levels Partnership, a group established in 2001, administers the NIA. The main aim is to create an internationally renowned, unique wetland landscape, supporting thriving communities, economy, ecosystem services and wildlife. Sadly, there is still no obvious recognition of the globally significant palaeo-heritage – the unique timeline profiles of the peat bogs and the fossil forest of ancient trees. In other countries, such as the United States of America, surely this would have been declared a 'National Monument' long ago.

This project is not about turning back the clock to when the Levels were an impassable wetland, an ancient and intractable swamp. Rather it will enhance existing internationally important wetlands (the Humber and the Humberhead Peatlands), other SSSIs and Local Wildlife Sites. These sites will be reconnected by working with local farmers to create ribbons of habitat on unproductive drain-sides, headlands and wet field corners associated with the important rivers and dykes that traverse the area. Wildlife will be free to move through adjacent farmland, and the land's economic values will be maintained and its resilience to climate change increased. This programme will create or restore at least 3,526 acres (1,427 hectares) of key wetland habitat. As part of the work, there will be progress towards the reinstatement of England's largest lowland mire system. Success here will increase the amount of carbon sequestered into newly forming peat and wetland soils, a vital ecosystem service.

Importantly, the NIA will begin to develop community capacity to get involved with the wildlife sites, something sadly lacking so far. The suggested approach will have three distinct facets. Firstly, there will be improved interpretation and face-to-face contact with visitors on five sites with existing visitor infrastructure. It is hoped that this will encourage an extra 6,000 visits to local wildlife sites over the next three years. Secondly, new environmental education programmes will operate from three different sites in the area to improve awareness and hopefully engagement. Thirdly, there will be targeted volunteer development and training to deliver an extra 3,910 hours of volunteer input to the projects. Improved integration of land use will make the region more resilient to climate change. Furthermore, closer partnership working will align farming with more sustainable flood defence, water supply and nature conservation. It is hoped that there will be impetus for the local 'green economy' through, for example, work on biomass to energy projects. Initiatives such as this might provide new jobs and sustainable development opportunities in the areas of 'multiple deprivation', such as around the town of Thorne. The project indicates that there will be work for conservation management contractors and for green tourism employees from café staff to nature guides. The aspiration is that connecting local communities to their wildlife sites will increase independence from central government funding and thus increase local pride and stewardship. This will foster social wellbeing and provide significant health benefits.

This is all good stuff but there are still major problems. The region lacks any main tourist attraction to draw visitors in and to become an economic growth-pole for the area. Indeed, a target of 6,000 new visitors is not significant and the area remains a tourism desert, lacking any joined-up tourism strategy. What visitors do come to Thorne and the surrounding areas spend little or no money in the local economy, since there are few places to spend it and little to buy. In this way, the area is trapped in a vicious cycle because the unemployed and economically deprived local community see little tangible benefit attached to the site and the recent influx of 'exotic' visitors to their patch.

These are difficult issues but need to be resolved if this wonderful area is ever to recover its potential. It is also worth noting that whilst the injection of cash for the NIA is to be welcomed, it is nowhere near enough. Perhaps a simple calculation of what has been taken out of the landscape, in terms of economic benefits attached to the destruction of the Northern Fenland over the last 200 years, might indicate the necessary levels of future reinvestment to get back the ecosystem services and more. In recent years, the great monolith of the modern Thorne Colliery grew to dominate the flat landscape. Never opened or operating, it was

THE NATIVE POOL FROG

One of the most bizarre stories of extinction in the Fens is that of the pool frog (*Rana lessonae*), the last English native populations of which went extinct in the late twentieth century. This was probably for a combination of reasons, but primarily caused by habitat loss (e.g. pond infilling) and habitat modification and destruction (notably large-scale fenland drainage in past centuries). Water abstraction and lack of site management were problems in the mid to late twentieth century. However, thus far, the story is not unique; but there is an ironic twist. Following its discovery there was little attention paid to the pool frog because it was assumed to be a non-native species, i.e. an introduction. The species lived anonymously in the fenlands and sadly, in recent centuries, faded from them in equal obscurity. Indeed, its true identity was only established internationally a few decades before its UK extinction in the wild. There were big questions to be answered. Firstly, was it a native species? Secondly, was the British population, like the edible frog, actually a hybrid of marsh frog (*Rana ridibunda*) and pool frog (both from Europe) and actually introduced from the continent in the nineteenth century? By the time these questions were answered, the animal had become extinct.

The last remaining site was near Thetford in Norfolk, with a population there until between 1993 and 1995. The last survivor from that population actually died in captivity in 1999. There followed a belated campaign to 'reintroduce' the now lost frog. Work was undertaken to assess its former status and, according to Jim Foster, then a vertebrate ecologist with Natural England, it proved to be a 'huge needle-in-a-haystack exercise'. A specially commissioned palaeo-zoologist painstakingly sifted through hundreds of ancient frog bones unearthed by archaeological digs. Eventually the remains found at Saxon settlement sites in Ely in Cambridgeshire, and Gosberton in Lincolnshire, were found to be of native pool frogs. So pool frogs existed in England more than 1,000 years ago and other evidence supporting this emerged after almost ten years' research across Europe, to unravel the mystery. There has since been a co-ordinated programme of reintroduction, with animals taken from the wild in Sweden, under special permission from the Swedish authorities and overseen by UK agencies. So according to the project website and authority Brian Unwin, the scheme is now underway '... to restore to the English countryside a creature that most people didn't know ever existed', and is now nearing completion.

then demolished, all at the expense of the taxpayer, with sums that dwarf the current levels of investment. A school end-of-term report was would say 'Trying hard, but could do better'.

POTTERIC CARR NATURE RESERVE

Potteric Carr was the greatest and most intractable of the Yorkshire carrs, but as described earlier it eventually succumbed to a major drainage scheme. It was the largest of the wetlands that surrounded the vast Humberhead Levels, and lies in a basin of low-lying land to the south-east of Doncaster. Historically, until drained in the 1700s and 1800s, it was mostly bog, carr and fen. Turned to agricultural use after the drainage, the area was then affected by Victorian coal mining and the emerging railways. These developed on parts of the carr and the numerous railway lines fragmented the land, making farming difficult and ultimately uneconomic. During the mid-1900s, mining subsidence occurred under a part of the carr and, within about twenty years, the land began to revert to something resembling its former fen and carr conditions. The associated plants, birds and insects began to reappear. Some had probably survived in the drains which criss-cross the area.

During the 1960s, a number of the mineral railway lines became disused, but in 1975 new lines were constructed in connection with the introduction of high speed trains on the East Coast Main Line in 1978. A key event was in 1968, when a small area of the carr was designated a nature reserve by the Yorkshire Naturalists' Trust. The reserve was expanded in the mid-1970s, and in recent years, guided by local enthusiasts and environmental campaigner Roger Mitchell, the site has been hugely increased to attract breeding bitterns to newly created reed beds. New areas of marsh and open water were created and improved facilities provided for the visiting public during the 1980s and early 1990s. The site has re-emerged to become the other big relict of the great Northern Fens, alongside Thorne Moors.

As noted, concurrent with railway development and closely allied to them, was the exploitation of the coalfields around Potteric Carr. This was mostly during the late nineteenth century. The Potteric Carr Nature Reserve began life in the 1950s, due to a coal working of the nearby Rossington Colliery penetrating under the carr and causing subsidence. This re-created conditions that had prevailed perhaps 200 years earlier, before the efforts of Smeaton and the other engineers. Soon there were extensive areas of open water and marsh with their associated plant and animal communities, particularly wetland birds. Local naturalists, particularly birdwatchers, quickly adopted the site. Then, at the instigation of Roger Mitchell, the reserve was established in 1968 on about 35 acres (14 hectares) of marsh (Low Ellers Marsh). The mining subsidence largely ceased by the late 1970s as the worked areas stabilised. In the early 1970s, the whole area was threatened by obliteration from the proposed routing of the M18 motorway through it; the threat was eventually averted but only after nearly four years of uncertainty and a public inquiry. It was here that the irascible William Bunting spoke. There followed proposals for further railway lines across the site, but the Potteric Carr Internal Drainage Board was also examining the possibility of using some of the reserve for flood relief for the expanding urban areas of south Doncaster. As in the Southern Fens, it was this realisation of ecosystem function which was to breathe new life into Potteric.

MANAGING WATER

The purpose of the proposed flood relief scheme was to relieve pressure on the downstream river systems. The original designs were not ideal for nature conservation but after discussions, and influenced by Mitchell's personal expertise in water engineering, the designs were amended. This addressed both conservation and flood relief issues. Construction took place from 1979 to 1981, and the system was brought into use. Land drains were re-graded and deepened, and there were two new pumping stations. The works caused considerable short-term disturbance to the site and its wildlife, but with the promise of future benefits. All land drainage water entering the reserve from the west and north was to be pumped from the lower level maintained in the drains under normal flow conditions. During floods, excess water was pumped into open water bodies of the reserve, and released later when any flood surge had subsided. The scheme included agreed limits to the extent of fluctuation of water levels in the reserve.

The changes resulted in a lowering of the water-table over the whole area. What had been a groundwater-dominated regime changed to be one with a perched water-table. However, during winter months with normal rainfall, all the water-bodies filled naturally and the clay substrate enabled the water to be retained on site. In summer, water levels dropped through evaporation and transpiration; but water from the Mother Drain, the only source of water throughout the year, could be used by agreement with the Internal Drainage Board and the Environment Agency. The Internal Drainage Board has pumps and the nature reserve has its own pumping system.

The recent development of land to the north and west of the reserve for housing, light industry and leisure has meant an increase in flood flows. This is due to pasture being converted to hard surfaces and hence more rapid draining following rainfall. However, guided by the team of locals led by Roger Mitchell, the Yorkshire Wildlife Trust has negotiated the funding and support to create a new and extensive addition to the earlier Potteric Carr Nature Reserve. This has meant an investment of nearly £2,000,000 from the Heritage Lottery Fund and the EU to create 185 acres (75 hectares) of new reed beds for bitterns from former farmland. This has made Potteric Carr into a 791-acre (320-hectare) area nature reserve of low-lying wetland only 2 miles (3.2km) from the bustling centre of Doncaster. So far, up to five bitterns have been recorded wintering at the site and more than seventy different bird species breed regularly. There is also a rich diversity of insects such as butterflies, dragonflies and damselflies, and there are mammals including water voles, bank voles, grey squirrels, brown hares, badgers, roe deer and bats. In 2012, the first bitterns to breed in South Yorkshire for around 100 years were at nearby RSPB Dearne Valley.

Like many of the sites discussed earlier, Potteric has lost its traditional uses and these will never return. However, it does give hope for a site that suffered so many setbacks to have re-emerged as it has. It also indicates potential new uses and new ways to connect these wetlands to local people. Around 25,000 visitors now come to the site annually and they help the local tourism economy. Potteric has been shown to be good for business as it provides a high quality and highly visible green profile, and a gateway to the emerging centre that is Doncaster. By establishing the carefully designed series of inter-connected reed beds, streams and lakes, a major function of the site is to provide a suitable breeding habitat for rare birds such as the marsh harrier, bearded tit, and the bittern. However, the reserve also helps clean waste water, 'polishing' effluent from 25,000 Doncaster homes and providing more than 200 'Olympic swimming pools worth' of floodwater storage.

THE FUTURE – AN EXAMPLE FROM SUFFOLK

In May 2007, cranes were found breeding in the East Anglian Fens for the first time in 400 years. These huge birds were nesting at the RSPB's Lakenheath Fen Nature Reserve in Suffolk. This was an arable field used to grow carrots until the Society bought it only eleven years ago to begin its transformation into a square mile of marsh and fen. The RSPB staff found the nest by chance whilst undertaking a routine site survey; the eggs were about to hatch. The nesting pair of cranes seemed to attract other cranes to visit the area.

LAKENHEATH FEN PLANS FOR THE FUTURE

There is more habitat creation on the way with the RSPB planning to create almost 20 square miles (5,000 hectares) of new wetlands in the East Anglian Fens over the next twenty years. They are a part of the Wet Fens Partnership that is promoting wetland creation, and, with a newly-opened £700,000 visitor centre at Lakenheath Fen, the Society hopes this will be a 'Gateway to the Fens' and will bring viewing opportunities of the wildlife for tens of thousands of people. The target is visitor numbers increasing per year, from 15,000 to 60,000. The main aim of Lakenheath Fen was to form a landscape-scale wetland suitable for breeding bitterns; the cranes are a fortunate accident. Between 1996 and 2002, the RSPB converted over 500 acres (200 hectares) of arable land into reed beds and damp meadows by carrying out extensive excavations and by planting a third of a million reeds.

OTHER WILDLIFE AT LAKENHEATH FEN

As well as common cranes, Lakenheath Fen has around six pairs of breeding marsh harriers and the area has long been the stronghold of the brightly coloured golden oriole. The re-created fen has over 100 species of aquatic plants, whose seeds had lain dormant in the cultivated soils.

WATCHING THE CRANES AT LAKENHEATH

The RSPB manage visitor access to the reserve to minimise disturbance to the rare birds, especially the cranes. Visitors have the opportunity to watch for them at a designated viewing point, with staff and volunteers on hand to provide information.

THE EAST ANGLIAN FENS

This wetland habitat formerly covered about 1,300 square miles approximately between Peterborough, Lincoln, Cambridge, and King's Lynn. The huge expanses of wetland were almost entirely drained in the seventeenth century. This, along with hunting, led to the disappearance of breeding cranes from England by about 1600. The RSPB now manages

wet grazing marshes at the Ouse and Nene Washes in Cambridgeshire. They are creat-
ing new freshwater wetlands at the Hanson-RSPB wetland project at Needingworth in
Cambridgeshire, and adjacent to the Wash at Freiston Shore and Frampton Marsh, both
in Lincolnshire.

This then helps with vital flood protection for valuable farmland and homes close-by and
further downstream.

FENSCAPE: A FUTURE NATURE

Gradually, like turning a great ocean-going liner or oil tanker, the fate of the Fens is changing course. As always, and as an environmentalist I am allowed to be a bit miserable, it is
rather too little too late. However, despite my concerns that we still do too little and we
are late acting to halt the catastrophic losses, there is much to celebrate. It is encouraging to
witness the new initiatives, but they must now continue to grow over the decades. Fads and
fashions have no place in this future fenscape vision; what we need is long-term application
and dedication. Having wrought the greatest destruction to nature that one could possibly
conceive, we are now beginning a process of reconstruction and rebirth. For success, these
new fenscapes must engage local people and the local economy and, through this, they
can help combat serious environmental challenges in the future. It is these areas, which
will alleviate floods and droughts, and will kick-start rural tourism. They will help mop
up excess carbon in the atmosphere and mitigate or buffer the worst excesses of climate
change. Their landscape scale will help nature conservation and especially the issues of biodiversity responses to massive environmental change – past, present and future. For species
to survive they will need joined-up fenscapes through which they can move and in which
they can adapt to new circumstances.

These are all 'good things'; but at the end of it all, we really have little choice. With rising
sea levels and increasingly extreme storm events across the region (affecting the coastal zone
in particular), we need to re-think our engagement with nature. The new fenscapes are a part
of this process of human adaptation for survival. This can be in a long-term vision where we
accept and plan for environmental change, as the Great Fens Project and the Wicken Fen
Vision do. In such a way, we can maximise benefits and minimise problems. The alternative is
like the Dutch boy with his finger in the hole in the dyke – it may be good in the short-term
but not sustainable.

LOST FENLANDS IN THE TWENTY-FIRST CENTURY

The story of England's lost fens is one of human attrition over many centuries, with the
virtual eradication of nature over entire landscapes. It is the removal of several thousand
square miles of wetland and a unique ecology. Furthermore, this eradiation applied to the

wider landscape as well, and so the total loss is beyond comprehension. None of us alive today has ever seen such a landscape and so, in the words of David Lowenthal, with 'the past being a foreign country', we can hardly imagine it. Here I have written about just those fenlands in the east of England. We could extend the story further to include wetlands in Somerset, in the Severn Valley, around Merseyside, Cheshire and Lancashire. The plot is always the same but the story of each has its unique twists. Beyond this, the demise of England's fens interacted with those across Europe, and through European settlement around the world, exported globally. What I describe here applies worldwide a thousand times over or more.

These landscapes were at once dark, dangerous, unpredictable black waters, but at the same time productive, rich, and a sanctuary from oppression or persecution. The Fens were, and indeed still are, contested spaces. Different stakeholders vie and compete with each other and with nature for possession of land and of water. In the last 200 years, a major change has been the move from local ownership of, and subsistence on, the resource, to capital-based industrial exploitation. To achieve this transformation has involved a remarkable piece of political and legal manoeuvring which was at the heart of William Bunting's objections in the Northern Fenland. In essence, through enclosure and improvement, they stole the commons from the commoner. As the old rhyme goes:

> The law doth punish man or woman
> That steals the goose from off the common,
> But lets the greater felon loose
> That steals the common from the goose.

It seems that today, in the twenty-first century, for all sorts of reasons, the geese are coming home to roost.

BIBLIOGRAPHY

Anon. *A discourse concerning the drayning of fennes and surrounded grounds in the sixe counteys of Norfolk, Suffolke, Cambridge, with the Isle of Ely, Huntington, Northampton and Lincolne* (London, 1629) Reprinted in 1647 under title: *The Drayner Confirmed, and the Obstinate Fenman Confuted*

Anon. *The History and Antiquities of Thorne with some Account of the Drainage of Hatfield Chase* (S. Whaley; Thorne, 1820)

Anon. *The Humberhead Peatlands National Nature Reserve. On the South Yorkshire / North Lincolnshire Border* (English Nature; Wakefield, 1997)

Anon. *The Humberhead: Turning the Tide of History* (English Nature; Wakefield) (undated)

Astbury, A.K. *The Black Fens* (The Golden Head Press Ltd; Cambridge, 1958)

Babington, C.C. *Flora of Cambridgeshire. Or, a Catalogue of Plants Found in the County of Cambridge, with References to Former Catalogues, and the Localities of the Rarer Species* (John Van Voorst, 1860)

Bain, C. & Eversham, B.C. (eds) *Thorne & Hatfield Moors Papers*, 2 (Thorne & Hatfield Moors Conservation Forum; Doncaster, 1991)

Bain, C. & Eversham, B.C. (eds) *Thorne & Hatfield Moors Papers*, 3 (Thorne & Hatfield Moors Conservation Forum; Doncaster, 1992)

Baldcock, D. *Wetland Drainage in Europe: The Effects of Agricultural Policy in Four EEC Countries* (International Institute for Environment and Development, and the Institute for European Environmental Policy; London, 1984)

Balfour-Browne, F. *The Aquatic Coleoptera of the Wicken Fen Area, Cambridgeshire*. In Gardiner, J.S. (ed.) *The Natural History of Wicken Fen. Part III.* (Bowes & Bowes; Cambridge, 1926)

Benfield, C. 'River that's causing flood of problems', *Yorkshire Post Country Week Magazine* (2012), pp. 6-7

Bevis, T. *Strangers in the Fens: Huguenot / Walloon communities at Thorney, Parson Grove, Guyhirn and Sandtoft, and some adherents* (Westrydale Press, March; Cambridgeshire, 1983)

Bircham, P. *A History of Ornithology* (New Naturalist, HarperCollins; London, 2007)

Birks, H.J.B. 'Contributions of Quaternary palaeoecology to nature conservation', *Journal of Vegetation Science*, 7 (1) (1996), pp. 1–144

Bloch, M. *Land and Work in Mediaeval Europe: Selected Papers By Marc Bloch (Translated by J.E. Anderson)* (University of California Press; Berkeley and Los Angeles, 1967)

Bloom, A. *The Farm in the Fen* (Faber and Faber; London, 1944)

Bristowe, W.S *The World of Spiders* (New Naturalist; Collins, London, 1958)

Buckland, P.C. *Thorne Moors: A Palaeoecological Study of a Bronze Age Site; a Contribution to the History of the British Insect Fauna*, Department of Geography Occasional Publication No. 8 (University of Birmingham; Birmingham, 1979)

Buckland, P.C. & Dinnin, M.H. 'The rise and fall of a wetland habitat: recent palaeoecological research on Thorne and Hatfield Moors' in *Thorne & Hatfield Moors Papers*, 4 (1997), pp. 1-18

Bunting, W. *An Outline Study of the Level of Hatfield Chase, Part Three* (Wm Bunting; Thorne, Doncaster, 1983)

Camden, W. *Britannia Sive Florentissimorum Regnorum, Angliae, Scotiae, Hiberniae, Et Insularum Adiacentium* (1590)

Cartwright, F.F. & Biddiss, M. *Disease & History* (Sutton Publishing; Stroud, 2004)

Caufield, C. *Thorne Moors* (The Sumach Press; St Albans, 1991)

Charnley, P.R. *Old Dykes I Have Known: A History of the North Level Part of the Great Level of the Fens* (Barney Books & P.R. Charnley; printed in Lincoln, 1994)

Chatwin, C.P. *British Regional Geology: East Anglia and Adjoining Areas* (HMSO; London, 1937)

Clarke, E. 'Potterick Carr', *The Field* (26 November 1887)

Cobbett, W. *Rural Rides*, expanded edition of the 1830 issue with appendices (London, 1853)

Coles, J. & Hall, D. *Changing Landscapes: The Ancient Fenland* (Cambridgeshire County Council, and the Wetland Archaeology Research Project; Cambridge, 1998)

Coones, P. & Patten, J. *The Penguin Guide to the Landscape of England and Wales* (Penguin Books; Middlesex, 1986)

Cornish, C.J. *Wild England Today* (Seeley and Co.; London, 1885)

Cory, V. *Hatfield and Axholme: An Historical Review* (Providence Press; Ely, 1985)

Darby, H.C. 'An Account of the Birds of the Undrained Fen', in Lack, D. *The Birds of Cambridgeshire* (Cambridge Bird Club; Cambridge, 1934)

Darby, H.C. *The Draining of the Fens* (Cambridge University Press; Cambridge, 1940)

Darby, H.C. *The Medieval Fenland* (Cambridge University Press; Cambridge, 1940)

Darby, H.C. 'The Draining of the Fenland', *The New Naturalist: A Journal of British Natural History*, 6 (undated), pp. 17-21

Darby, H.C. *The Changing Fenland* (Cambridge University Press; Cambridge, 1983)

Darby, H.C. and Maxwell, I.S. (eds) *The Domesday Geography of Northern England* (Cambridge University Press; Cambridge, 1962)

Davis, J.V. & Lees, P.A. *West Yorkshire: An Account of its Geology, Physical Geography, Climatology and Botany* (London, 1878)

Day, A. *Turf Village: Peat Diggers of Wicken* (Cambridgeshire Libraries & Information Service; Cambridge, 1985)

Day, A. *Farming in the Fens: A Portrait in Old Photographs and Prints* (S.B. Publications; Seaford, 1995)

De La Châteaubriant, A. *The Peat-Cutters*, translated by Robinson, F.M. (The Dial Press; New York, 1927)

De La Châteaubriant, A. *La Brière* (Le Livre de Demain; Paris, 1926)

De La Pryme, A. *The Diary of Abraham De La Pryme: The Yorkshire Antiquary* (Andrews & Co.; Durham, 1870)

De La Pryme, A. (1699) Letters as quoted in Dinnin in Van de Noort, R. and Ellis, S. *Wetland Heritage of the Humberhead Levels: An Archaeological Survey* (Humber Wetlands Project, University of Hull, 1997)

Defoe, D. *A Tour Through the Whole Island of Great Britain* (1724-6)

Dinnin, M. 'The drainage history of the Humberhead Levels' in Van de Noort, R. and Ellis, S. *Wetland Heritage of the Humberhead Levels: An Archaeological Survey* (Humber Wetlands project, University of Hull, Hull, 1997)

Drayton, M. *The Complete Works of Michael Drayton, Now First Collected. With Introductions and Notes by Richard Hooper*, published in three volumes (John Russell Smith; London, 1876)

Duffey, E. *Nature Reserves and Wildlife* (Heinemann Educational Books Ltd; London, 1974)

Dugdale, W. *The History of Imbanking and Draining of Divers Fens and Marshes, both in Foreign Parts and in this Kingdom, And of the Improvements Thereby* 2nd edition revised and corrected by Charles Nalson Cole (W. Bowyer and F. Nichols; London, 1772)

Dunston, G. *The Rivers of Axholme with a History of the Navigable Rivers and Canals of the District* (A. Brown & Sons; London, 1912)

English, B. *The Great Landowners of East Yorkshire 1530-1910* (Hull Academic Press; Howden, 1990)

Ennion, E. *Adventurers Fen* (Methuen & Co., 1942)

Eversham, B.C. 'Thorne and Hatfield Moors: implications of land use change for nature conservation' in *Thorne & Hatfield Moors Papers* (1991) pp. 2, 3-18

Fedden, R. & Joekes, R. *The National Trust Guide* (Book Club Associates & The National Trust, London, 1980)

Firth, C. *900 Years of the Don Fishery: Domesday to the Dawn of the New Millennium* (Environment Agency; Leeds, 1997)

Forster, J. *Lives of Eminent British Statesmen*, Vol. 6 (Longman, Brown, Green & Longmans; London, 1838)

Friday, L. (ed.) *Wicken Fen: The Making of a Nature Reserve* (Harley Books; Colchester, Essex)

Gardiner, J.S. & Tansley, A.G. (eds) *The Natural History of Wicken Fen, Part I* (Bowes & Bowes; Cambridge, 1923)

Gardiner, J.S (ed.) *The Natural History of Wicken Fen, Part II* (Bowes & Bowes; Cambridge, 1923)

Gardiner, J.S. (ed.) *The Natural History of Wicken Fen, Part III* (Bowes & Bowes; Cambridge, 1923)

Gardiner, J.S. (ed.) *The Natural History of Wicken Fen, Part IV* (Bowes & Bowes; Cambridge, 1923)

Gardiner, J.S. (ed.) *The Natural History of Wicken Fen, Part V* (Bowes & Bowes; Cambridge, 1923)

Gardiner, J.S. (ed.) *The Natural History of Wicken Fen, Part VI* (Bowes & Bowes; Cambridge, 1923)

Garnett, A. *From Pennine High Peak to the Humber*, in Mitchell, J. (Ed.) *Great Britain Geographical Essays* (Cambridge University Press; London, 1961)

Giblett, R. *Postmodern Wetlands, Culture, History, Ecology* (Edinburgh University Press; Edinburgh, 1996)

Gilpin, W. *Observations on Several Parts of the Counties of Cambridge, Norfolk, Suffolk, and Essex, also on Several Parts of North Wales; Relative Chiefly to Picturesque Beauty, in Two Tours, the Former Made in the Year 1769, the Latter in the Year 1773* (Published by his Trustees, printed in London, 1809)

Godwin, H. *Fenland: Its Ancient Past and Uncertain Future* (Cambridge University Press; Cambridge, 1978)

Goodchild, J. (ed.) 'The Peat-cutting Industry of South Yorkshire' *The South Yorkshire Journal*, Part Three (May 1971), pp. 1-5

Goodchild, J. (ed.) 1973) 'The Peat-cutting Industry of South Yorkshire, part two' *The South Yorkshire Journal*, Part Four (April 1973), pp. 11-19

Grove, A.T. 'Fenland' in Mitchell, J. (ed.) *Great Britain Geographical Essays* (Cambridge University Press; London, 1961)

Gurney, J.H. *Early Annals of Ornithology* (H.F. & G. Witherby; London, 1921)

Hanson-Smith, C. *The Flemish Bond: East Anglia & The Netherlands – Close & Ancient Neighbours* (Groundnut Publishing, Diss, Norfolk, 2004)

Harris, L.E. *Vermuyden and the Fens: A Study of Sir Cornelius Vermuyden and the Great Level* (Cleaver-Hume Press Ltd; London, 1953)

Harrison, K. & Rotherham, I.D. 'A memory re-discovered of South Yorkshire's Fens: map-based reconstruction of the region's former wetlands', *The Yorkshire Naturalists' Union Bulletin*, 48 (2007), pp. 1-8.

Heathcote, J.M. *Reminiscences of Fen and Mere* (Spottiswoode & Co.; London, 1876)

Hill, J.W.F. *Medieval Lincoln* (Cambridge at the University Press; Cambridge, 1948)

Hills, R.L. *Machines, Mills & Uncountable Costly Necessities: A Short History of the Drainage of the Fens* (Goose & Son; Norwich, 1967)

Hills, R.L. *The Drainage of the Fens* (Landmark Publishing Ltd; Ashbourne, 2003)

Hogan, D.V. & Maltby, E. *The Potential for Carbon Sequestration in Wetlands of the Humberhead Levels*, Technical Report (Royal Holloway Institute for Environmental Research, Royal Holloway University of London; London, 2005)

Humphreys, M. 'Malaria: "Evil" Air and Mosquitoes' in Kiple, K. (ed.) *Plague, Pox & Pestilence: Disease in History* (Weidenfeld & Nicholson; London, 1997)

Hywel-Davies, J. & Thom, V. *The Macmillan Guide to Britain's Nature Reserves* (Macmillan; London, 1986)

Jackson, N. & Eversham, B. (eds) *Nature Atlas of Great Britain* (Pan Books Ltd; London, 1989)

Jeffrys (1772) *Map of the County of Yorkshire* (Harry Margary; Lympne, 1973)

Jenkins, J. & James, P. *From Acorn to Oak Tree: The Growth of the National Trust 1895-1994* (Macmillan; London, 1994)

Johnstone, J. *An Account of the Mode of Draining Land, according to the system practiced by Mr Joseph Elkington*, Second edition corrected and enlarged (For the Board of Agriculture; London, 1801)

Jones, M. 'Deer in South Yorkshire: An Historical Perspective' in Jones, M., Rotherham, I.D. and McCarthy, A.J. (eds) Deer or the New Woodlands? *The Journal of Practical Ecology and Conservation, Special Publication*, No. 1, November 1996

Kerridge, E. *The Farmers of Old England* (George Allen & Unwin Ltd; London, 1973)

Kingsley, C. *Prose Idylls New and Old* (Macmillan and Co.; London, 1889)

Korthals-Altes, J. *Sir Cornelius Vermuyden* (Williams & Norgate and W.P. Van Stockum & Son; London and The Hague, 1925)

Lack, D. *The Birds of Cambridgeshire* (Cambridge Bird Club; Cambridge, 1934)

Latham, J., Edwards, D. & Daniles, A. *South of the Wash: Tydd St. Mary to Spalding* (Battleford Books, 1995)

Limbert, M. 'An Early Visit to Thorne Moors' *The Lapwing*, 13 (1983), pp. 18-26.

Limbert, M. (ed.) *Thorne & Hatfield Moors Papers*, 1 (Doncaster Naturalists' Society; Doncaster, 1987)

Limbert, M. (ed.) (1998) *Thorne & Hatfield Moors Papers*, 5 (Thorne & Hatfield Moors Conservation Forum; Doncaster, 1998)

Limbert, M. & Eversham, B.C. (eds) *Thorne & Hatfield Moors Papers*, 4 (Thorne & Hatfield Moors Conservation Forum; Doncaster, 1997)

Limbert, M., Mitchell, R.D., & Rhodes, R.J. *Thorne Moors Birds and Man* (Doncaster & District Ornithological Society; Doncaster, 1986)

Lindley, K. *Fenland Riots and the English Revolution* (Heinemann Educational Books; London, 1982)

Lowenthal, D. *The Past is a Foreign Country* (Cambridge University Press; Cambridge, 1985)

Lunn, D. 'Kings, Canals and Coal: Some Account of the Parishes in and around Hatfield Chace' *Volume Two of the History and Topography of Parishes of the Diocese of Sheffield* (1993)

Lysons, D. & Lysons, S. *Magna Britannia Volume 2 Part 1 Cambridgeshire* (T. Cadell & W. Davies, 1808)

Mais, S.P.B. *This Unknown Island* (Putnam; London and New York, 1932)

Manning, S. & Green, S.G. *English Pictures Drawn with Pen and Pencil* (The Religious Tract Society; London, 1885)

Martins, S.W. *Farmers, Landlords and Landscapes: Rural Britain, 1720 to 1870* (Windgather Press; Macclesfield, 2004)

Miller, K. 'The Isle of Axholme: Historic Landscape Characterisation Project' Unpublished Report, Countryside Commission, Leeds (1997)

Miller, S.H. & Skertchly, S.B.J. *The Fenland Past and Present* (Longmans, Green & Co.; London, and Leach and Son; Wisbech, 1887)

Moore, N.W. 'The Fenland Reserves' in Friday, L. (ed.) *Wicken Fen: The Making of a Wetland Nature Reserve* (Harley Books; Colchester, 1997)

Oldfield, E. *Topographical and Historical Account of Wainfleet and the Wapentake of Candleshoe, in the County of Lincoln. With Engravings* (Longman, Rees, Orme, Brown & Green; London, 1829)

Peck, W. *A Topographical History and Description of Bawtry and Thorne with the Villages Adjacent* (Printed by Thomas and Hunsley; Doncaster, 1813)

Peck, W. *A Topographical Account of the Isle of Axholme, being the West Division of the Wapentake of Manley, in the County of Lincoln* (Printed by Thomas and Hunsley; Doncaster, 1815)

Pennant, T. *A Tour in Scotland 1769* (John Monk; Chester, 1771)

Pryme, G. (edited by Alicia Bayne) *Autobiographic Recollections of George Pryme Esq., M.P.* (Deighton, Bell & Co.; Cambridge, 1870)

Pryor, F. *Flag Fen: Prehistoric Fenland Centre* (B.T. Batsford Ltd; London, 1991)

Purseglove, J. *Taming the Flood: A History and Natural History of Rivers and Wetlands* (Oxford University Press; Oxford, 1988)

Rackham, O. *The History of the Countryside* (J.M. Dent & Sons; London, 1986)

Richards, W. *The History of Lynn* (R. Baldwin; London, 1812)

Rimington, E. 'Butterflies of the Doncaster District' *Sorby Record Special Series*, 9 (1992)

Rippon, S. *The Transformation of Coastal Wetlands* (The British Academy, Oxford University Press; Oxford, 2000)

Roberts, C. & Cox, M. *Health & Disease in Britain: From Prehistory to the Present Day* (Sutton Publishing; Stroud, 2003)

Rotberg, R.I. (ed.) *Health and Disease in Human History: A Journal of Interdisciplinary History Reader* (The MIT Press; Cambridge, 2000)

Rotherham, I.D. 'Floods and Water: A Landscape-scale Response' in Rotherham, I.D. (ed.) *Flooding, Water and the Landscape* (Wildtrack Publishing; Sheffield, 2008), pp 128–37

Rotherham, I.D. 'Landscape, Water and History' in Rotherham, I.D. (ed.) *Flooding, Water and the Landscape* (Wildtrack Publishing; Sheffield, 2008), pp. 138–52

Rotherham, I.D. *Yorkshire's Forgotten Fenlands* (Pen & Sword; Barnsley, 2010)

Rotherham, I.D. & Harrison, K. *History and Ecology in the Reconstruction of the South Yorkshire Fens: Past, Present and Future*, proceedings of the IALE Conference, *Water and the Landscape: The Landscape Ecology of Freshwater Ecosystems* (2006), 8–16.

Saunders, W.H.B. *Legends and Traditions of Huntingdonshire* (Simpkin, Marshall; London, 1888)

Saxton, C. *Map of the County of Yorkshire* (1577)

Saxton C. & Goodman W. *Map of Pottrick Carr near Doncaster*, Local Archives, Doncaster MBC Libraries (1616)

Scarfe, N. 'A Frenchman's Year in Suffolk: French Impressions of Suffolk Life in 1784', *Suffolk Records Society*, Vol. XXX (The Boydell Press; Woodbridge, 1988), pp. 226 & xxxvii

Scarfe, N. *Innocent Espionage: The La Rochefoucauld Brothers' Tour of England in 1785* (The Boydell Press; Woodbridge, 1995)

Scarfe, N. *To the Highlands in 1786* (The Boydell Press; Woodbridge, 2001)

Shakespeare, W. *King Lear* (Oxford Standard Authors; Oxford, 1905), pp. ii, iv, 169

Sheail, J. *Nature in Trust* (Blackie; Glasgow & London, 1976)

Skempton, A.W. (ed.) *John Smeaton FRS* (Thomas Telford Ltd; London, 1981)

Skidmore, P., Limbert, M. & Eversham, B.C. 'The Insects of Thorne Moors', *Sorby Record*, No. 23, Supplement (1985)

Skidmore, P. 'Balaam's Donkey and the Hairy Canary: Personal Reflections on the Changing Invertebrates of Thorne and Hatfield Moors' *Thorne & Hatfield Moors Papers*, 3 (1992), pp. 66-70

Smallhorn, T. *Most Brute and Beastly Shire* (Richard Kay; Boston, 1987)

Smith, R. *Enjoying the Humberhead Levels* (Halsgrove; Tiverton, 2004)

Smith, R. (ed.) *The Marsh of Time: Saving Sutton Common* (Halsgrove; Tiverton, 2004)

Smiles, S. *Lives of the Engineers* (John Murray; London, 1904)

Smout, C. *Nature Contested – Environmental History in Scotland and Northern England since 1600* (Edinburgh University Press; Edinburgh, 2000)

Somerville, C. *Britain & Ireland's Best Wild Places: 500 Ways to Discover the Wild* (Allen Lane, Penguin Books; London, 2008)

Strong, R. *The Story of Britain* (Hutchinson; London, 1996)

Summers, D. *The Great Level: A History of Drainage and Land Reclamation in the Fens* (David & Charles; Newton Abbott and London, 1976)

Summers, D. *The East Coast Floods* (David & Charles; Newton Abbot, 1987)

Taylor, M. *Thorne Mere and the Old River Don* (Ebor Press, 1987)

Thompson, P. (1856) *History and Antiquities of Boston* (John Noble Jun., Boston, Longman & Co.; London, 1856)

Tomlinson, J. *The Level of Hatfield Chace and Parts Adjacent* (John Tomlinson; Doncaster, 1882)

Van de Noort, R. and Davies, P. *Wetland Heritage: An Archaeological Assessment of the Humber Wetlands* Humber Wetlands project (University of Hull; Hull, 1993)

Van de Noort, R. and Ellis, S. *Wetland Heritage of the Humberhead Levels: An Archaeological Survey* Humber Wetlands project (University of Hull; Hull, 1997)

Van de Noort, R. *The Humber Wetlands: The Archaeology of a Dynamic Landscape* (Windgather Press; Macclesfield, 2004)

Vermuyden, C. *Map of Hatfield Chace before the Drainage* (1626)

Walker, N. & Craddock, T. *The History of Wisbech and the Fens* (Richard Walker; Wisbech, 1849)

Waterson, M. *The National Trust: The First Hundred Years* (BCA; London, 1994)

Wells, S. *The History of the Drainage of the Great Level of the Fens, called Bedford Level; with the Constitution and Laws of the Bedford Level Corporation* (R. Pheney; London, 1830)

Wentworth-Day, J. *History of the Fens* (George Harrap & Co. Ltd; London, 1954)

Wheeler, W.H. *The Drainage of Fens and Low Lands by Gravitation and Steam Power* (E. & F.N. Spon; London, 1888)

Wheeler, W.H. *A History of The Fens of South Lincolnshire, being a Description of the Rivers Witham and Welland and their Estuary, and an Account of the Reclamation, Drainage, and Enclosure of The Fens Adjacent thereto*, second edition (J.M. Newcombe, Boston, and Simpkin, Marshall & Co.; London, 1897)

Whitehouse, N.J., Dinnin, M.H. & Lindsay, R.A. 'Conflicts between paleoecology, archaeology and nature conservation: The Humberhead Peatlands SSSI' in Rotherham, I.D. and Jones, M. (eds) *Landscapes … Perception, Recognition and Management: Reconciling the Impossible?* Proceedings of the conference held in Sheffield, UK, 2-4 April, 1996 *Landscape Archaeology and Ecology*, 3 (1998), pp. 70-8

Wilcox, H.A. *The Woodlands and Marshlands of England* (University Press of Liverpool, Hodder & Stoughton; London, 1933)

Woodruffe-Peacock, E.A. 'The Ecology of Thorne Waste', *Naturalist*, 45 (1920-21)

Woolley, B. *The Herbalist: Nicholas Culpeper and the Fight for Medical Freedom* (HarperCollins; London, 2004)

Young, A. *Political Essays* (W. Strahan and T. Cadell; The Strand, 1772) (Re-printed 1970 by Research Reprints Inc., New York)

Young, A. *General View of the Agriculture of the County of Norfolk* (The Board of Agriculture; London, 1804)

Young, A. *On the Husbandry of Three Celebrated British Farmers: Messrs Bakewell, Arbuthnot, and Ducket* (1811)

If you enjoyed this book, you may also be interested in…

Lincolnshire Villains: Rogues, Rascals and Reprobates
DOUGLAS WYNN

In addition to the pirates, coastal criminals and countryside rogues, there was murder and mayhem aplenty in such cities as Lincoln, Grimsby, Boston and Stamford. Moreover, Lincolnshire was a haven for highwaymen and footpads – even the infamous Dick Turpin had a Lincolnshire connection. With exciting and dramatic tales featuring the worst of Lincolnshire's villains, this book will inform and fascinate everyone interested in the county's criminal past.

978 0 7524 6611 8

Norfolk Villains: Rogues, Rascals and Reprobates
NEIL R. STOREY

Discover the darker side of Norfolk with this remarkable collection of true-life crimes from across the county. Featuring tales of some of the most notorious characters from the county's past – including pirates, poachers, thieves, murderers and bodysnatchers – all factions of the criminal underworld are included in this macabre collection.

978 0 7524 6001 7

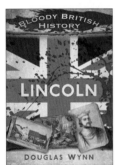

Bloody British History: Lincoln
DOUGLAS WYNN

Containing medieval child murder, vile sieges of (and escapes from) the castle, the savage repression of the Lincolnshire Rising by King Henry VIII (who had the ringleaders hanged, drawn and quartered) and plagues, lepers, prisons, and terrible hangings by the ton, you'll never see the city in the same way again.

978 0 7524 6289 9

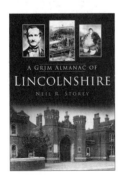

A Grim Almanac of Lincolnshire
NEIL R. STOREY

Full of dreadful deeds, macabre deaths, strange occurrences and heinous homicides, this almanac explores the darker side of Lincolnshire's past – from highwaymen, smugglers and poachers to giants, witches and rebels. Also featured in this remarkable collection of true-life crimes are accounts of prisons, bridewells and punishments – read on if you have the stomach for it.

978 0 7524 5768 0

Visit our website and discover thousands of other History Press books.

www.thehistorypress.co.uk